Routledge Revi

The Welsh in their History

This book, first published in 1982, is a sequence of interrelated essays and aims to redirect attention to some critical moments in Welsh history from Roman times to the present. Each of the essays breaks new ground, argues for a new approach or opens a new discourse.

The Welsh in their History

Gwyn A. Williams

Routledge
Taylor & Francis Group

First published in 1982
by Croom Helm Ltd

This edition first published in 2022 by Routledge
4 Park Square, Milton Park, Abingdon, Oxon, OX14 4RN

and by Routledge
605 Third Avenue, New York, NY 10017

Routledge is an imprint of the Taylor & Francis Group, an informa business

© 1982 Gwyn A. Williams

Publisher's Note
The publisher has gone to great lengths to ensure the quality of this reprint but points out that some imperfections in the original copies may be apparent.

Disclaimer
The publisher has made every effort to trace copyright holders and welcomes correspondence from those they have been unable to contact.

A Library of Congress record exists under ISBN: 0709927118

ISBN: 978-1-032-27300-6 (hbk)
ISBN: 978-1-003-29288-3 (ebk)
ISBN: 978-1-032-27459-1 (pbk)

Book DOI 10.4324/9781003292883

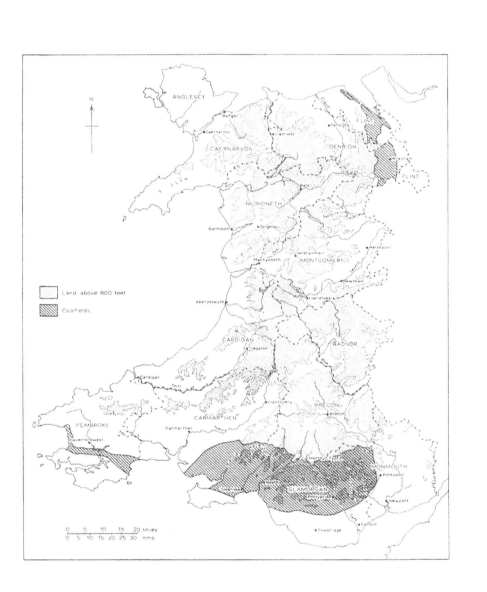

ANGLESEY

N

•Bangor

•Caernarfon

CAERNARVON

•Llanrwst

•Denbigh   FLINT

DENBIGH

Bala

FLINT

MERIONETH

Barmouth•   •Dolgellau

Welshpool

Llanbrynmair

•Machynlleth   MONTGOMERY

•Newtown

□ Land above 800 feet

▨ Coalfields

•Aberystwyth   •Llanidloes

CARDIGAN   RADNOR

•Tregaron

•Cardigan   Teifi

•Llandovery   BRECON

•Brecon

PEMBROKE   CARMARTHEN   Towy

Haverfordwest•   •Carmarthen

Merthyr Tydfil   MONMOUTH

•Pontypool

Neath   GLAMORGAN

•Swansea   Pontypridd   •Newport

•Cowbridge

•Cardiff

0   5   10   15   20 Miles
0 5 10 15 20 25 30 Kms

The Welsh in their history

Gwyn A. Williams

CROOM HELM
London & Sydney

© 1982 Gwyn A. Williams
Reprinted 1985

Croom Helm Ltd, Provident House, Burrell Row,
Beckenham, Kent BR3 1AT

Croom Helm Australia Pty Ltd, Suite 4, 6th Floor,
64-76 Kippax Street, Surry Hills, NSW 2010, Australia

British Library Cataloguing in Publication Data

Williams, Gwyn A.
    The Welsh in their history.
    1. Wales—History
    I. Title
    942.9   DA714

    ISBN 0-7099-3651-6 (Pbk)

Printed and bound in Great Britain by
Biddles Ltd, Guildford and King's Lynn

CONTENTS

For
Eric J. Hobsbawm,
Master Craftsman

INTRODUCTION

In Wales today, historical work of major significance appears with the speed, regularity and decision of the guillotine during the Terror. The historian, strenuous at his sullen craft, sees his words pressed into immediate political service by the committed. Nothing so concentrates a people's mind as the prospect of its imminent execution.

I have therefore decided to follow the advice of those who for some time have been urging me to collect and broadcast work of mine which has appeared in publications they consider obscure. This practice has generally seemed to me prematurely posthumous. In the Wales I live in, it now seems appropriate.

I have chosen those writings which seemed to me to break new ground, to suggest a new approach or to open a novel discourse. Of the nine pieces which appear here, three have not appeared in print before; the others, with one exception, were published in Wales. They differ widely in character; some are lectures, some essays and some scholarly articles as the profession understand the term. I have indicated their original provenance and have retained their original documentation, whether it were nil or overpowering. There is some overlap between a couple of them and the final essay courses over all that has gone before, but I have tried to reduce verbal repetition to the minimum without mutilating the originals.

In work which ranges from Vortigern to Neil Kinnock, I have obviously incurred many debts. I am a marxist who believes that marxism needs no hyphen, but my obligation to Antonio Gramsci, the Sardo who made himself a European, will be clear. In more immediate terms, I owe much to Cardiff colleagues, past and present, to David Smith and Matthew Griffiths of the Department of the History of Wales here and to its accomplished director Gwynedd Pierce; to Hywel M. Davies who has reversed traditional Welsh procedure and has been called to Aberystwyth from Jesus. I am particularly indebted to my friend and comrade Brian Davies, formerly of the Universities of York and Swansea and the National Museum of Wales who, with his companions of the Niclas Society, is engaged on an historical enterprise of an audacity comparable to that of John Evans who set off alone up an unknown eighteenth-century Missouri with one dollar and seventy-five cents in his pocket.

I am most deeply indebted, in ways which cannot be listed or sometimes even expressed, to two decidedly mature research students of Cardiff, my friends, comrades and companions through a bad time, Carole Harwood and Kevin Littlewood.

I would like to offer these essays, without permission, as a tribute to a man whose work has been for me one continuous stimulus and challenge over a quarter of a century and who is one of the finest historians to have graced the Island of Britain, nursery of historians.

Gwyn A. Williams, University College of South Wales, Cardiff

ACKNOWLEDGEMENTS

For kind permission to reprint to the editors of the journals *Welsh History Review* and *Llafur,* to the editors and publishers of *A People and a Proletariat: essays in the history of Wales 1780-1880* (Pluto Press and *Llafur,* London, 1980); *Pioneers of Welsh Education* (Faculty of Education, University College, Swansea, 1964); *Culture, Ideology and Politics: essays in honour of Eric Hobsbawm* (Routledge and Kegan Paul, London, 1982) and to the presses of University College, Cardiff and the British Broadcasting Corporation. I thank Professor Harold Carter and the Department of Geography at the University College of Wales, Aberystwyth, for supplying me with the map.

BY WAY OF PREFACE: THE PRIMITIVE REBEL AND THE HISTORY OF THE WELSH*

Classics, it is said, are great books which are never read. Eric Hobsbawm's *Primitive Rebels* came out in 1959, was marginally revised in 1963 and has attained the status of a classic.[1]

I hesitate to say it is never read. There was a period, clearly, when it was read intensely. But it is a book which, no less than Edward Thompson's classic, *The Making of the English Working Class,*[2] created a new genre of historical writing, particularly since, in practice, it worked in harness with George Rudé's classic anatomical study of crowds which, at one time, bid fair to erect the crowd into a cosmic phenomenon.[3] Such gales of fashion, such revolutions in historical interpretation, reminiscent of Karl Marx's German philosophers of the 1840s, are characteristic of our historiography and one indicator of its essentially petty-bourgeois predicament.

I suspect that, by this time, Eric Hobsbawm's book is actually read, even by, or perhaps I should say especially by, certified specialists in primitive rebellion about as often as Jean Jacques Rousseau was read by *sans-culotte* militants in the Paris of 1793.

These remarks are inspired in part by Hywel Francis's comment in his programme notes to this series of classes, that for many of the Welsh movements which would occupy us under this head, Sophisticated Rebels would be a more suitable title. Precisely. Over the years, Hobsbawm's title has been severed from his content. In his book, of course, he makes this particular point repeatedly. In his introduction, he puts primitive in quotation marks. Since a whole corpus of historical writing has been created from this original life-giving impulse, it is important now, I think, to grasp first what Hobsbawm actually meant when he used the term primitive, sometimes varying it with archaic, without quotation marks, that is, out-of-date.

In the first place, he did not mean primitive in time. All the movements he dealt with, which were mainly Italian, were movements

---

*Unpublished. A lecture delivered in October 1979 at the South Wales Miners' Library, Swansea (Director: Hywel Francis) to launch a course of extramural classes on Primitive Rebels in modern Welsh history. I have inserted a few references to books and have updated a few comments.

of the nineteenth and twentieth centuries. Plenty of them, like banditry in Sardinia, are still happening. What Hobsbawm was concerned with, in using this word primitive, was what technical historians call heuristic, the craft of the historian. It is to the historian's craft, his skill, his mystery, his trade if you like, that the term Primitive Rebel was directed. It is not the rebellion which is primitive, but our understanding of it.

Hobsbawm was determined to conquer for history a whole continent which had been lost like Atlantis. As a marxist, he was also concerned to mobilise a vital sector of that usable past which it is the function of marxist historians to make available to the organic intellectuals of the working-class movement and of marxism. He observed that there was a gap in the historical treatment of many movements among the popular classes.

We knew something about popular action in the fairly remote past, in classical and medieval times; slave revolts, mass heresies, heretical sects, peasant rebellions. They had generally been treated as incidents, anecdotes, curiosities or as forerunners of later, more familiar movements.

We had a well-established discipline of study of modern labour, trade union and socialist movements, in Europe dating normally from the late eighteenth century and in our own day, extending over the whole world. Usually this work had been done within a socialist set of assumptions and it had created a pattern which was, half-consciously, assumed to hold good everywhere. These movements were regarded as having their primitive stages, such as Luddism or Utopian anarchism and socialism, but the norm which fixed standards of judgement was the familiar working-class movement of recent times.

A crippling weakness of this kind of history — a populist version of the Whig interpretation and often enshrined in the bastard concept of 'labour history' — is that it is teleological, it thinks of phenomena as fulfilling some inbuilt purpose, like an acorn which cannot escape its destiny as an oak. The ultimate goal of all these movements was the familiar labour movement. A labour movement existed as some kind of holy ghost within them. In an extreme form of this history, the ultimate goal of British popular history, for example, appeared to be the British Labour Party, presumably on the marxist assumption that history repeats itself, first as tragedy and then as farce.

This attitude, in slightly more sophisticated form, persists among non-socialist historians uninterested in labour movements. They make a distinction, for example, between what they call the political and the non-political. A grain action, a price-fixing action or a food riot, machine-breaking, under this head become non-political: no committees, no agenda, no platform, no Mr Chairman-on-a-point-of-order ... It is rather difficult to maintain a clear-cut distinction, since a price-fixing crowd action, of course, is a direct expression of a certain view of social life, social obligations and social justice and therefore cannot help being in some important senses highly political. We tend to fall back on useful words like sub-political.

This word is particularly useful since no one knows quite what it means. It can convey an impression: there is something political lurking there. Hobsbawm himself in his book uses the word pre-political, which is more precise. This describes the actions and statements of people who have not found or do not command or conceivably do not want or need, a specific set of political concepts and a specific political language to express their perception of and aspirations in the world. This is perhaps useful. Hobsbawm himself in 1959 (I'm not sure he'd say the same today) talks of people who have 'not *yet* found' such a language (my italics). This seems to imply that they are looking for one, like blind white fish in a barrel. It lets in the teleological demon by the back door. It seems to imply that there is some recognisable route towards such a language, which is certainly not proven.

But what Hobsbawm wanted to do was precisely to avoid that kind of thinking, to move into these movements in their own right, not as half-baked labour movements.

There were understandable reasons for their exclusion from history, particularly left-wing history. They *were* pre-political; they existed in a world where classes did not seem to exist or at least could not be defined in the same way as classes in mature industrial society; they were largely illiterate and therefore difficult of access. They were steeped in pre-capitalist modes of production and existence, to which kinship groups and other 'tribal' phenomena were central. They were very odd altogether, like a crazy old grandfather who keeps coming downstairs when you have important visitors.

The movements and phenomena Hobsbawm studied all appeared in societies which were pre-capitalist or only imperfectly capitalist or in transition into capitalism. He began with what he considered a basic form, banditry, and particularly that form of it which could express social protest or predicament. He later elaborated this into an extraordinarily stimulating book, *Bandits,* where he refined his analysis.[4] He discussed who became bandits, the economics and politics of banditry, their relation to peasant revolution, if any, their status as symbols, 'the men who made themselves respected', the men who stood upright in a society of bent backs.

He outlined three type-figures of the social bandit: the cruel and merciless avenger of wrongs; the Balkan *haiduks* who were almost a resistance movement and, of course, the universal Noble Robber, Robin Hood. He even constructed a brilliantly argued model of a universal Robin Hood under nine heads, the Nine Faces of Robin Hood. Some of his work here proved controversial, but as with everything Eric Hobsbawm ever writes, it is hugely stimulating.

What you have to remember is that he is dealing with a tiny minority. Hobsbawm repeatedly stresses that no more than ten per cent of all bandits, if that, were or are social bandits. Among them, the cruel avengers are often worse than the wrongs they are avenging. It has become necessary to reaffirm that ninety per cent of bandits are plain common or garden bandits, that the social protest expressed, for example, by a gang clobbering an old woman for her handbag is directed primarily against old women with handbags. It can, of course, be interpreted as a sub-political revolt by depraved elements (depraved on account a they're deprived) demanding equality in the distribution of handbags. That way madness lies.

In his *Primitive Rebels,* Hobsbawm moves on from the social bandit to the Mafia, the parallel counter-state family. Then comes a whole section on millenarian movements, mass movements believing in the Second Coming or a Messiah, or some passionate religiose creed which found mass expression in action. Here, in the face of some criticism and more recent work, he has modified his position a little. He recognises the need to make an analytical distinction between mass and explosive millenarian upheavals, often fleeting, and millenarian *movements* which cohered into organised sects, like the followers of Joanna Southcott or Robert Brothers, or the rather terrifying Israelites of Ashton-under-Lyne, or some of the heretical forms of Methodism during the formation of a British working class. The recent work of John Harrison, not to mention the remarkable studies of an earlier period by Dame Frances Yates, have enormously enriched our understanding of such people.[5]

Hobsbawm then moves on, in one of the most brilliant historical essays I have ever read, to the city mob, existing in close symbiosis with city government, a form of collective urban social banditry systematised into a way of life. His analysis of Parma offers the best approach to the English Hustings; he says more about the mob in a few pages than most of the weighty tomes that now press down upon our bookshelves and our brains. Here, of course, his work ran into confluence with George Rudé's seminal study of the crowd. Since their springtime days, work on the crowd and the mob has become virtually a sub-sector of historiography in its own right.

Finally, Hobsbawm closed in on two related phenomena within labour movements, the labour church or sect and ritual in early social movements, the kind of secret and terrifying ceremonies associated with the first trade unions which left such an imprint on their first banners, the iconography of labour, generally imitative of the Freemasons.

What Hobsbawm was anxious to do was to establish these as problems in their own right to be studied in their own terms. He wanted, also, to situate them as contemporary with developed labour movements and to identify them as movements which could in fact recur in modern times in different forms. What he was anxious above all to avoid was to locate them as stages in some natural progression.

It is a belief common to marxists and Christians that men's efforts often produce results opposite to those intended. The paradox is that *Primitive Rebels* has produced precisely the consequences it sought to exorcise.

What makes these movements primitive in Hobsbawm's terms? It is not their chronological time. It is not their inner quality: many of them were highly organised, highly intelligent and highly effective — in Wales witness the Rebecca Riots and the Scotch Cattle; the former actually won their immediate objectives. No, it is precisely their pre-political character. They do not marshal a working-class consciousness. They are primitive in the same way as Utopian Socialisms are utopian. Utopian Socialisms, many of them, of course, were not utopian at all in the common usage of the word. Utopian Socialisms are not utopian but defeated. It was Marx and Engels who dismissed them as Utopian, in contrast to their own self-styled scientific socialism. Since marxism won the ideological struggle within European working-class movements and achieved a kind of vicarious prestige in Britain, the label stuck. Having been defeated, non-marxist socialisms found themselves Utopian. A partisan term has become a category of clinical description. History to the defeated may cry alas but cannot pardon.

Primitive in this sense is not a partisan term, but what it has come to mean in the work of many is non-marxist. Hobsbawm analysed these movements in marxist terms, but imitators, and they have been legion, have been cruder; the movements simply become pre-marxist. If we aren't careful, we diminish them once more into people in the waiting rooms of 'real' history, hanging on for Godot.

I think this has happened because people who think of themselves as marxists seem unable to apply any marxist categories except those elaborated to analyse the nineteenth and twentieth centuries; the only classes they seem to recognise are those of industrial capitalism. Take the *sans-culottes* of the French Revolution. They act as one tends to expect a working class to act, in terms of politics. They are not working class, many of their ideas are classically petty-bourgeois, but it's hard to think of them as a lower middle class either. So their ideologies are treated as incomplete, unfinished, unrealised, somehow on the way towards a working class. It does not seem to occur to commentators that in the eighteenth century, under a merchant capitalism operating within a landowning oligarchy based on an increasingly productive agriculture and generating its own rural proto-industrialisation, ranges of society might well have constituted a class, in relation to a plurality of modes of production, in a way that has been lost to modern society.

Such analysts tend to conceive of class as a thing or object. As Edward Thompson repeatedly argues, they see no process in it. Edward Thompson's own concept of class is inadequate and self-defeating; G.A. Cohen's cogent exposition of traditional marxism demonstrates the necessity of a traditionally structural explanation.[6] But neither concept of class can be sufficient unless it is firmly located within that essential marxist concept, a mode of production (which is rather more flexible and comprehensive, I think, than Cohen will allow).

The mode of production has once again become central to marxist argument in philosophy and economics, but it remains peculiarly an absentee from marxist history. Some years ago, I read an essay in a Spanish marxist journal, then published in Parisian exile, which analysed the bourgeois revolution in nineteenth-century Spain in terms of this original and classic definition. It provoked a storm of protest from fellow-marxists and a special editorial comment. This, they said, is not how we normally think of a bourgeois revolution; their terms, though broad, were essentially political and couched in the language of political power and its appropriation. Since Lenin, the Bolshevik Revolution (regarded as a success) and the invention of a mode of discourse and practice called Leninism, much marxist analysis has become a form of political art or science, focusing on the dynamics and mechanics of power in a bourgeois society and its practice. However sophisticated such analysis, it tends to reduce revolution to merely one of its marxist meanings; revolution becomes an act, an event, or more frequently, a complex of political conjunctures; the other, more basic marxist sense of revolution, a long process of dialectical development, has shrivelled. Gramsci and other marxists of the 1920s often took as their model the Christian Revolution which, over centuries, succeeded in transforming society totally and in achieving the internal assimilation of its ideology as 'custom'; in Gramsci's work, but also in that of other communists, this perspective remained central. This was, after all, Marx's own original and basic conception; the bourgeois revolution had taken three hundred years. Today, many marxists seem to respond to the very notion of a Christian Revolution by going into a state of incredulous shock.

This perspective on historical development demands of historians a different approach. It demands in particular that we *start* from a mode of production and, more important still, that we grasp what has been a normal condition through much of human history, the fact that within any social formation, a number of modes of production can coexist. One may be becoming dominant, but others persist — and are sometimes even stimulated by the establishment of that dominance. This is obvious enough in a country like Italy. But think of Wales. At many points in its history, this small country, scarcely 200 miles from end to end, has been the theatre for several modes of production simultaneously. This condition is, in truth, far more common in history than the ubiquity of a single dominant mode.

Each mode of production will produce its own relations of production and its own social relations, its own cluster of ideologies which exist in autonomy, with serious consequences for the structure of any state. This means that whole groups, classes and sub-classes, will live on different time-scales. Time, or rather the perception of time, is no more unilinear than a sequence of modes of production. In any one chronological period, whole 'societies' within a society will be operating to different time-scales and different perceptions of time, with different classes being formed and forming themselves in different ways and with different perceptions of reality. It is surely here that one response to creative art registers?

And surely it is precisely here that the notion which 'primitive rebels' tries to embrace should operate? Dafydd ap Siencyn in the Teifi valley in 1830 lived on a different time-scale from his cousin in Merthyr (to judge from evidence thrown up by the Merthyr Rising of 1831, the latter would actually own *a watch*); one's rebellion could be 'primitive', the other's could be Chartism. In late eighteenth-century Wales, at one and the same time, merchant capitalism with its rural proto-industrialisation was, over whole tracts of the Welsh countryside, abolishing 'peasants', while industrial capitalism was beginning its sweep, raising cloth factories along the Severn to disrupt rural villages of industrial workers, commandeering the minds of improving landowners to make even the marginal agriculture of Wales a capitalist industry, planting the continuously innovative iron industry in the south-east, among a population whole sectors of which lived informally according to the half-remembered laws of Hywel Dda of a 'tribal' society.

To understand such a situation, to quote Lenin, concretely to analyse a concrete conjuncture, it is necessary, first, to try to establish just what the modes of production actually were and just what their interaction actually implied. This is very difficult indeed, but only in this way can we locate in history and make sense of, any rebels we are tempted to label primitive. What one cannot do is simply to draw up a shopping list of 'characteristics of the primitive rebel' and then 'apply them . . . 1, 2, 3 . . .' to particular Welsh experiences.

Such 'application' can be very sophisticated, raiding psychology, anthropology, sociology and quantitative methodology for ideas. A whole continent *has* been uncovered. The study of the crowd, of crime as a social phenomenon, medical history, the analysis of popular beliefs, the study of weather, have all been pressed into service and have widely extended our understanding. But very soon, the consumer of this kind of history begins to feel frustration. The study of 'rebels' is beginning to follow the study of 'the crowd' straight up a blind alley. In the end, beyond a certain point, if you go on applying Rudé's anatomy of a crowd, you reach the terminus of a cul-de-sac. In these terms, in the end, a crowd is a crowd is a crowd, a conclusion designed to hurl the assiduous researcher into paroxysms of rampant apathy.

If you reach out to the fuller and richer world opened up by Hobsbawm's study of rebels, you may, in the terms in which it is customarily conducted, end up with insights useful to sociology but rarely to history There is a sense of stasis, stagnation, immobility, the death of history. For history, you need a dynamic to break out from what becomes a closed, self justifying, self-perpetuating circular system. The only break-out lies in a full, conscious exercise in the marxist and materialist conception of history.

What does this mean in practice? (1) it means, firstly, trying to establish what the modes of production *were* in any society.

(2) This means trying to see society *whole*. What do they know of rebels who only rebels know? What do they know of workers who only workers know? You can't understand a working class unless, at the very least, you understand the bourgeoisie in constant daily interaction and conflict with which the working class defines itself. You can't understand the bourgeoisie unless you understand the society in which all classes function. Marxist history has to be, at least in ultimate perspective, totalising history.

This is obviously terribly difficult. What it means in practice is that one has to be constantly aware in one's work of that totalising perspective. We must realise that all our partial, sectoral, limited histories are just that. What they are *not* is microcosms of a macrocosm. They are not microcosms, not representative samples. They are what Sorel called *diremptions,* slices ripped from living tissue which die as they are ripped. Think not for a minute that in one of your sectional histories you have a little test-tube sample of the whole. Think not for a minute that if you build up enough of them, you just add them up to get a whole. You do not. The whole lies in the interactions, in the mediations as a marxist would say. Totality resides not in aggregation but in mediation.

(3) If you have managed to work out some sense of modes of production and their interaction, you have to move into relations of production and their social relations. This means moving into a world of real people as they actually existed in their own and in 'common-sense' perception: people often shaped by ideas, perceptions, traditions deriving from older modes of production and living, sometimes dead for centuries, sometimes non-rational, sometimes irrational. Things change, words remain.

First of all, you have to learn *their* language; you don't make them talk in yours. To work on Spanish history, said Marx, first learn Spanish... and first learn the verbs, said Lenin. It's harder when people use English, because they don't use our English. Friendship in the eighteenth century did not mean what it means today. You have to learn a new English.

More important still, you have to immerse yourself in *their* ideologies, not lock them into yours. Over great tracts of Welsh history, it is necessary to know what Sabellianism was and how it differed from Arianism, constructive, conglomerate and concurrent; it is important to know whether an Arminian was related to a

Campbellite: we have to place Muggletonians and Swedenborgians, differentiate between what seems an infinity of Calvinists and an eternity of Baptists. Over whole stretches of our history, ordinary working people, for sound historical reasons, found meaning in their lives precisely in such, to us, or to me anyway, alien and often alienating notions. People defined what we would call their class status by their attitudes to a particular set of Biblical texts; they defined their lives in that way, explained themselves to themselves in such terms. Before we can start applying any of our brilliant analytical techniques we have to learn the language in which the subjects of our inquiry conducted theirs. We need to cultivate humility before our subjects. We do not stand outside history. We are not gods, we are only apprentices to a craft.

(4) Beyond that lies the whole onerous task of relating such modes and realities of living to action or the lack of it. For we also have to analyse apathy. What is apathy? Apathy is a pejorative word, like mob. Historians tend by nature to be political beasts, we don't really understand the absence of a political sense; we see it as a negativity, it is apathy. Apathy as a word has precisely the same status as mob used to have; we need a George Rudé of apathy.

Beyond that, we have to relate the forms of politics to everything we have learned. And if we are marxists, of course, we have to relate that, in turn, to our present. In the process we have to locate ourselves in history, to historicise ourselves, shed the illusion of the historian commenting on the past from some mythical limbo of a juror's seat. No man squats outside history, said Marx. No historian does, even if the practice of his craft sometimes seems to force that posture upon him. Seeing oneself as history, of course, is the most difficult of all our undertakings.

This programme is one of daunting difficulty. We will probably need teams and teams are being formed. The most important duty is not to waste time, to do the right jobs and find the right questions.

I was 54 yesterday; everything I do now is a race with the undertaker. I cannot waste any more time; I've wasted enough. I'm about to publish two books which are really one extended essay on the 1790s, which I see as a starting point for modern Wales and, indeed, modern Britain.[7] I now face two major enterprises. I think a 'working class' emerged in Britain over the critical period 1829-34, the time of the Merthyr Rising here in Wales, the point at which Edward Thompson stopped. We need to understand that particular moment. I need to creep up on it crabwise, which I am going to do via the Infidel working class, the free-thinking, Deist and atheist militants among working people. At the moment I do not think that at that time British working people had an ideology of their own. Bronterre O'Brien told a Co-operative Congress in 1831 that working-class militants had no doctrines of their own, they simply mouthed middle-class nostrums in a harsher accent. This is a polemical expression of a truth. The nearest working-class spokesmen had to an ideology was Thomas Paine democracy, which they shared with others. That democratic tradition splintered between 1790 and 1830 under the hammer of class formation, even as the single culture visible in *Hog's Wash* of 1793, the first popular political journal collapses into the pages of the *Poor Man's Guardian* of 1831 which look like volcanic eruptions, as writers try to wrestle with a language which can no longer express what they wish it to express. The word radical appeared in 1819, the word liberal in 1820, much to the rage of Richard Carlile who protested against the disintegration of the democratic tradition and tried to maintain the old and honourable word of republican. I believe one operative substitute for an ideology was the intransigence of Infidelity and I'm going to explore the implications of that.

I will start on Wales in the same period. I will begin with that British civil war which was the American Revolution and which coincided with the population explosion and the first impact of industrial capitalism. David Williams the Deist from Caerphilly and the friend of Condorcet, who may have provided Robespierre with his Festival of the Supreme Being, said that Jacobinism, that is militant democracy, was born in 1782 and born not in France but in Britain; certainly Welshmen from Glamorgan presided at the birth. In 1782, William Owen a central figure in the Welsh revival, joined the London-Welsh Gwyneddigion, generator of a new Welsh nation and peopled from that Denbighshire which was being transformed by industrial capitalism. And in 1787, Peter Onions invented the puddling process, as good a birthday for modern Wales as any.

That is where I mean to start and, to the best of my ability, I mean to work in the ways I have tried to outline. The two books which come out next year in effect try to clear the ground and map out a programme of work. For I found that the 1790s were a climacteric moment in the history of the Welsh people. You have but to glance at that decade to see that it positively teems with primitive rebels; it is overpoweringly over-populated by primitive rebels. Social bandits, millenarians by the score, labour sects, ritualistic revolts, you name it, we had it, with recurrent and pungent whiffs of a transatlantic mafia. Turn but a stone in the 1790s and half a dozen primitive rebels scuttle out like bats out of a Baptist belfry. But I swear to you on the blood and bones of Iolo Morganwg that if I ever use the word again or think the thought again, I will retire in shame and sackcloth to Upper Corris in the rain or some other salubrious spot.

The concept of a Primitive Rebel was a very valuable tool with which Eric Hobsbawm broke open a Pandora's Box for us. After twenty years of overuse and abuse, it has broken in our hands. It has come to resemble one of those relations of production originally creative which become a fetter on further production. Throw it away. Who needs a charcoal burner when we've got a puddling furnace?

The idea of the primitive rebel was exhilarating and productive in its time. So no doubt was a castiron bedpan. But when we become men and women, we must put away primitive things. Brothers and sisters, put such thoughts as primitive rebels from you. If you ever hear me use the words again or even suggest the idea again, you have my permission to cut out my tongue. You can always donate it to St Fagan's Folk Museum as an outmoded relation of production.

Notes

1. E.J. Hobsbawm, *Primitive Rebels* (Manchester University Press, Manchester, 1959; revised edn 1963 and 1971).

2. Edward P. Thompson, *The Making of the English Working Class* (Gollancz, London, 1963; revised edn Penguin, Harmondsworth, 1968).

3. George Rudé published several books and many articles analysing crowds in action. His work is usefully summarised in his *The Crowd in History* (Wiley, New York, 1964; revised edn Lawrence and Wishart, London, 1981).

4. E.J. Hobsbawm, *Bandits* (Weidenfeld and Nicolson, London, 1969; Penguin, Harmondsworth, 1972).

5. J.F.C. Harrison, *The Second Coming: popular millenarianism 1780-1850* (Routledge and Kegan Paul, London, 1979); Dame Frances Yates published several remarkable books on sixteenth-century themes; the most immediately accessible to beginners is perhaps her *The Occult Philosophy in the Elizabethan Age* (Routledge and Kegan Paul, London 1979).

6. G.A. Cohen, *Karl Marx's Theory of History: A Defence* (Clarendon, Oxford, 1978); and see also Perry Anderson, *Arguments within English Marxism* (New Left Books, London, 1980).

7. Published in 1980: *The Search for Beulah Land: the Welsh and the Atlantic Revolution* (Croom Helm, London) and *Madoc: the making of a myth* (Eyre Methuen, London).

1 WELSH WIZARD AND BRITISH EMPIRE: DR JOHN DEE AND A WELSH IDENTITY*

In April 1576, Sir Humphrey Gilbert published his *Discourse* on a North-West Passage which initiated the great cycle of semi-official exploration, colonisation and piratical enterprises of Elizabethan England and launched the first serious British essay in American settlement. No-one did the book excite more than Dr John Dee, London-Welshman, mathematician and magician of European stature, scientist, Welsh patriot and *Arch Conjuror* of England, whom Elizabeth I called 'hyr philosopher' and who was central to the Elizabethan Renaissance as he was to the first British break-out into the oceans and the New World.[1]

Brooding in his magnificent library at Mortlake, one of the focal centres of the Platonic and Hermetic learning of the European Renaissance, Dee recalled an 'Atlanticall discourse' of his own on Atlantis, as he called America, the *Reipublicae Britannicae Synopsis,* written in English in 1565 and now lost and, during six days in August 1576, constructed an impressive text, the *Pety Navy Royall,* devoted to the Brytish Monarchie and its Incomparable Islandish Empire. He ran straight on into three more massive volumes, all grouped under the rubric *General and Rare Memorials pertayning to the Perfecte Arte of Navigation:* a book of Tables Gubernatick for the Queen's Navigators grounded in his new invention the Paradoxicall Compass (now lost), another which he burned as too dangerous, probably because it developed the Christian interpretation of the Jewish Cabala, and a fourth which he completed in the early summer of 1577, the *Great Volume of Famous and Rich Discoveries* on British projects towards Cathay through the arctic seas of the North-East, in which, fulfilling a promise in the *Pety Navy Royall,* he presented evidence of an early British dominion in the north in the days of the British-Welsh hero Arthur and summoned Elizabeth to rebuild a great British maritime empire in the high latitudes extending from Novaya Zemlya in the

---

*Delivered as the third annual Gwyn Jones Lecture at University College Cardiff in April 1980 and published by University College Cardiff Press, with assistance from the Welsh Arts Council (Cardiff, 1980). I have inserted notes at key points, derived from my research into *Madoc: the making of a myth* (Eyre Methuen, London, 1980).

Russian Arctic through the Orkneys, Iceland and Greenland to the very shores of Atlantis. His evidence, though supported by material of Venetian and Icelandic and Flemish provenance, was essentially British-Welsh.

Under the monstrous shadow of Habsburg and Counter-Reformation Spain, the Elizabethan court trod as delicately as Agag, but in response to pressure Dee published his first volume in a strictly limited edition of one hundred in August 1577. It was graced by a gorgeous and allegorical engraving of Elizabeth at the helm of a European imperial ship, restoring the twenty kingdoms of the British Empire and establishing a quasi-mystical, quasi-scientific, quasi-religious world order, under that British-Protestant fraternity of chivalry which Sir Philip Sidney was to personify and Edmund Spenser to celebrate. The drawing is occult in the Hermetic, Platonic and Cabalistic tradition. It belongs to a family of symbols, signs and semiological constructs which Dee created and whose central *figure* was his celebrated *Monas Hieroglyphica* of 1564, which he said summed up his philosophy. This Monas was an arithmetical, geometrical, alchemical, astral, zodiacal and above all cabalistic *sign* of a new world order. It was to become the badge of a European movement which Dee launched from Prague in the 1580s, with occult support (in both senses of the term) from the Elizabethan court, a movement of radical religious and political reform, to be led by England and the Palatinate against the Counter-Reformation, the Habsburgs and above all the Jesuits. It was to create its own anti-Jesuit Order, on the model of Sir Philip Sidney's, in the Knights of the Rose Cross (the Cross of the Tudor Rose), *Rosencreuz,* with their invisible colleges and Christian Unions and Jewish sympathies.

Crushed by the Battle of the White Mountain, which also expelled the Czech people from history for two centuries, by the Thirty Years' War and by the grotesque epidemics of witch-hunting in the religious wars, the Order went underground to live an occult and increasingly weird existence as Rosicrucianism. It re-surfaced during the eighteenth-century Enlightenment and the Age of Revolution as one of the formative forces in a radical and international Freemasonry and to generate those secret circles of *Illuminati* which spokesmen of the Counter-Revolution like the Abbé Barruel, John Robison and Edmund Burke identified as the motor-force of the entire cycle of revolutions after 1790.

By this strange and aberrant route, the ghost of Dr John Dee returned to his homeland. For it was through the *Illuminés* of Avignon and their relationships with the millenarian and Swedenborgian circles of the London poet, artist and *Jacobin* William Blake that Dee's Cabalistic and Patriarchal conceptions came to infuse the thinking of the London-Welsh *Gwyneddigion*, William Owen and Iolo Morganwg, the Welsh *Jacobins*. This second historically significant cluster of organic Welsh intellectuals who worked and lived in and through the English language followed the same route as those contemporary Czech revivalists who were also creating a new nation out of old legend and reaching back beyond the Battle of the White Mountain to make the past into an instrument with which a present could build a future. The Welsh *Jacobins* were working in precisely the same manner and in Iolo's Druids who pre-dated Jews and Christians, his Order of Bards who were their inheritors and were to be the directive intelligentsia of a Welsh nation conceived in liberty, in his revived Madoc epic of American discovery and his Welsh Zion in a New World, Dr John Dee's British Israelism was transmuted into a Cambro-British Israelism, to give birth to the first modern Welsh Nation, snuffed out in its turn by the twin Counter-Reformations of political repression and evangelical secession.[2]

Such a future was hardly visible in 1577, but a more immediate potential was certainly apparent to Sir Humphrey Gilbert, who visited Dee on 6 November and, the very next day, presented Elizabeth with nakedly anti-Spanish projects for America and the Caribbean. Before the month was out, Dee was summoned by Gloriana herself. 'I spake with the Queen hora quinta . . . I spake with Mr Secretary Walsingham...I declared to the Queen her title to Greenland, Estotiland and Friseland . . .' By June 1578 Gilbert got his patent of colonisation . . . 'I told Mr Daniel Rogers', noted Dee, 'Mr Hakluyt of the Middle Temple being by, that King Arthur and King Maty [another mythical British-Welsh hero] both of them did conquer Gelindia, lately called Friseland, which he so noted presently in his written copy of Geoffrey of Monmouth, for he had no printed book thereof'. Hakluyt the Younger, compiler of the celebrated *Principall Navigations, Voyages, Traffiques and Discoveries of the English Nation,* was to use the Comelinus Heidelberg edition of Geoffrey of Monmouth of 1587: most of the classics of Welsh tradition, including all the seminal geographical work of Humphrey Llwyd, were being printed at this time in Germany and the Low Countries (where the celebrated illustrator of American exploration, Theodore de Bry, himself a Palatine Rosicrucian in contact with Dee, was to propagate the Madoc story).[3]

And in August 1578, at her summons, Dee went before the Queen at Norwich with twelve scrolls of vellum setting out her title to Atlantic empire. They are lost, but if another set he presented two years later was in truth a summary of them, they would have argued for British dominion over most of the Arctic and the North Atlantic based on the conquests of Arthur and other British-Welsh heroes and, in particular, over the whole eastern American coast, known as *La Florida,* based on Madoc's alleged twelfth-century journeys. The Queen discussed her Title with Dee at Richmond.

Within days, however, Dee had to record that he had succumbed to a fit. For Gilbert's first venture failed and Dee's fellow London-Welshman, William Cecil Lord Burghley, Elizabeth's great statesman, viewed Dee with that hooded-eyed Welsh suspicion which I normally associate with Aberystwyth but which perhaps came appropriately to a man from the Welsh-speaking district of Herefordshire confronted by one from English-speaking Radnorshire. Dee had nightmares of Burghley burning his books. He became paranoid. He stripped to stare at himself in the mirror, 'my skin all overwrought with work like some kind of tuft mockado with crosses blue and red'. He was plagued by the whispering campaign against him as a black magician and conjuror. His marriage and the birth of a son (called Arthur naturally) he records in passing in a journal gloomily obsessed with his great imperial project.

During 1580, matters improved. Simon Fernandez, the Azores pilot and pirate often based with his fellow John Callice at Cardiff and Penarth, went on a quick reconnaissance to *Norumbega,* the New England area, and returned to report to Dee at Mortlake. Gilbert revived his colonisation project and promised Dee vast grants of land north of the 50° degree latitude, which would have given him much of modern Canada. On 3 October 1580, Dee was once more summoned to court. There he presented the Queen formal and powerful claims to the North Atlantic evidently serviced by a small team of cartographers. One set survives; it is a superbly executed map with a full and formal Title Royal worked out on the dorse.[4]

This Title Royal, in which Madoc first enters historical discourse, is the first pronunciamento of British Empire, a term which Dee himself is said to have coined.

It was, then, a London-Welshman, a Welsh patriot acutely conscious of his Welshness, who seems to have invented the expression *British Empire.* This was appropriate. Since at least the tenth century, the century of Hywel Dda and his One Law for One Wales, this tiny and marginal people the Welsh have survived by anchoring themselves in variant forms of Britishness. Hywel Dda was the second of those High Kings which the Welsh, like their cousins the Irish, created in crisis. The first, the ninth-century Rhodri Mawr, Dr John Dee was to claim as his ancestor. But Hywel it was who defined a political Wales and defined it as a junior partner of a Britain loosely controlled by the new 'English' dynasty of Wessex. Not until the tenth century did the peoples to the west of Offa's Dyke even begin to think of themselves as Welsh. Up to that point, they conceived of themselves essentially as British, deprived of their Britain by the Treachery of the Long Knives of landless Saxon pirates. As late as that tenth century, *Armes Prydein*, a polemical poem written by a south Wales cleric in opposition to Hywel's pro-Wessex policy, forced on him, of course, by the Viking menace, concentrated anti-Saxon minds not on a Welsh but on a British identity. The longest and most fecund tradition in Welsh history, from the moment of visible birth of Welsh writing in the sixth century in the verse attributed to Aneirin, which is British verse written in what is today Scotland about battles in what is today Yorkshire in defence of Romano-British polity against Northumbria, is the British and Arthurian tradition, shot through with those memories of Romano-Celtic Britain which so infuse that magnificent collection of stories whose survivors were grouped in the nineteenth century under the title *Mabinogion*. It was this which governed the mind of the Welsh: a tradition of mythical history, Heroic Age values, redemptive prophecy, a hard, jewelled, mosaic tradition, already old in the sixth century and remote from that Celtic Twilight which later Welsh writers tried to live up to, after the English had invented it. Under the Tudors that British-Arthurian tradition became virtually official state doctrine. For of all the British identities within which this tiny people anchored itself, Tudor Britain was inevitably the most Welsh.[5]

A story current at the Tudor court had St Peter reduced to despair by a sudden influx of Welsh into Heaven, driving everyone mad with their incessant talk. He arranged for an angel to stand outside the gates and cry in a loud voice, *'Caws Pôb'* (toasted cheese, evidently the original Welsh rarebit). The Welsh thundered out in a stampede after their national delicacy and the gates were slammed shut behind them, to everyone's intense relief.

Henry Tudor, of course, was a descendant of those great survivors, the Tudurs of Anglesey, stock of Ednyfed Fychan, seneschal to Llywelyn the Great. Henry, reared for his first fourteen years at Pembroke, spoke Welsh and spoke English with a Welsh accent. When he landed at Milford Haven in 1485, his agents drenched Wales in the old Arthurian traditions in their novel political persona. Henry took pains to consult a celebrated Welsh diviner near Machynlleth; he depended utterly on a Welsh rally to carry him into England. At Bosworth, he unfurled the Red Dragon of Cadwaladr the Blessed. 'A worthy sight it was to see', says the Ballad of the Rose of England, 'how the Welsh rose wholly with him and shogged them to Shrewsbury.' And to his victory Te Deum in London, the Welsh came shogging in herds, for Merlin's prophecy had at last come true. Henry VII made sure it would: he called his eldest son Arthur. 'The Welsh', said the Venetian ambassador, first professional in that craft, 'may now be said to have recovered their former independence for the most wise and fortunate Henry VII is a Welshman'.

This was politic play-acting, but the accession of Henry VII initiated that Tudor century which liberated the Welsh from colonialism, introduced them as junior partners into the merchant capitalism of the sixteenth century, at the price of the expulsion of their language from the state and official life, its segregation into a sacral, sacred area of experience which by the eighteenth century was becoming marginal. An immediate consequence was a major migration of the Welsh to the centre of power. Dafydd Seisyllt from the Welsh-speaking region of Herefordshire (old Erging-Archenfield of the Silures, potent and creative marcher land of the Welsh) went up to London as a sergeant of Henry's guard; he bought land and installed his son as court page. His grandson was William Cecil, Lord Burghley, whose kinsfolk still lived in Erging. The Seisyllts, in a transfiguration which was to become commonplace, transmuted into the Cecils who are, as we all know, all too much with us still, late and soon. Morgan Williams from Glamorgan set up as a brewer in Putney, prospered, married a sister of Thomas Cromwell, Henry VIII's powerful minister; in three generations, after the customary mutations, the family under its new name produced Oliver. Spotting these somewhat diluted 'Welshmen' among the elite became as much of a national pastime among later stay-at-homes as it was among those British Jews whom in some respects they resemble.

There were hordes of lesser imitators. The London-Welsh emerge as the surrogate capital of their invertebrate homeland and the process reached its climax under Elizabeth I, 'that red-headed Welsh harridan' as A.L. Rowse called her, presumably in what passes for wit in Cornwall, when Blanche Parry from Welsh Herefordshire and cousin to John Dee, ran her household and acted as focus for a whole Welsh

curial coterie in legal, naval, academic and professional circles, when
Welsh intellectuals concentrated in such force around the Queen's
immediate entourage and behind the first thrust for naval growth and
American colonisation. Under Elizabeth, for the first time in centuries,
the Welsh Church ceased to serve as outdoor relief for deserving and
destitute Europeans. Many Welsh bishops had previously been unable
even to speak English (admittedly a disability they shared with most of
their flock) but under the Virgin Queen thirteen of the sixteen bishops
appointed to Welsh sees were Welshmen. In 1571 Jesus College Oxford
was created as a specifically Welsh college, apt symbol of the whole
movement.

The impact was no less powerful in the intellectual field. For a
Protestant England had to struggle for its Protestantism, for its
independent 'empire', for its place in the sun, against that Counter-
Reformation Spain which was monopolising the new-found lands in
America. Intellectually and emotionally central to this enterprise was
the assertion of an aboriginally independent and imperial British
identity. The historical roots of this island polity, of necessity, had to be
sought in those remote ages, the time of giants, when Albion was an
empire and its Christianity free from Rome. The mythical British
history of the Welsh, which established Brutus the Trojan as the
progenitor of Britain, Joseph of Arimathea as the founder of its
independent Christianity and, buried at the same Glastonbury, Arthur
of Britain as its great hero, grew to become quasi-official doctrine
under Elizabeth. Geoffrey of Monmouth's *British History* of the
twelfth century, with its Welsh and Breton roots, its gigantic King
Arthur straddling the European and much of the extra-European
world, became an ever-extending heartland of patriotic ideology.
Protestantism was derived from the ancient seventh-century struggle
of the Celtic church in Wales against St Augustine and his Roman
corruptions. This new Britishness inevitably took much of its tone and
colour from those Welsh who had been its first celebrants and were still
its most direct inheritors. The Tudors necessarily devoted much time
to legitimising genealogies tracing their line back through Welsh and
British kings to Arthur and Brutus. In this new Britain, the Welsh with
their British tongue, could recover a respectable and central identity,
the English create a new and useful one, under those Tudors who *were*
the Return of Arthur prophesied by Merlin.[6]

It is no accident that this British and Arthurian cycle reached its
climax, in learning, poetry, public ritual and propaganda, in the late
1570s and 1580s, the days of Spenser's *Faerie Queene,* when relations

between England and Spain degenerated into open war, when the
excommunication of Elizabeth brought down repression on English
Catholics, when the voyages of Drake, Hawkins, Gilbert and Raleigh
culminated in the crisis of the Spanish Armada. It was to this imperial
construction that the *Worthiness of Wales,* to quote one of its English
celebrants Thomas Churchyard, and Welshmen like Dr John Dee
were central.

Born in 1527 to a Welsh court official, John Dee became one of the
foundation Fellows of Trinity College Cambridge in 1546. He moved
to Louvain because English humanism was inadequate in science and
established intimate contact with some of the seminal minds in
mathematics and geography: Gemma Phrysius the Flemish
Cosmographer to the Emperor, Gerard Mercator the great map-
maker and Abraham Ortelius of Antwerp. Dee was an astounding
polymath. The lectures of this 23-year-old at Paris were a sensation; he
was to be courted by princes all over Europe. He returned to England
with navigational devices like the balestila or cross-staff, was taken up
by the Queen, established himself among the Dudleys, the retinue of
the Earl of Leicester and the Sidneys, and at the heart of the
Elizabethan Renaissance. A brilliant mathematician like Robert
Recorde of Pembrokeshire before him, he published an augmentation
of Recorde's *Grounde of Artes,* a mathematical textbook which ran to
26 editions by 1662 and wrote his own seminal Preface to the English
translation of Euclid. With his remarkable library at Mortlake, this
Mechanicien of the Plat Politicall of the Brytish Monarchie became the
thinker behind most of the ventures of the English in their search for
the North-East and North-West Passages to Cathay, pouring out
treatises, maps, instructions, in his characteristic blend of technology,
science, imperialism, speculation, fantasy and the occult.

He was also, of course, like Kepler after him, as much magician as
scientist, a caller of devils holding converse with angels, the Arch
Conjuror of England. He was once imprisoned under Mary for trying
to 'enchant' the Queen and when he left for Poland and Prague in 1583,
the London crowd sacked his library as the den of a black magician. He
is said to have been the model for both Shakespeare's white Prospero
and Marlowe's black Faust: 'tis magic, magic which hath ravished
me...

Although she may sometimes have pursued her remarkable
researches with a perhaps Rosicrucian passion, it is Dame Frances
Yates who has restored John Dee to his full Renaissance stature. He
falls into place not only among the Hermetic and neo-Platonist

thinkers but among the practitioners of that older Jewish Cabala brought to Christian Europe by the Sephardic Jews expelled from Spain in 1492, a tradition earlier than the more widespread Lurian Cabala of the Diaspora. This was a Cabala which focused understanding on the concept of number and proportion, on the manipulation of the sacred letters of the language which God gave to Moses, and on the secret, divine language hidden within it, on the penetration to truth through numerology and the multiple Names of God. Transmitted through the Florentine Pico della Mirandola, the Venetian Francesco Giorgi and the German Henry Cornelius Agrippa and drawing on a tradition of Christian Cabala derived from the Catalan Ramon Lull and the German Reuchlin, this in the high noon of Renaissance audacity transmuted into a creed which strove to transcend not merely Protestantism and Catholicism but Christianity and Judaism themselves, which married numerology and mathematics, astrology and astronomy, magic and science. Before it was extinguished in the hideous religious wars, it was evolving a concept of a universe of three spheres: the elemental world which could be assimilated through medicine and philosophy, the physics of Agrippa's curriculum; the celestial, the stars, intermediaries between the human world and the Creator with his angels, which could be assimilated through astrology and mathematics, the mathematics of Agrippa's curriculum; finally the super-celestial, the realm of those angels who were intellectual concepts and could be approached only through the study of religious ceremonies and above all the Jewish Cabala, key to the original language which God gave mankind. Cabala, linked with the magic which embraced all three spheres and could enable the Magus to converse with angels directly, was the key to a world-renovating belief which would transcend the ferocity of doctrinal war on earth.

In all this, of course, there were the seeds of a genuinely scientific outlook, though the magic frame had to be broken before that outlook could emerge. John Dee's Preface to Euclid is a landmark in mathematical thought . . . 'By number a way is to be had to the searching out and understanding of every thing able to be known...' He had a grasp of abstract mathematical theory, particularly that of proportion based on the work of the Roman architect Vitruvius; he applied it in practice with his navigators, artisans and technicians. But he also summoned angels and held conversations with them through the medium Edward Kelley and the mystical Polish prince Laski. He built on Agrippa and the German artist Albrecht Dürer and through number reached out to the super-celestial world by means of the Jewish Cabala. His diagram the Monas which was so secret he feared he had committed a mortal sin by publishing it, combines signs of the seven planets, the zodiac Aries for fire, a species of alchemy, a strong mathematical thrust and above all the Cabala, 'the stupendous fabric of the Hebrew letters'. He ended as a proponent of a world science-cum-magic expressed in a politico-religious Empire opposed to that of Rome, the Habsburgs and the Jesuits, grounded in that Elizabethan Empire which had such ancient British roots, stretching back into Patriarchal times themselves.

Such an Empire was bound to be Welsh in origin. Dee was totally committed to the old British and hence Welsh traditions of island empire. He steeped himself in those traditions: 'the origins and chiefe points of our ancient British histories . . .' was the title he gave many of his laboriously constructed texts which are now lost. He traced his own genealogy to Rhodri Mawr, claimed kinship with the Tudors, immersed himself in the new chorography, the detailed topographical survey which was to culminate in a definitive British history and which gave birth to William Camden's magnificent *Britannia.* In secular reality, or rather, to be precise, in that secular mythology which *was* historical reality to his age, such an empire could only be Arthur's.

'O Glastonbury! O Glastonbury!' Dee wrote in his *Pety Navy Royall,* 'that Apostle-like Joseph, that triumphant British Arthur!'. What Britain needed were a Christian Aristotle and a Christian Alexander; these Dee as a British Philosopher, modestly offered to provide. In his campaign for the building of a British navy of sixty tall ships and the mobilisation of British resources in the service of overseas expansion, he could summon up from strictly English precedent only that peaceable King Edgar, who had 4,000 ships according to the decidedly innumerate author of the *Flores Historiarum.* Dee quoted Edgar's obituary, but added 'and why not Arthurus Brytanis?' Why? Because Arthur had been a thorn in Saxon eyes and had defeated them twelve times. Edgar after all had been 'but a Saxon'; his progeny qualified for General Empire only because Albion was now (now underlined) the greater part of British Empire. 'But yet', said Dee, 'there is a little lock of LADY OCCASION, Flickering in the Ayre, by our hands, to catch hold on: whereby, we may, yet ones more (before all be utterly past and for ever) discretely and valiantly recover and enjoy, if not all our Ancient and due Appurtenances to this Imperiall Brytish Monarchy, yet, at the least, some such Notable Portion thereof.'

For the British Arthur had enlarged his realms much further long before the days of Edgar. Dee, as Elizabeth's British Philosopher, was about 'to open the door of his philosophical and political British furniture' to reveal to the Queen, herself descended from Arthur, the true foundations of her English or rather British state. For if sea power had been the stay of the Athenian state, how much more was this true of the British Empire, 'O Albion, O Britain, O England and I say thrice times over, O Brytan yet again.'

And in his *Famous and Rich Discoveries,* Dee went on to thunder out a roll-call of Arthur's great conquests in the North. He used two major sources. One was William Lambard's *Archaionomia* of 1568. Lambard was a celebrated jurist versed in Arthurian lore and, using an 'ancient text', he said of Arthur, 'His kingdome was too little for him and his mind was not contented with it'; so he subdued 'all Scantia [now called Norway] and all the Islands beyond Norway, to wit Iceland and Greenland which are appurtayning to Norway', and he went on into a sonorous chant, listing all Arthur's kingdoms which ranged from Lapland and Russia through Scandinavia into the Arctic and to the Pole.[7] There had evidently been a massive extension of Arthur's mythical conquests; Geoffrey of Monmouth in the twelfth century had contented himself with Iceland and 'the Six Islands of the Ocean Sea'. This roll-call of Lambard's reverberates through the sixteenth century and seems to have its origin in French texts. William Worcestre, a Bristol antiquarian familiar with that city's ventures into the Atlantic in search of the magic island of Brazil which might have taken Bristol men to America before Columbus, certainly knew of such Arthurian conquests from French manuscripts.[8] This testimony Dee fused with that of the apocryphal journeys of the Zeno brothers of Venice, published in 1558 and best known in England from Ramusio's collection of voyages of 1574. The Zeni peopled the fourteenth-century Arctic with imaginary islands which were duly to figure in the great world maps of Mercator and Ortelius and which Dee allotted to Arthur.[9]

The critical moment, however, came in the summer of 1577, after he had finished his *Famous and Rich Discoveries*, when, in a reply to a query from Dee about his mapping of the polar regions, the great cosmographer Gerard Mercator sent him a letter summarising the testimony of the Flemish or Dutch explorer Jacob Cnoyen of s'Hertogenbosch. Cnoyen cited a mysterious but evidently fundamental text, the anonymous *Gestae Arthuri*, Deeds of Arthur.[10] This was very knowledgeable about the Arctic and quite patently drew heavily on the massive knowledge of the Icelanders (with their admixture of Celts) who had been sailing those seas as far as Markland (Labrador) and Vinland (Newfoundland) in America for centuries. The *Gestae* organised this knowledge in an Arthurian pattern; it had Arthur's great army penetrating the northern seas from Scotland in the sixth century, losing thousands of people but colonising the polar and American islands, thrusting Britain right up against the Pole. This *Gestae* was evidently rather late; it uses the travels of Marco Polo and recalls the fifteenth-century maps of the Dane Claudius Claves Swart, the first to depict Greenland, and themselves based on the explorations of the Icelanders; they were no less a source for the Zeni text. The *Gestae* attributed to Arthur the peopling of a mythical island Grocland, which in terms of the geography then known to Mercator, Ortelius and Dee, had to lie in the immediate vicinity of America. More startling still, Cnoyen asserted that in 1364, eight survivors of 'these people' including a Fleming by five generations' descent, had turned up in the court of the King of Norway at Bergen and had given an account of the polar journeys of an English friar who had presented yet another lost geographical text, the *Inventio Fortunatae*, to King Edward III. The latter book had certainly existed; it had been used by Martin Behaim for his first great globe and by Johannes Ruysch for his early maps; John Day had mentioned it in his famous letter to Columbus.[11]

This information, which was characteristically a blend of genuine geographical knowledge and fantasy, massively supplemented Dee's evidence on early British empire, 'Gestae Arturi', he wrote, 'a rare testimony of great importance to the Brytish title to the Septentrional Regions, Atlantis in particular'. But this information also stopped him in his tracks. These people of 1364 could not possibly have been descended from Arthur (his margins fill with entertaining calculations). Where then did these British or Welsh come from? Dee opened the door of his British furniture still further, in a search for Welsh adventurers later in date than Arthur. And in a history composed by Humphrey Llwyd, a celebrated Tudor geographer who was a protégé of the seminal Netherlands school, he came across Madoc, that Welsh prince who in 1170 was said to have sailed away from civil wars in Wales, to have found a marvellous land, returned for colonists, sailed off again to disappear. This land, Llwyd said, 'must needs be . . . by reason and order of Cosmographie' that American land the Spaniards claimed to have discovered.[12]

A Welsh seafarer Madoc had actually entered European discourse three centuries earlier, in a thirteenth-century romance by Willem of Ghent, the Fleming who composed the superb Dutch version of that medieval best-seller *Reynard the Fox*. His romance was probably based on historical personalities, on the exploits of those Welsh half-Vikings who had appeared in the Celtic-Scandinavian world of the Irish Sea since the tenth century. One such, a Freeman of Wales who raided their settlements from Lundy Island, had registered in the sagas of the Icelanders themselves in the middle of the twelfth century. For Dee, this clinched it. According to his friend John David Rhys, another of these Welsh Europeans, who had taught at Siena, Venice and Padua, travelled in Crete and Cyprus and published best-selling books on Italian grammar and pronunciation in Italy, Dee unearthed a map showing the tracks of Madoc and the Oxford astronomer far out in the Atlantic. Dee at one time was speculating that Madoc might have reached Bermuda, which was itself possibly a model for Prospero's island in *The Tempest*.[13]

It was Madoc who knit Dee's British Empire together. In the Title Royal presented to Elizabeth in 1580, he heads the list. Thence, Madoc swept into British and European discourse, to lodge in the very first pre-eminence, supported by all those other heroes surging up out of the Welsh pre-history of Britain, in that very voice of the new British imperialism, Richard Hakluyt's classic *Principall Navigations* of 1589.[14] For one brief generation, the Worthiness of Wales reached its Tudor climax in Madoc and all his kin as the symbolic spearpoint of the first British thrust into a New World. John Dee's mystical British world empire was translated into an earthier reality.

Dee himself did not witness this directly. In 1583, he took off on his vast but abortive mission to Europe, to return to a Jacobean England which had turned chilly to the kind of thinking he represented, to be banished to an English Siberia in Manchester, to die in poverty and neglect and to suffer three centuries' scorn as an eccentric and a fraud.

The point about Dr John Dee is that, striking as he was as an individual, he was also in some senses representative. He and that whole cluster of Welsh Tudor humanists to which he belonged (for there were dozens of them) were also the organic intellectuals of a class; that class we lumber with the unhelpful description *gentry*, a class which had climbed through two centuries of colonialism over the ruins of Welsh principality and aristocracy alike, to be hoisted to their summit by Thomas Cromwell with his Welsh brother-in-law and his Acts of Union. They were the first Welsh intellectuals fully to enter an English language cultural universe through a British identity. Their entry marks a decisive bifurcation in Welsh tradition. At the very moment when John Dee was carrying this new British Welshness to its climax, the Welsh-language poets Edmund Prys and William Cynwal were locked in an enervating combat, the eisteddfodau at Caerwys were failing to regenerate the poets' guild and its culture. A culture which had been buoyant and innovatory in the fifteenth century stammered before the Renaissance and the new frontiers even as it was brutally expelled from political life in the first attack by the English state on the Welsh language. It now seems to me that the experience of the first major constellation of Welsh writers in English is in some, perhaps limited but nevertheless central, senses, *exemplary.*

Welsh historiography, like Welsh history and the Welsh landscape itself has been grotesquely mutilated. Welsh historiography is almost as hallucinatory as Spanish historiography has been until recently. G.M. Trevelyan once called social history, history with the politics left out. The history of Arnold Toynbee has been called history with the history left out. A great deal of Welsh history has been Welsh history with the Welsh left out.

One crippling deformation has been the fairly recent divergence in language which has become mutually exclusive and sometimes hostile. In recent generations, this, as it were, extended backwards in time, to create multiple historiographies which are in some vital senses no less mutually exclusive; they have sometimes been quite alien to each other, like the 'memories' of two mutually insulated 'nations'. They are both totally inadequate. We lack an effective and credible history of the Welsh intellect, of Welsh writing and of the condition of production of Welsh writing.

Two models seem to me helpful. One is Gerald Brenan's remarkable history of the literature of the Spanish people. In order to write a history of the literature of the Spanish people, Brenan had to deploy eight languages. Any serious and effective history of the Welsh intellect will need to deploy at least four (leaving out of account Caernarfon Welsh and Cardiff English) and, moreover — and infinitely more exacting — to give adequate weight to each in historical context and in a complex inter-acting totality. In this respect, the second model seems to me the seminal work (work of a European and indeed world significance) of Raymond Williams. I am thinking in particular of his essays on *The Long Revolution, Keywords, Marxism and Literature* and his testimony in *Politics and Letters.* There is no socio-cultural work on Wales of comparable calibre and scope in either English or Welsh, though some recent studies demonstrate an approach to it. The production of such work has become an urgent necessity. To no people's history are the concepts of Antonio Gramsci more relevant, whichever of the four historic languages is involved.

Here, I think the experience of this Tudor generation may prove exemplary. They were deeply Welsh, Welsh patriots who knew no conflict of languages. They used English as centrally as Latin. They were peculiarly *European* in formation; the content and drift of their thinking were quite distinctly European rather than narrowly English. This had been true of successive generations of Welsh organic intellectuals of course since the twelfth century, when the Normans prised Wales out of the Celtic-Scandinavian world of the Irish Sea and inserted it into Latin Europe.

The Normans also drew a frontier across the bony face of Wales. Consider that frontier. It lasted for five hundred years. Nations have been born, lived a span and died in less time. That frontier, the frontier between March and *Pura Wallia*, has appeared and reappeared throughout our history. Merchant capitalism, Puritanism, Old Dissent as opposed to Methodism, industrial capitalism, the English language, all rooted themselves in the easier, more accessible lands of the March. Today that frontier is a frontier in matters great and small, between two languages (where it can sometimes seem like a Berlin Wall between two civilisations), between a Wales which is dry on a Sunday and a Wales which is wet, a Wales which is radical and a Wales which is conservative. Consider the Serbs and Croats, two people biologically close, indeed biologically one, split by a political demarcation line which subjected them to the radically different disciplines of Habsburgs and Turks. They evolved into two mutually hostile nations. The line was never so hard in Wales. It was constantly crossed; it constantly served as a zone of interaction. It was repeatedly swept away by those upsurges from the Welsh people themselves, whatever rulers they were subjected to, upsurges of an irreducibly Welsh identity whose survival over a millennium and a half constitutes one of the minor miracles of history. Nevertheless the persistence of a line first drawn through this few and fragile people in the twelfth century suggests a certain historical congruity.

The March drew most of the Welsh into Europe, made the Welsh a European people. In response, the Welsh turned their rich oral traditions into a scintillating written literature simultaneously Welsh and European. They gave Europe one of its most formative literary-historical experiences. The Arthurian traditions were transmitted into Europe and the Crusader states as coveys of interpreters, Welsh, English, Breton, Norman, Fleming, transformed the conditions of literary production. Welsh knights, Welsh towns, Welsh merchants appeared; Welsh shipping nosed into the Gironde. Henry le Waleys of Chepstow could serve as mayor of London and Bordeaux; Welsh students could move to Paris where John of Wales shone, and to its offshoot Oxford. The Welsh moved more often into a mainstream of European rather than specifically English creativity.

This is even more striking in the Tudor generation of course. These men were now free of the English language, indeed masters of it some of them, but they were so only because the Tudors had liberated them and made England into *Britain*. They were very noticeably *European* in their formation and style. This was even more true of their less numerous but no less brilliant Catholic rivals, of the tragic saga of the Catholic exiles, when Gruffydd Robert could produce his Welsh grammar on St David's Day in the Milan of his patron Carlo Borromeo, when Morris Clynog could publish his Welsh Christian Doctrine in Rome. The Welsh students in Rome, Milan, Douai and Valladolid were not strong enough to carry clout and they became, interestingly enough, as anti-Jesuit as any John Dee; their Europeanism is of a similar quality.

Moreover and possibly more striking still, this characteristic remains true of that second cluster of organic intellectuals in and through English at the end of the eighteenth century, Iolo Morganwg, William Owen and their kin. These new Welsh, in both periods, used English in their creative work, were European in formation and style, intensely *British* but not English in their identity, and American in their ultimate focus.

That pattern I find to be recurrent from the sixteenth century into the *Jacobins*. I cannot say as yet whether it survives as anything more concrete than metaphor after the earthquake from the 1790s. I do not know whether this peculiar formation survives the passage across the most dramatic dividing line in the history of the Welsh, when the Welsh population graph becomes a right angle, when two-thirds of the people are sucked into an English-speaking and continuously revolutionising south-east, when a new imperial and democratic industrial civilisation is created and a new Welsh populist identity claws its way into existence. Nevertheless, when one considers the highly distinctive pattern of Welsh industrialisation, far more American than English in its rhythm and manner, when one broods over the all-pervasive

American character of its so-called 'anglicisation', when one thinks of its massive British commitment and explores whatever of Europe there might be in it (a sight more than might appear at first inspection) and when one further recalls that this Americanism, Europeanism and Britishness all appear to be in incipient dissolution, some serious exploration of a possibly exemplary generation in Tudor times at the point of cultural bifurcation seems called for. Raymond Williams, in his latest writing, has begun to call himself a Welsh European and in a distinctive, differentiating, indeed distancing sense.

I conclude, then, by suggesting that this generation of Dr John Dee, this first major generation of Welsh writers who used English as their creative medium, European in formation, non-English British in identity and American in ultimate focus, may repay a study different in form and purpose from any they have yet been subjected to. This would not only be a worthwhile project in its own right; it would help to re-set the historical analysis of collective mentalities among the Welsh, an analysis which is at present badly skewed. It might establish a method and a style which could prove of wider application.

I personally believe that this generation of John Dee can serve as a symbol, a sign, a *monas*, if you like; a *monas* to exemplify the process by which what was a condition of creative work for a fistful of intellectuals has become the historical predicament of a people.

Notes

1. On John Dee, I have used his own work, *Famous and Rich Discoveries,* British Library Reference Division, Cottonian Ms. Vitellius C.vii and his writing in Augustus I,1,i and in Caligula A.vi; his printed *General and Rare Memorials Pertayning to the Perfecte Arte of Navigation* (London, 1577); *The Private Diary of Dr John Dee,* ed. J.O. Halliwell (Camden Society, London, 1842); among secondary works, central of course, is the brilliant scholarship of Dame Frances Yates, in many volumes, of which perhaps her *The Occult Philosophy in the Elizabethan Age* (Routledge and Kegan Paul, London, 1979) is most relevant; see also a stimulating work in the same tradition, P.J. French, *John Dee: the world of an Elizabethan Magus* (Routledge and Kegan Paul, London, 1972).
2. See Chapter 2 of this volume, Druids and Democrats.
3. Apart from the works already cited, see the magnificent *The Hakluyt Handbook,* ed. D.B. Quinn, 2 vols. (Hakluyt Society, London, 1974); E.G.R. Taylor, *Tudor Geography 1485-1583* (Methuen, London, 1930); D.B. Quinn, *England and the Discovery of America 1481-1620* (Allen and Unwin, London, 1974) especially part III.
4. This beautiful map may be found in British Library Reference Division Cottonian Ms. Augustus I,1,i; it is analysed in detail in W.F. Ganong, 'Crucial Maps, IX', *Proceedings and Transactions of the Royal Society of Canada,* ser. 3, xxxi (1937) section 2, pp. 113-16; discussed in D.B. Quinn, *Voyages and Colonising Enterprises of Sir Humphrey Gilbert,* 2 vols., (Hakluyt Society, London, 1938), pp. 52-3 and reproduced in part in the end-pocket; there are relevant illustrations and text in the superb compilation,

W.P. Cumming, R.A. Skelton and D.B. Quinn (eds.), *The Discovery of North America* (Elek, London, 1971) esp. pp. 174, 177, 215; on Fernandez, D.B. Quinn, 'A Portuguese pilot in the English service', *England and the Discovery of America*, Ch. 9.

5. This account of the Welsh in Tudor Britain, derived from multiple sources, is taken from my *Madoc: the making of a myth* (Eyre Methuen, London, 1980).

6. These themes are explored in many texts, notably T.D. Kendrick, *British Antiquity* (Methuen, London, 1950); Glanmor Williams, *Welsh Reformation Essays* (University of Wales, Cardiff, 1967); Frances Yates, *Astraea: The Imperial Theme in the Sixteenth Century* (Routledge and Kegan Paul, London, 1975); Charles B. Millican, *Spenser and the Table Round* (Harvard University Press, Cambridge, Mass., 1932, Cass, London, reprint 1967) and P.J. French, *John Dee*.

7. On Lambard, W. Dunkel, *William Lambard, Elizabethan Jurist 1536-1601* (Rutgers, New Jersey, 1965).

8. J.H. Harvey (ed.) *William Worcestre, Itineraries* (Oxford, 1969) introduction and Lambard insertion on p. 390; critical comments by D.B. Quinn, *England and the Discovery of America*, pp. 7-8, 31n, 57-8, 73.

9. The literature on the Zeni or pseudo-Zeni narrative is considerable; see T.E. Armstrong in *The Hakluyt Handbook*, p. 259 and the accounts, accompanied by maps, including sections of Mercator's, in *The Discovery of North America* pp. 213 and 271 ff.

10. For this remarkable letter, E.G.R. Taylor, 'A letter dated 1577 from Mercator to John Dee', *Imago Mundi*, xiii (1956), 56-68, which translates and comments on the original in Dutch and Latin in British Library Cottonian Ms. Vitellius C.vii, fo.266-269v; Tryggvi J. Oleson, *Early voyages and northern approaches 1000-1632* (Oxford University Press, Oxford, 1964) pp. 105-10; B.F. da Costa, *Inventio Fortunata* (reprint from *Bulletin of the American Geographical Society*, New York, 1881); D.B. Quinn, *England and the Discovery of America*, pp. 83-4, 106-9.

11. E.G. Ravenstein, *Martin Behaim, his life and his globe* (London, 1908); D.B. Quinn, *England and the Discovery of America*, pp. 83-4; B.F. da Costa, *Inventio Fortunata*, pp. 22-3; *The Discovery of North America* p. 214.

12. A manuscript copy of Llwyd's history which was made for John Dee, with marginal comments and interstitial corrections in Dee's hand, is in British Library Cottonian Ms. Caligula A. vi(1); the Madoc section is on fo. 150v-151; information on Llwyd's history is provided, of course, in the celebrated 'augmentation' of it by one of Dee's circle David Powel, in his *Historie of Cambria* (London, 1584). Llwyd's own *Breviary of Britayne*, first printed in Latin at Cologne in 1572 and Englished by Dee's friend Thomas Twyne in 1573 also has a little relevant material.

13. The key material is in E. Colledge (ed.) *Reynard the Fox and other medieval Netherlands secular literature* (London, 1967); J.W. Muller and J.D. Wolters on *Vos Reinaerde* (Leiden 1939 and Groningen, 1959): W.G. Hellinga, *Wie was Willem die de Reynaert schreef?* (1950?); J.F. Willens (ed.) with essay by O. Delepierre, *Le Roman du Renarde, traduit depuis un texte flamand du xii siècle* (Brussels, 1837); *The Orkneyingers' Saga*, trans. G.W. Dasent from ed. by G. Vigfusson (Rolls Series, London, 1887); Gwyn Jones, *The Norse Atlantic Saga* (Oxford, 1964); I have argued the case at some length in my *Madoc: the making of a myth*.

14. D.B. Quinn, introduction to photolithographic facsimile of Richard Hakluyt's *Principall Navigations* of 1589 (1965); the original of the *Principall Navigations* of 1598-1600; D.B. Quinn (ed.) *The Hakluyt Handbook*; E.G.R. Taylor (ed.) *The Original Writings and Correspondence of the two Richard Hakluyts*, 2 vols., (Hakluyt Society, London, 1935).

2 DRUIDS AND DEMOCRATS: ORGANIC INTELLECTUALS AND THE FIRST WELSH NATION*

'I am giving you the Patriarchal religion and theology, the Divine Revelation given to Mankind, and these have been retained in Wales until our own day': it was Iolo Morganwg speaking in 1792, a stonemason Bard of Liberty from the Vale of Glamorgan and a leading figure, along with the vivacious societies of the London-Welsh, in a Welsh literary-historical revival. He was announcing to the Welsh the rediscovery of their ancient Druidic tradition; he was giving them, for the first time in centuries, a coherent vision of their own past, to inform and direct the re-creation of their Nation. He was offering them in his newly-minted *Gorsedd*, or Order of Bards of the Island of Britain, a democratic organisation of their intelligentsia, a cadre of People's Remembrancers, as its instrument.[1]

A few months earlier, at one of the *eisteddfodau*[2] which the London-Welsh had revived in order to re-engage an interrupted tradition, in Llanrwst, a north Wales market centre of the remarkable stocking trade of an intensely poor and intensely Welsh mountain people, William Jones, a follower of Voltaire who lived in the village of Llangadfan as a teacher and country healer among the Welsh and Independent weavers of Montgomeryshire, circulated a dramatic Address. It announced that the Lost Brothers, the Welsh Indians descended from that brave and peace-loving Prince Madoc who had discovered America three hundred years before Columbus, had been found on the Far Missouri 'a free and distinct people . . . who . . . have preserved their liberty, language and some trace of their religion to this very day'. William Jones read the whole history of the Welsh as one long struggle against English oppression. He was composing a Welsh National Anthem, *Toriad y Dydd, Daybreak*, as a counter to *The Roast Beef of Old England* and he called on the Welsh to quit their Egyptian slave-masters and join their Lost Brothers to re-create Wales in the new Land of Liberty.[3]

---

*Unpublished until now. Written for a volume of essays in honour of Eric Hobsbawm, edited by Raphael Samuel and Gareth Stedman Jones and published by Routledge and Kegan Paul in 1982, *Culture, Ideology, Politics*.

A few months later, in 1793, Morgan John Rhys, a Baptist minister of Pontypool in the industrialising south, who published the French free-thinker Volney in Welsh translation and would have published Voltaire had not his printers taken fright, brought out the first political periodical in the Welsh language: *Y Cylchgrawn Cymraeg, The Welsh Journal.* Morgan John had launched a crusade for Protestant liberty in the revolutionary Paris of 1792. As the self-appointed Moses of the Welsh Nation, he was to ride the entire length of the new American Republic in 1794-5, to fight for a black church in Savannah, Georgia and for Indian identity at the peace talks at Greenville, Ohio which expelled the Iroquois from history. In 1795, he was to stand on 'the unbroken grass' west of that Ohio and, on Bastille Day, claim the American Frontier as a National Home for the Welsh People, a *Gwladfa.* In his *Journal,* he printed an Exhortation from a newly-resurrected and Jacobin Madoc to the renaissant Welsh: *Dyma ni yn awr ar daith ein gobaith,* Here we are now on the journey of our hope.[4]

In the 1790s, a handful of intellectuals in Wales, in common with men like them from other 'non-historic' peoples in Europe, those antiquarians, historians, poets, of the Czechs, the Catalans, Serbs, Croats, who were stamping nations out of the ground and weaving new tricolours out of old legends, summoned the Welsh to the re-creation of a Nation they had rediscovered. When they encountered indifference, hostility and repression in the Great Britain of the age of Atlantic revolution, they tried to transport that nation across the Atlantic.

This Welsh Nation of the intellectuals was born of an alternative society which had been slowly forming in Wales under the carapace of the gentry-parson squirearchy and which, no less than that *ancien régime,* was a product of Great Britain with its Atlantic dimension.

Welsh in a Great Britain

Great Britain took shape around the union of England and Scotland in 1707 and was built on merchant capitalism, imperialism, naval power and liberal oligarchy. In its sweep to maritime supremacy, its hegemony over the Atlantic trade with its slave economies, its agrarian modernisation with its unparalleled productivity, in its monstrously dominant capital of London, it evolved a highly unusual, indeed probably unique structure, in which what was in fact a multi-national state achieved a British uniformity and created a British nation, sanctified during the traumatic experience of the generation-long war against revolutionary and Napoleonic France, when Wellington and Nelson were erected into *British* heroes and *God Save Great George Our King* into a *British* national anthem.

The battles of the seventeenth century had destroyed absolutism and demystified monarchy, had established a Bank of England, religious toleration, a governing aristocracy which directed the state to mercantile and increasingly bourgeois objectives. They had created a powerful civil society and a parliament which could hire kings from the Dutch and the Germans. When the partisan conflicts of the later Stuarts were over, this polity, after disarming the English provinces and putting through a prudent restriction of the franchise, was able to ride commercial and agrarian growth into an extraordinarily relaxed and informal pattern of government.

It had to tolerate a licensed area of popular anarchy in times of dearth. It erected a law in defence of property and oligarchy which was terrifying in its severity but, except at moments of crisis, tolerant in its application.[5] It won a 'moment of consent' which lasted over a century and which acquired popular depth and resonance during the wars against revolutionary France. The government of this Great Britain reduced politics to the play of predatory faction around a Whig core under a broad, flexible, ruthless, semi-capitalist and innovatory oligarchy, which, in its hustings, its licensed mobs, its flexible web of libertarian traditions and its Freeborn Englishman mentality (systematised into an ideology in confrontation with American and French Revolutions) permitted the commons a voice.

This remarkable state, out of which a British *nation* emerged into historic existence, seems to be taken for granted by English historians. Frustrated and aspirant Europeans of the eighteenth century certainly perceived it as extraordinary; many took this modern 'Republic of Venice' as their model. Within it, the Welsh, like the Slovaks during the Austro-Hungarian Empire, had 'disappeared' into the dominant partner. Their pattern of response, in both assimilation and resistance, was not un-Slovak either, though the organic intelligentsia which the growth of this Great Britain created in its Welsh province at the end of the eighteenth century behaved more like Czechs. For the effects of this almost insensible growth of Great Britain and its Atlantic dependency on Wales were far more serious than those of the seventeenth-century struggles, for all the latter's drama.

The economy of Wales, essentially a Tudor creation, experienced subtle but significant change. Poor and marginal in general terms, it may have been one of the few regions of Britain which still had 'peasants' (though this is becoming increasingly doubtful). What has been overlooked, however, is the extent to which it had already been penetrated, and was increasingly being directed, by merchant capitalism of an imperial character, with its attendant rural proto-industrialisation. Even the tiny and scattered charcoal furnaces of south Wales were producing a sixth of British pig iron in 1720. The Shropshire iron industry, going over to coal, pulled well ahead and by 1788 was producing twice as much. In that year, however, south Wales, still accounting for a sixth of British output, had seen the first giant and integrated plants raised by London and Bristol capital, derived essentially from the Atlantic slave trade and the Indian Empire, and by Midlands technology, on its hill-country coalfield, it was beginning to use coal and, in the puddling process, the 'Welsh method', it had just acquired the key to its meteoric expansion in the 1790s, when it established, and maintained for two generations, a 40 per cent grip on the pig iron production of Britain. In the mid-eighteenth century it was in no sense the virginal land which the celebrated ironmaster dynasties of Crawshay and Guest allegedly deflowered.

Far more striking were copper, tinplate and their related industries. British production centred almost wholly on the Swansea-Neath area in the south, which was in turn linked to the mines of northern Anglesey, where Thomas Williams had established virtually a world monopoly. Copper, brass, tinplate (with a base in south-eastern Monmouthshire and its Pontypool japanning plants as well) were directed almost wholly to Atlantic export, particularly to the West Indies and the world the slave empires fed. The ultimate destination of south Wales iron is less visible, with Ireland looming large as an early customer, but this whole sector of the economy was essentially mercantile-imperialist in character.[6]

This was no less true, however, of more traditional, less organised and less capitalised trades which were turning whole tracts of rural Wales into networks of 'factory parishes'.[7] The cloth trade had migrated to mid and north Wales since Tudor times and was subjected to the Shrewsbury Drapers. Its farm-based production was turning the country people of a great tranch of Wales, running from Machynlleth on the west coast, in a broad arc through Merioneth and Montgomeryshire in the north and north-centre to Denbighshire and the English borderlands, into a population of rural industrial workers with demographic and life-chance rhythms radically different from those of 'traditional peasants'. Most of that production went out through Blackwell Hall to Europe and the Americas. Even the poorer quality cloth of rock-ribbed Merioneth, and above all its intense stocking trade which could produce sales of £18,000 at markets in Bala and Llanrwst, went through the busy little port of Barmouth to Charleston and the Gulf of Mexico, to serve British soldiers, poor whites and American slaves.

Shropshire, whose technicians were revolutionising iron production in Glamorgan and Monmouth, was also stimulating growth on the north-eastern coalfield which, while ultimately abortive, was at first of a southern intensity and turned Denbigh and Flint into potent centres of innovation. In the late eighteenth century, in fact, the largest concentration of people in Wales was in the parishes of Wrexham in the north-east around the biggest fair in the Principality; 8,000 lived there. There were only 6,000 in Swansea which had developed, however, into a fully-articulated if miniature, mercantile, social and intellectual capital. The whole south, like Denbighshire, had a scatter of industry and improving landlords; the Vale of Glamorgan and south Pembrokeshire were the nearest approach to the champion farming country of southern England. There was a cluster of lively little towns, over-supplied with artisan crafts, professional men and printers, in Carmarthen, Brecon, Haverfordwest, Neath, Denbigh and Caernarfon, and a brisk if forgotten fraternity of seamen, particularly numerous on the western coasts facing Ireland and the Atlantic. Even the 'peasant' society of allegedly self-subsistent hill-farmers had developed a major drovers' trade in store cattle which sent great herds into England, Wales's 'Spanish silver fleet', bringing back currency, breeding banks and its own peculiar guild of organic intellectuals, who were to prove of some cultural significance.

This lively if porous mercantile capitalism was transforming much of rural Wales, had created pockets of modernisation and reservoirs of technical skills and had turned the economy of a country measuring scarcely 200 miles from end to end into a plurality of modes of production. Major work has still to be done in this field, but it would appear at present that merchant capitalism had not effected any profound structural change before the explosive impact of industrial capitalism in the 1790s. To the human beings subjected to it, it appeared to operate on the margins and in the interstices of a population of about half a million who were still penned to the mountain core of Wales's hollow heart. The stockings which went out to the Gulf of Mexico from Merioneth were knitted by a poverty-stricken people who used to gather *en masse* over the winter in chosen farmhouses to save money on candles; entertained by harpists and singers, they turned the area into a legendary stronghold of Welsh vernacular culture, as it was later to be of Dissenting ministers and craggy polemicists over Biblical texts in the Sunday Schools. There was a very similar stocking-trade concentration in the south-west around Llandovery and Tregaron in that land no less legendary in the history and mythology of Welsh-language popular culture and Dissent, the land which lived by seasonal migration to the lowlands and England, the Galicia of Wales and the district in closest human contact with the America of the Nonconformists. North Wales was passing from the control of Shrewsbury to that of Liverpool; Bristol enmeshed the south; the London-Welsh were still the main source of native funds and enterprise. Many of the Welsh, on their upland farms and at their treadmill of loom and spinning wheel, were trapped in a back-breaking poverty and an economy of unremitting colonial dependence.

Nevertheless, there was a panic over American Independence in Dolgellau in 1775 and it was when Barmouth was closed during the French wars that Merioneth, like Montgomeryshire and Denbighshire, lurched into its *Jacobin* crisis of proletarianisation, pauperisation, radicalisation and millenial emigration. Merchant capitalism, with its multiplying rural dependents, its small concentrations of urban industry, its colonies of skilled workers, its little shipping fleets, its merchants, salesmen and hucksters and above all, perhaps, in the crafts and professions it called into existence or nurtured to service it, was sending ripples of insistent change through slow-moving parishes. Throughout the eighteenth century there is a shuffling but visible rise in the numbers of artisans, craftsmen, professional agents of the service sectors, many of them 'on tramp', a notable increase in the strength of the professions, lawyers, teachers, doctors, a surprising number of them of relatively humble origin.

This steady rise of what later generations would call a 'lower middle class', moreover, accompanied a dramatic fall in the status of that numerically strong lesser gentry of Wales, a product of its old kindred social structure and a characteristic feature of its distinct identity. From the late seventeenth century, landholding became once more an aristocratic and thrusting business. Under the spur of agricultural change and commercial growth, the great estate made the running. The lesser gentry of Wales could not stand the pace. They lost their traditional anchorage in the universities and the Inns of Court, in politics and Parliament; they lost their toe-hold in the dominant culture. They shrank back into a merely local and precarious prestige and even there, they were challenged by the multiplying 'middle orders'. The consequences were serious for Wales's political structure and its sense of identity.[8]

By the eighteenth century, some 30 to 40 parliamentary families, worth perhaps £3000 - £5000 a year, monopolised Commons seats and the patronage which went with them.[9] Beneath them, the local gentry, the £500-a-year men, perhaps 25 to 50 families a county, served as JPs with their parsons and ran the place through their country club of a Quarter Sessions. In some relatively affluent counties like Glamorgan and Denbigh, as many as 1,500 men could vote and the forty-shilling freeholder was a force. The tiny boroughs, forty villages in the squires' pockets, were well under control; voters could be created virtually at will to ward off local malcontents or some new rich 'nabob' horning in. Before the constitutional conflicts of the late eighteenth century, genuinely political issues were largely absent and rarely disturbed the even tenor of traditional practice among the 20,000 to 25,000 Welshmen who possessed the franchise, though a challenge could turn elections into Eatanswill orgies and precipitate bankruptcies. Encrusted with its dependent interest groups, buttressed by its myriad hungry servitors and lubricated by deferential but robust Church-and-King ideologies which could find room for Welsh sentiment or sentimentality if safely antiquarian or anodyne in cultural content, the system worked well enough for its purposes and was to prove durable.

During the eighteenth century, however, there was a visible constriction in this system which opened up a kind of vacuum in Welsh society. A handful of great families came to exercise a virtual monopoly: Dukes of Beaufort in Monmouthshire, the Earl of Pembroke in Glamorgan, the Marquis of Powys in mid-Wales. A profusion of Welsh heiresses, traditionally marketed during the Bath season, led to the installation of a striking number of Anglo-Scottish houses, Butes, Campbells and their kin. Together with the greater Welsh clans, Morgans in the south, Vaughans and Pryses in mid-Wales, Middletons in the north-east, Wynns and Bulkeleys in the north-west, they established in the early eighteenth century a political monopoly which lasted nearly two hundred years.

This process, coupled with the drop-out of the lesser gentry from serious political life, emptied that political life of any recognisably Welsh content. In 1830, Wales's own judicial system, the Great Sessions, could be abolished with scarcely an eyebrow raised. Within the church the situation was, from this point of view, probably even worse. The church was a broad-bottomed and Whig corporation; one of its bishops was accused of atheism by his clergy. The poor Welsh dioceses, treated as stations of the cross in a clerical progress towards cross-border redemption, saw absenteeism and pluralism spectacular even for this century. Clergy in the lower and middle ranges and the occasional bishop were in no way as indifferent to the Welsh as the Nonconformist nineteenth century was to claim, but much of the ecclesiastical establishment became marginal to its flock. Lesser clergy followed lesser gentry into a kind of limbo within their own country.

Several historians have suggested that there is a connexion between this driving back of lesser gentry and clergy into a provincial obscurity and the growth of Dissent, the acceleration of the Methodist movement and the upsurge of interest in Welsh antiquities, language and history, all of which become visible by mid-century and intensify rapidly from the 1780s. Men of short purse, long pedigree and diminished status cherished local roots and developed an alternative system of values.

But an alternative system of values, alternative local leaderships, alternative ideologies, alternative societies in embryo, already existed in the quite literally trans-Atlantic world of Dissent and its fellow-travellers, in the strengthening communities of artisans, tramping craftsmen, local professional groupings and commercialised farming families with cultural aspirations. The peculiar development of Great Britain in this, one of its marginal yet mercantile and Atlantic-oriented provinces, was slowly but remorselessly prising its society apart, opening a gulf between classes and social groups, depersonalising it and creating social and intellectual space for alternatives. In the late eighteenth century, this Great Britain, with the loss of its American colonies, suffered its first post-colonial crisis which was also in some respects a British civil war of the mind and heart, at the very moment when economic growth accelerated, industrial capitalism massively penetrated Wales and quantitative change became qualitative.

At that moment, a freemasonry of organic intellectuals from the excluded classes equally abruptly proclaimed the rebirth of a Welsh nation. They were unconscious heralds of a generation of explosive change which actually created one.

An Alternative Society

One major source for an alternative society lay in the scattered groups of chapels, societies and schools of Dissent, those inheritors of the

Puritan Revolution of the seventeenth century who rejected the State Church.[10] Originally Calvinist, they had been granted limited toleration after the Glorious Revolution, but were denied full citizenship. The major affiliations had formed an effective pressure group, with a London committee directed at the Whigs and Parliament, around the 'Three Denominations' of Independents (Congregationalists), Baptists and Presbyterians. In Wales, they were a small minority but an influential one, rooted in people of the humbler classes who were of some substance and independence.

Those 'common people' of Wales, the *gwerin* (folk) as they were later to be called in idealistic salute after their conversion to Nonconformist radicalism, were largely monoglot Welsh, though an instrumental knowledge of English, spreading from the borders and the market towns, was more widespread than has been assumed. They lived a Welshness in which the old language, excluded from official life, was dissociating into local patois, but in which survivals of the traditional skills of the highly-trained and exclusive guild of poets continued to exist among local groups and in local prestige, in country poets as the Welsh call them *(beirdd cefn gwlad)* and in which popular practice enshrined traditions, Catholic and pagan in origin, now shaping into a way of life strongly 'folkloric' in character: muscular games and sports, ballads, story-tellings, wordplay, complex contrapuntal harp-song, the *penillion*, distinctive communal and marriage customs of informal vigour, popular and generally picaresque festivals erratically punctuated by beery and incoherent 'eisteddfodau' and penetrating a literature marginal to polite discourse through almanacs and 'interlude' popular drama.

Out of this world grew artisan crafts and some of the new professional groups and interpenetrating with it was Dissent, cultivating an ambiguous, occasionally sympathetic but generally patronising attitude towards it. If Dissent were to grow it needed to colonise and ultimately to control these people, but it was conscious of what it considered superior intellect (a consciousness which strengthened as it absorbed eighteenth-century science) and to a lesser extent (at least before its explosive expansion from the 1790s) its character as Calvinist Elect. To join Dissent was to distance oneself.

From the early eighteenth century, a time of relative agrarian prosperity which touched those service sectors of the 'middle orders' from which the sects drew some sustenance, Dissent turned in on its own intense intellectual life. This was in fact an immersion in the European Enlightenment which was to produce startling results when its evangelical passion was renewed in the challenge presented by Methodism and abrupt social change, which made the 1790s into an intellectual cauldron of competing ideologies in Wales.

Such proselytising energies as it possessed went into education and this carried it into the developing world of the Anglo-American polity. The Puritan regime had created the first state schools in Wales; out of their ruins and motivated by much the same impulses, handfuls of Dissenters and Anglicans of evangelical temper resumed the campaign, even under repression. In 1678 such people sponsored a new Welsh translation of the Bible which was distributed free in its thousands. Individual Dissenters like Samuel Jones in Glamorgan launched those Academies which during the eighteenth century grew into distinguished educational institutions, running behind the universities of Scotland.

From the early eighteenth century, these efforts meshed into a major evangelical drive for literacy in the service of saving souls which was strictly an Anglo-American phenomenon in a human Atlantic being created by British commercial and naval power and the transplantation of British communities. The Society for the Propagation of the Gospel and the Society for the Promotion of Christian Knowledge, together with societies for the 'improvement of manners' embraced Wales within their missionary and Atlantic compass. They achieved some success, but were limited in their effect because of their use of the English language as the vehicle of enlightenment.

It was from these endeavours, however, that a remarkable circulating school movement emerged, so striking in character that it caught the attention of Catherine the Great of Russia. Griffith Jones, an Anglican clergyman of Carmarthenshire, grounded his schools in the Welsh language; with a minimal reading and Biblical curriculum and the use of mobile teacher-apprentices, he geared his schools effectively to the rhythms of living and working of hill communities of the poor. By 1761, his people claimed to have taught nearly 160,000 children and anything from 300,000 to 450,000 adults over fourteen, when the population of Wales could hardly have exceeded 500,000. However inflated these claims, the movement clearly scored a success comparable to some of the more spectacular literacy drives of our own day. A supporter, Madame Bevan, maintained the schools after Jones's death, but on her death in 1779, her will was challenged and the system collapsed, to be replaced by the sporadic, if intense, work of the Sunday Schools of both Methodism and Dissent.

There were to be major losses in the first manic sweep of industrial capitalism, but a central fact of the eighteenth century is that by its final quarter, a majority of the adult population had become technically literate in Welsh. It was in that century that the Welsh learned to read. From the same period dates the real emergence of the Welsh press, that no less remarkable phenomenon which left Wales 'over-producing' printers, as it was later to 'over-produce' ministers and schoolteachers, which equipped almost every little country town in Wales with its press, to bombard the Welsh with a myriad journals, 'over-produced' in total sectarian dedication, to make the Welsh a People of the Book.

The Book of course was Holy. The Welsh learned to read in an almost totally religious context; they learned to express themselves in the language, imagery and concepts of the Bible and of Protestant sectarianism. And they learned to read during the Atlantic Revolution, that great tide of revolutionary aspiration and ambition which swept the entire Atlantic basin, from the thirteen colonies to France, the Rhineland, the Low Countries, Spain, Ireland and the Americas north and south.

This was one, though not the only or a major, root of the Calvinistic Methodist movement in Wales. Its origins in the 1730s, though located in the same stir of 'moral improvement', were independent of those in England. The instincts it shared with such movements everywhere and not least in the American colonies — where the revival led by Jonathan Edwards in 1739 occurred at much the same time and interpenetrated with it — were the more powerful in a Wales whose established church seemed remote and cool and whose people were robustly indifferent or hostile. The movement began within the Anglican church and for long remained within it, distancing itself from the older, and somewhat disconcerted, Dissent.

Young Anglicans, whether ordained or not, started to stand up in the open air and to bear witness, to ram home awareness of sin and, employing every device known to reach the senses as well as the intellect, to achieve that cataclysmic conversion, which had men and women 'born again'. Howell Harris, an outstanding preacher and organiser and a towering personality of somewhat psychopathic temper, started in Breconshire; Daniel Rowland, who could throw thousands into those public ecstasies which earned them the nickname of Holy Rollers, in Cardiganshire; William Williams, Pantycelyn, probably Wales's finest lyric poet, found his outlet in hymns which have become irredeemably central to a 'Welsh way of life'.

They did not become a way of life, however, until several generations later. The movement's growth was slow and molecular, though highly organised from the start, through its local *seiat* (society) and its *sasiwn* (session) into a federal structure, a church within the Church, plagued by repeated heresy and secession, but firmly controlled from the centre (they were, after all, 'precisians' as well as 'jumpers'). Methodists remained resolutely within the Church of England, despite growing strain and despite the hostility they encountered, especially in north and west, where the gentry could organise mobs against them. Their Calvinism was largely accidental, stemming from Harris's service as deputy to George Whitefield during the latter's American missions, but it hardened into a tribal identity, with orthodoxies, witch-hunts and sectarian fragmentation. When the Arminian (Wesleyan) Methodists penetrated the Calvinist fief of Wales early in the nineteenth century, the theological thunder deafened Welsh ears; the myriad documentary relics have since populated the dusty shelves of Welsh second-hand book shops.

As Methodism gradually accumulated a people devoted to 'vital religion', Dissent drifted in the opposite direction. As late as the early 1800s, a Baptist minister in the mushrooming industrial town of Merthyr Tydfil was hooted in the streets for trying to *introduce* hymns into chapel. Dissent's academies were open to the trade winds and the currents of Enlightenment, to Newtonian science and political theory. Their founding fathers had cut a king's head off, on principle; legally they were second-rate citizens. However respectable they became, their stance had necessarily to be somewhat political; their London committees were the first organised extra-parliamentary pressure groups.

The Carmarthen Academy of the Welsh Independents succumbed early to heresies, to Arminianism with its relative autonomy for the human will, to Arianism, a partial denial of the divinity of Christ, to Socinianism, a total denial. Its controllers moved the academy about Wales in an effort to stamp them out, in 1743 it split again and in 1755 the Congregational Board in London temporarily excommunicated it. It was in 1726 that Jenkin Jones from Carmarthen took over a church in south-east Cardiganshire and began the process that was to turn a particular south-western district on the river Teifi into a persistent seedbed of rationalist heresy, the *Black Spot* of Calvinist demonology.

The schoolmaster-ministers of this tendency, which tended to breed or to appeal to mathematicians and scientists, exercised an influence out of all proportion to the group's tiny number. It carried the small Presbyterian denomination, whose name came simply to signify liberalism in theology (and politics). A particular conquest were the Independent communities (total in their congregational autonomy) of fairly affluent and literate Glamorgan and Gwent, with their comfortable Vale causes and their craggier hill-country chapels being taken over by workers from the new iron industry. Over a single generation, the *Presbyterian* families of the south-east, largely commercial and artisan in character, with a flow of recruits from the south-west, clustered so strongly around the new iron town of Merthyr Tydfil that they made it the base for the launching of a new Unitarian denomination in 1802. Out of the Unitarianism and the 'unitarian' impulses in other denominations, which developed considerable power through the industrialisation of south-east Wales and the central textile districts, emerged a new political tradition. In 1831, Unitarian democrats captured local control in Merthyr, Wales's first industrial town; they were to be central to the first phase of the Chartist leadership. It was two Unitarians who published Wales's first working-class journal in 1834.

Most of the people in Merthyr, however, came from south-west Wales and while Methodism was a minority creed in south and east, these people came in hot for 'vital religion'. As Methodism grew, particularly in the last years of the eighteenth century, its modes and practices penetrated a resurgent Dissent. Within the Old Dissent, the 'methodised' current ran harder than the 'unitarian' and in the opposite direction, away from science and politics, towards passionate proselytising and systematically censorious personal reformation. Blank if not hostile to popular politics, its leadership, particularly among the Methodists themselves, could become a bilious form of intransigent Toryism. In the last quarter of the century, the older sects went into crisis. The Baptists, in particular, who in their upsurge rivalled Methodists as missionaries among the poor, entered a prolonged crisis from 1779 which twenty years later ended in schism.

The crisis was a crisis of growth. From the third quarter of the century, the pace of growth within Methodism accelerates; from the 1780s or so, Old Dissent follows. During the 1790s there were campaigns which resembled mass mission drives and in the first years of the nineteenth century, growth was torrential. When the Methodists were driven out of the Church by persecution in 1811, Nonconformists old and new may have accounted for perhaps 15-20 per cent of the population. By the first religious census of 1851, they outnumbered Anglicans on average by five to one; in many places the ratio was seven and even ten to one. In the early nineteenth century, the sects of Dissent threatened to become as much of a 'national church' for the Welsh as Catholicism had become for the Irish; their breakneck advance seemed to be turning the Church of England in Wales into a sick historic joke.

This is one of the most remarkable cultural transformations in the history of any people. A people which around 1790 was still officially overwhelmingly Anglican and Tory, over little more than a generation, became a Nonconformist people of radical temper. A major irony is that, in the process, an old frontier, that between the March and Welsh Wales, for five hundred years the frontier between innovation and conservatism, reappeared in Wales. For the victory of Nonconformity was the product of a crusade from the south and east into the north and west. In the early eighteenth century, there were some 70 Dissenting congregations on record; only ten were in the north and those mainly in the north-east. The Methodist leader Thomas Charles who rooted his sect in north Wales and gave the Welsh Sunday Schools their characteristic form (a species of directed democracy of exacting catechismic self-education) made Bala in Merioneth the capital of the creed, but he had come up from southern Carmarthenshire. At the great Baptist *gymanfa* or preaching festival in Nefyn in the northern Llŷn peninsula in 1792, a climax of the crusade, seven of the nine preachers were from the south. The greatest Baptist preacher of his day, Christmas Evans, another southerner, made hitherto infidel Anglesey his fief. In the Dissenter breakthrough, it was Methodists who made the running in north and west, outstripping Baptists and Independents. The consequences were striking.

In 1823 Thomas Clarkson, the anti-slavery crusader, went on tour in Wales. As soon as he crosses from south-east Wales (where Independents, Baptists and Unitarians were legion) into Cardigan-shire, the tone of his journal abruptly alters. Dissenters now mostly Methodists, were much more under the shadow of an oppressive and aggressive Establishment; the gentry would not sit with them on committees. The social strain grew worse as he moved north. In Caernarfonshire, John Elias a Methodist leader who towered over many Welsh minds like a Pope, with his Bulls of Bala, dared not meet Clarkson at home; they had to meet in secret in Chester. Not until he reached north-east Wales could Clarkson relax. He was shattered by the experience. Eastern Wales, he claimed, was fifty years behind England in its politics; western Wales fifty years behind the east.[11]

What does this mean, this re-emergence of an old frontier? It means that Methodist advance, with Dissent following up, visible from the 1790s, synchronises with the advent of rapid economic change in general and with the advent of industrial capitalism in particular.[12]

By 1796, the iron industry of Glamorgan and Gwent, with its mushrooming coal dependency, had outstripped Shropshire and Staffordshire, to produce 40 per cent of British pig iron. Some of the largest and most advanced plants in the world ran in a clamorous belt along the northern rim of the south-eastern valleys. The 1790s saw a canal mania in both counties, and ribbed them with tramways. Along one of the latter Trevithick's steam locomotive, first in the world, made its run in 1804. Exemptions granted the port of Newport spawned a sale-coal industry run by Welsh entrepreneurs on a shoestring. Entirely novel communities sprouted on the coalfield, sucking in population from the rest of Wales and starting the process which was to wrench its centre of gravity into the south-east. Monmouthshire's population increased at a rate faster than that of any other county in England and Wales; Glamorgan came third on the list. Already the dissident south-west, with its riotous little capital of Carmarthen, was being transformed into the human matrix and the service centre of a new industrial society in the south-east. At this stage, the transformation of the north-eastern coalfield was scarcely less decisive, with Denbighshire and Flintshire moving rapidly into industrial capitalism.

The most unhinging impact, however, was on rural west and north. The acceleration of industrial growth in England brought factors from Liverpool and Lancashire into the cloth country, to break the hold of the Shrewsbury Drapers. The consequences were complex: the emergence of petty local entrepreneurs, a sharp increase in pauperisation during the French war, a fairly rapid proletarianisation. 'Machines are eating people', shouted old William Jones in Llangadfan; Voltaire's prophecy was coming true, soon there would be nothing but tyrants and slaves. The first cloth factories rose along the Severn, at Newtown, Llanidloes, Welshpool, even in Dolgellau. Rural centres of production, like the Llanbrynmair which was a stronghold of Independency, went into prolonged crisis.

The crisis was immeasurably intensified by the War of 1793 with its taxes, levies, press gangs and militia lists; its merciless inflation the closure of Barmouth. Capitalist rationality moved in massively on even this marginal agriculture. During the long wars, cultivation marched higher up the hillsides in Wales than it did during even Hitler's War. Modernisation meant enclosures, the annual lease, rack-renting, the disruption of traditional community. The 1790s were a decade of virtually continuous disturbance in the Wales which lay outside the coalfields, building up to dramatic peaks during the terrible years of famine prices in 1795-96 and 1799-1801. Waves of revolt broke across rural west and north in an arc of tension which follows the curve of the cloth country; Machynlleth, Denbigh, Llanbrynmair saw large scale civil disobedience. Troops were repeatedly marching and counter-marching through Bala, the tiny Mecca of Calvinistic Methodism and there were Jacobin toasts in its pubs.[13]

The crisis of the south-west was more occult, a surface deference and quietism in matters political masking a society riddled with tension, secret societies and the growing alienation of an increasingly Nonconformist people from all establishments. Cardiganshire was hit harder by the population explosion than any county in Wales. With its smallholders, hill farmers, frustrated artisans, lead miners and squatters encroaching without cease on the two-thirds of its stubborn soil owned by the Crown, it became a community of land-hunger and inching self-improvement, as were its sister societies in upland Carmarthenshire and northern Pembrokeshire. In the post-war period, this region was to be the most disturbed in Wales; this was the homeland of the later Rebecca Riots, the celebrated guerilla struggle of small farmers, the 'Mau Mau of West Wales'. And this, too, was the prime recruitment zone for workers in the new industries on the coalfield to the east. It was the secret societies of the south-west, organised around the *ceffyl pren* — the wooden horse marched around villages to the accompaniment of 'rough music' in enforcement of communal and extralegal discipline — which helped to shape the equally celebrated and notorious guerilla movement of the Scotch Cattle, the 'industrial Rebecca' of the colliers of Monmouthshire.[14]

This was, above all, a region of strong and living American connexion. It became a major source of that distinctive migration movement which was one highly visible symptom of the crisis. From that sweep of rural and semi-industrial Wales they went, the curve of social tension from Cardigan and Carmarthen up through William Jones's country into Denbighshire, with the farmers and fishermen of the northern Llŷn peninsula in revolt against enclosures decimating the population of their community in an independent movement into upstate New York, as their compatriots drove for the new Welsh liberty settlements struggling into life in Pennsylvania and Ohio. From 1793, there was a small scale but steady flow, led essentially by artisans, rural industrial workers and above all, Dissenters, swelling into major movements during the crises of 1795-6 and 1800-1. It was men of some small substance who went, while behind them thousands trapped in poverty clamoured to get away. The first native-born Governor of the State of Ohio in the USA was the son of a man from the rebellious Independents of Llanbrynmair.[15]

Millenarian in tone, this migration was peculiarly Dissenter in spirit, leadership and substantially in personnel. This may have been a contributory factor to the marked regional differentiation between the sects of Nonconformity which becomes a factor of major significance from this period. While the denominations were competitively present everywhere in Wales, it was the richly productive hinterland of Carmarthen in the country of the Rebecca Riots, the textile districts around Llanidloes and Newtown (birthplace of Robert Owen) and, above all the south-eastern coalfield, which emerged as the centres of the more liberal, more combative, more rationalist and more radical doctrines, Unitarians, quasi-Unitarian chapels among the traditional denominations, radical Baptists, Welsh revivalists, a fringe of Deists. In Merthyr Tydfil, in its Unitarian Association of 1802, its Cyfarthfa Philosophical Society of 1806 and its burgeoning world of *patriot* eisteddfodau and chapel verse and musical festivals, such people were establishing some kind of institutional base.[16]

To north and west, however, it was Methodism and its kin which won a local and popular hegemony. This defined a distinct people no less, but defined it in a kind of defensive withdrawal. It tended to lock its people away in a bunker. Not until it was forced to by the repression of 1811 did Methodism leave the Church; for long it remained respectful. The consequences were long-lasting. It was the Old Dissent which was to produce Wales's first serious Welsh-language journals, to turn Carmarthen-Merthyr-Llanidloes into a permanent radical triangle in the frontier years of the nineteenth century. Not until 1843 did the Dissent of rural Wales acquire a questioning and radical press; not until then, in response to an Anglican counter-offensive, did it move to the attack, in its turn to create a new and different Welsh 'nation' which formed along a religious line which was also a language and a class line. Frequently in the nineteenth century, the line ran between brothers. To put it crudely, among a people whose mind was being formed by preacher-journalists, the Methodist was apolitical and quietist, the Independent or Baptist a 'politician'. This is why the complex phenomenon embraced in the catchphrase 'the radicalising of the Methodists' was so central to nineteenth-century Welsh politics.

One would hardly think so, however, from the correspondence of the gentry of north Wales during the 1790s when the process of differentiation began. According to one distraught curate in Anglesey, whose report was passed to the King, 'hordes of Methodists' were 'overrunning north Wales' and 'descanting on the Rights of Man' (indeed some of them, in that place at that time, might well have been).[17] For what both Methodists and Dissenters offered, in the vacuum which had opened in Welsh life, was an alternative local leadership in a time of economic change widely experienced as human cataclysm.

What made this particular dislocation potentially the more serious was that this embryonic alternative society was being offered a new Welsh national ideology of radical temper together with some new Welsh institutions to serve it.

A Jacobin Intelligentsia

The new Welsh nation was manufactured in London.[18] The first *Gorsedd* (order) of Iolo's directive elite of people's remembrancers was held on Primrose Hill; Jac Glan y Gors, Wales's Thomas Paine, kept the King's Head, Ludgate.

Since the carpet-bagger Tudor migrations, the London-Welsh had become central to the economic and the cultural life of Wales. Waves of seasonal migrants, drovers, tramping hosiers, even poorer weeders and transient labourers, were accompanied by more permanent residents. Out of them had emerged the premier London-Welsh society dedicated to a revival and purification of Welsh life and letters, the *Cymmrodorion.*

An interest in Welsh history, language and antiquities had been growing, even as their practice shrivelled back home (a recurrent feature of Welsh life). Edward Lhuyd, second keeper of the Ashmolean Museum in Oxford, had established a Welsh classical scholarship in the early eighteenth century, to be followed by individuals in colleges and gentry houses, patrons like the Pennants and the Williamses of Aberpergwm, Henry Rowland who resurrected the Druids. It became something of a cultivated hobby for enthusiastic if ignorant gentlemen, parsons and, increasingly, artisans, professional men and small merchants of lively if sometimes quirky minds.

It was Welsh London (a minority of course among London Welshmen) which powered such interests with money, commitment and the skills which found a natural focus in the capital. The celebrated Morris brothers of Anglesey, particularly Lewis, together with the poet Goronwy Owen, who characteristically found his way to

America, established an Augustan school of poets, antiquarians and writers. They used the Cymmrodorion to rescue, edit and publish forgotten texts and to re-establish a literary and historical tradition.

The Cymmrodorion were in reality a bunch of commercially successful and frequently wall-eyed philistines afflicted with the Welsh *pietas* of self-satisfied expatriates and adorned by a few aristocratic drones. In the 1780s they yielded, with some abruptness, to the *Gwyneddigion.* These were much more active and populist. They drew their recruits in particular from Denbighshire, in its throes of capitalist modernisation. A crowd of bright young men came bustling through from Denbigh and elsewhere to people London's merchant houses, literary societies, intellectual taverns. A surprising number found a niche in the printing trade.

They reflect in a little Welsh mirror what was happening all over the Atlantic world in the shift from academies to *sociétés de pensée* in France, the *amigos del pais* of the Spanish Empire, the literary societies and debating clubs of the Anglo-American polity. Central was Owen Jones, *The Scholar* (Owain Myfyr) born in Denbighshire in 1741, who laboured for years as a currier in the fur trade and ended owning a business and a wealthy man. That wealth he poured out in the service of Welsh literature and history. He spent £180 on the society's edition of the medieval poems of Dafydd ap Gwilym, over £1,000 on its massive collection *The Myvyrian Archaiology.* He helped send the brilliant Walter Davies, *(Gwallter Mechain)* to Oxford, subsidised Iolo Morganwg and a host of others. The hardest worker was William Owen, *(Gwilym Dawel),* Will Friendly, a Merioneth man educated at Manchester, a freelance writer and something of a minor polymath in eighteenth-century style. An FSA, he edited the early poems *Llywarch Hen* in 1792, produced a Welsh dictionary between 1793 and 1803, published a *Cambrian Register* and *Cambrian Biography,* translated *Paradise Lost* and was a pillar of the *Archaiology.*

Around such men gathered an extraordinarily lively coterie of antiquarians, poets, intellectuals: John Edwards *(Sion Ceiriog),* musician, astronomer, wit and professional gadfly; David Samwell *(Dafydd Ddu Meddyg),* surgeon to Captain James Cook on the *Resolution* and the *Discovery,* accomplished botanist, amateur anthropologist and professional womaniser, who had made the first written record of the Maori language at Queen Charlotte Sound; John Jones, Jac Glan y Gors, who brought out pamphlets in 1795 and 1797 which were Thomas Paine in Welsh and who coined the celebrated expression *Dic Sion Dafydd* to describe that familiar type of Welshman who, on crossing the Severn, becomes so English he makes the English feel foreign.

This extraordinarily congenial crew hits the historian like a sunburst. Meeting constantly in pubs, often riotous, sometimes raucous, always felicitous, their discourse at its best had something of the flavour of the correspondence between John Adams and Thomas Jefferson. They were the last, warm, free-thinking, sometimes pagan glow from an old but awakening Wales before the Calvinist curtain came down.

And while Edward Jones, harper to the Prince of Wales, informer to Pitt's anti-Jacobin Privy Council and 'silly young man' according to Fanny Burney, was a Tory, most of them were radical. Swept into a millenarian politics by the French Revolution following so hard on the American, they had the engraver to the French National Assembly strike their competition medals when they revived the eisteddfod as an embryonic Welsh academy in 1789. At a time among 'non-historic' peoples when to publish a dictionary could be a revolutionary act, they poured out dictionaries, registers, biographies, translations and established Welsh scholarship on a new (if distinctly shaky) basis. Credulous, pre-scientific and unscholarly by twentieth century standards they undoubtedly were, but on their massive tomes, now safely embalmed in the British Museum, a new Welsh nation was built. And a radical one: when the Gwyneddigion set up a political club during the euphoric early 1790s, Jac Glan y Gors wrote its initiation song; it was a hymn to Madoc who had taken his people out of an old, brutal and corrupt world into a spring-fresh land of liberty, to find a new start in freedom for an old people.

It was precisely here that the Gwyneddigion's collaboration with Iolo Morganwg was so crucial. 'Why take needless alarms?' Iolo once asked his long-suffering wife Peggy who used to comment on his vagaries in pungent verse, 'I do not intend to publish my petition for the Abolition of Christianity until long after I have finished with the work in hand...'[19] The stonemason from Glamorgan's Vale, who went on incredible tramping journeys all over southern England, stands out now as one of Wales's most fecund if maimed geniuses. His family would have interested the early D.H. Lawrence. His father, intelligent and literate, was a working stonemason, his mother, frail, aloof and a dreamer, was the poor kinswoman of a distinguished gentry family and a descendant of one of Glamorgan's ancient dynasties of Welsh poets. She never let Iolo forget his twin cultural inheritance. Taught lexicographical and antiquarian skills by local gentlemen, Iolo plundered libraries and collections wholesale and built himself into the most learned man of his day on Welsh literature and history. He was much cherished by Southey and the English Romantics who saw in him an Original Bard out of the Celtic Twilight, an image he unscrupulously cultivated. His imagination was no less unscrupulous. A romantic and a forger in an age of iconoclastic poets and high-minded forgers in a good cause, the age of Wordsworth, the Noble Savage, the Druid, the Bard and William Blake, Iolo wove fabrications without number into his genuine discoveries; he invented Welsh traditions the world had never seen. It has taken the heroic work of a dedicated Welsh scholar of this century to cut him free from his fantasies.[20]

In that process, however, Iolo is not seriously diminished. His very forgeries embody a certain logic, convey a vision of which no-one else would have been capable. He called for a Welsh national library, a national museum, a national eisteddfod; he was one of the first serious folklorists in Wales. He had an intuitive grasp of the *historical* function of Welsh traditions and of their functional utility to the starved, neglected and often self-despising Welsh of his own day. Welsh poets, he observed, had not been poets as the English used the term; they had been the rib-cage of the body politic, remembrancers, a collective memory honed for historic action. So he invented a *Gorsedd*, a guild of those 'Bards' who would be so much more than mere poets, antiquarians or historians, a directive and democratic elite of a new and democratic Welsh nation, conceived in liberty, deploying a usable past in order to build an attainable future.[21]

Many of the Londoners had the same instinct. The foremost Orientalist of the time Sir William Jones, was a Welshman; his researches seemed to suggest that the Celtic tongues were related to Sanskrit. Was Welsh the degenerate descendant of Earth's Mother Tongue? William Owen, who became a close confidant of the millenarian Joanna Southcott, joined with his friends to purify the language of centuries of servitude and corruption, to invent a new orthography (in which he did not differ much, after all, from those typical new Americans, Noah Webster who wanted to turn old Gothic English into the Esperanto of Liberty or Dr Benjamin Rush who wanted to make New World medicine into a new world medicine).[22]

These obsessions ran into confluence with many of the bohemian fashions of the time. The ghost of their distant compatriot, that Dr John Dee the Elizabethan polymath and magus who had created the historical Madoc, returned to his homeland.[23] His vast and cosmic scheme for sixteenth-century regeneration, defeated in the Counter-Reformation, had gone underground to live an increasingly weird life as Rosicrucianism. In the eighteenth century, a version of it resurfaced on the fringes of Freemasonry and those societies of *Illuminati* which the Counter-Revolution, the Abbé-Barruel, Robison, Edmund Burke, were to identify as the generator of the French and the world revolution. The London Swedenborgians made contact with the *Illuminés* of Avignon in the late 1780s and these Welsh Londoners moved on the fringes of the circle of William Blake and the radical artisanry of the capital.

A whole new dimension was added to the misty perception of the past which Iolo and the Gwyneddigion were cultivating. Iolo came to see Druids as Patriarchal figures of vast Celtic lands, charged with the Jewish Cabala, key to the language which God gave to Moses, antecedent to both Christianity and Hebraism. Theirs was a version of Rousseau's natural religion, purged of superstitition and priestcraft, unitarian in its belief in a single God, Masonic in its descent through secret societies of Enlightenment to the present. The medieval guilds of Welsh poets thus became the last living representatives in Europe of that libertarian Druidism. Their descendants, the Jacobin Bards of the Welsh, must resume the march towards freedom and justice.

This millenarianism ran in harmony with the more measured, scholarly millenarianism which was coursing through orthodox religion, notably Dissent and of which Dr Joseph Priestley himself, philosopher and martyr to democracy, was such an exemplar. Morgan John Rhys, an original and imaginative Baptist in Glamorgan and Gwent, was possessed by it. A committed American in spirit, active in the campaign against the slave trade and in all manner of reform causes, he like many others saw the French Revolution coming hard on the heels of the American as the precursor of the Last Days. Liberation had become an urgent necessity. He crossed to France to preach it. Driven home by the outbreak of European War, he mobilised the Baptist Association of south-west Wales in a project to translate the old Puritan and unorthodox Bible of John Canne into French and *en masse.*

Inevitably, the Gwyneddigion, launching its freedom eisteddfodau from 1789, its first *Gorsedd* in 1792, supporting Morgan John Rhys's *Journal* in 1793, shuffled into loose alliance with men like Rhys and a scatter of individuals across the brittle and bitter parishes of Wales. An unstructured but active collective intelligentsia began to form, spiritual Americans to a man, and were swept into millenarianism by the new dawn of 1789. For the London-Welsh were up to their eyes in the radical London of the Corresponding Societies, of Blake, of that John Thelwall who used to preach democracy to a hostile world in fire, fury and a cudgel-proof hat. Their millenarian vision could act as a unifying factor; Unitarianism and Freemasonry run as underground currents through this first phase of Welsh re-creation. It was a new and possessed nation which reached out to its half-aware adherents back home.

Heavy weather they made of it. Hardly had their eisteddfodau and their *Gorsedd* got off the ground when Britain went to war with the Revolution and drowned them in successive waves of repression and John Bull jingoism. It was precisely at that point, however, that they found a new focus. The Nootka Sound crisis between Spain and Britain over legal title to North America in 1790 had sparked off, as such crises invariably did, a revival of the old myth of Madoc the Welsh prince who was said to have discovered America three hundred years before Columbus. In 1791, Dr John Williams, a learned Welsh divine of Sydenham, published a scholarly study of the claim. Within a year he had to bring out a new edition. For the consequences were startling. All the interests of this heterogeneous but dedicated fistful of organic intellectuals of the Welsh and of their growing band of followers, came to a sudden focus on the Ohio and the Missouri. Over there, after all, a free and liberal Dissenter Wales already existed.

An American Dimension

Welshmen were everywhere in the New World, from the West Indies to furthest Canada and had been since John Dee's Madoc.[24] During the eighteenth century, a number made for Spanish North America. There were a handful of Welsh merchants in New Orleans and a Rees family was prominent in New Madrid. The most amazing of them made St Louis his base. This was Charles Morgan, a Welsh West Indian known as Jacques Clamorgan, who was the driving force in Spain's last great enterprise in North America, the Missouri Company thrusting up the unexplored Missouri to win control of the fur trade, break through to the Pacific and pre-empt the oncoming British and Americans.[25]

Most Welsh migrations, however, went into the British colonies in denominational groups. The first serious migrations had followed the Restoration, when John Miles, founder of the Welsh Baptists, took his people to Swanzey (Swansea) in New England. Such movements tended to be Puritan, millenarian in temper, with a vision of a *gwladfa,* a national home for the Welsh. Pennsylvania rapidly became a focus. The Quaker *gwladfa* in Penn's promised Welsh Barony never materialised, but Welshmen were very prominent in the colony, Thomas Lloyd of Dolobran, Montgomeryshire, serving as Penn's deputy. Compatriots overflowed into the Welsh Tract in Delaware and there was a cluster of settlements bearing Welsh names and served by Welsh churches in an arc from Meirion to Pencader. Arminian Baptists from mid-Wales moved to the colony and around 1700-1 were followed by an important influx from south-west Wales where the mother church of Rhydwilym had its roots. Calvinistic Baptists, they quit the Arminians to people the Welsh Tract and Pencader. From these nuclei the Welsh grew in considerable strength, planting offshoots in the Carolinas, particularly at the Welsh Neck of the Peedee river.

Pennsylvania remained the Welsh heartland. A St David's Society was launched in Philadelphia as early as 1729; Welsh books were published there, including the first Welsh Biblical concordance. The only English translation of a Welsh classic, Theophilus Evans's *Drych y Prif Oesoedd,* Mirror of the Early Ages, appeared in Ebensburg, Pennsylvania, itself the product of the Madoc fever of the 1790s and was made by George Roberts, a Llanbrynmair Independent. For although migration faded out in the mid-eighteenth century, the Welsh-American population grew substantial. American Baptists in particular were for long notably Welsh in character. Their oldest church, Pennepek near Philadelphia, was served by a succession of Welshmen, having been founded by one; Jenkin Jones opened Philadelphia First Baptist as its daughter. Many churches in the Great Valley and Pencader were Welsh in spirit and served by ministers from Cardiganshire; Abel Morgan ran their celebrated academy and from the middle of the century, the Baptists entered another cycle of growth. A prime mover was Morgan Edwards, a Monmouthshire man who rode thousands of miles on circuit and wrote their history.

From 1762 Edwards was central to the creation of the Baptists' own college, Rhode Island College, later Brown University. The core of the college's library was books bequeathed to it by William Richards of Lynn, a Baptist from south-west Wales who was an ardent partisan of America and published a defence of the atheism of the French Revolution. Edwards's colleague in the launching of Rhode Island College was an even more remarkable Welsh-American, Dr Samuel Jones, a Glamorgan man in origin, who served Pennepek from 1762 to

1814. The real author of the College's charter, Samuel Jones came to rank as 'a sort of bishop among the Baptists'. In 1770 there were said to be 300 Baptist churches in America; by 1786 Samuel Jones was claiming that numbers had tripled, with the south and newly settled Kentucky as particular conquests. The mother organisation in Philadelphia embraced 50 churches and there were twelve other Associations, with Welshmen and Welsh-Americans prominent in the leadership.

Moreover, the Baptists remained in close contact with the homeland. Morgan Edwards returned to Wales to solicit funds for the College and established links with Joshua Thomas, a fellow-historian. Americans frequently demanded Welsh preachers. During the late 1780s Samuel Jones opened a correspondence with leading Welsh Baptists at home which brings to light a remarkably intense transatlantic world. There was a constant two-way traffic in books, letters, information and ultimately people. This Baptist International had its own ships, four or five favoured vessels, notably the *Pigou* and the *Benjamin Franklin* of the Loxley family, pillars of Philadelphia First Baptist, intermarried with the Welsh and London-Welsh Baptists at home and headed by Captain Benjamin Loxley, who had run the Continental Arms Laboratory during the War of Independence and had been Benjamin Franklin's technician.[26]

It was during the 1790s that Samuel Jones's correspondence suddenly turns into the chronicle of a diaspora; it abruptly fills with letters of dismission and warnings of the arrival of 'another seven score' from Pontypool, Newcastle Emlyn or Llanbrynmair. George Lewis from Caernarfon proposes to transplant the Independents of north Wales as a body to the Ohio. Jedidiah Morse, the famous American geographer starts to send massive information on immigration prospects to Wales, listing the places which needed ministers. It was the Philadelphia Baptist Association which revived the Welsh Society of the city (embracing most of its elite as honorary Welshmen) in 1795 precisely to deal with the sudden inflow from Wales. During the 1790s Samuel Jones found himself acting virtually as an unofficial Welsh consul in the USA as the Baptist network was mobilised and as it began to look in the middle of that revolutionary decade as if half the Welsh nation was ready to transplant itself.

For it was at that critical moment, with Welsh people, particularly in the north and west, going under the harrow of industrial capitalism and the little Jacobin 'nation' of the Welsh butting head-on into the first storms of counter-revolution in Britain, that Dr John Williams's learned book restored Prince Madoc, mythical Welsh discoverer of America and founder of a Welsh nation in the New World, to his people.

The story of Madoc, rooted in Welsh seafarers and European romances of the thirteenth century, had been promoted as a discovery of America, essentially by Dr John Dee, in the first Elizabethan imperialism. It had been transmuted into a myth of Welsh Indians in the seventeenth century. Madoc was reborn in another conflict of imperialisms, this time the rivalry over the lucrative fur trade of the Far West between Americans, Spaniards and British out of Canada.[27]

In 1792 a French trader from Spanish St Louis came across a tribe on the Upper Missouri, key to the vital Pacific route, the Mandans, and pronounced them 'white like Europeans'. The Welsh West Indian Jacques Clamorgan organised St Louis to despatch expedition after expedition up the difficult river to secure this miraculous tribe and get to the Pacific ahead of Spain's enemies. For years there had been rumours of such a tribe, the White Padoucas. Filtering back into the settled areas of the east, they fused with a revival of the old yarns of Welsh Indians in the Carolinas, given 'warrant' by the Madoc myth lodged in such official and semi-official Elizabethan texts as Hakluyt's authoritative *Principall Navigations . . . of the English Nation*. By the 1780s a tidal wave of Welsh Indian stories was breaking on English-speaking America and in the last years of the century, there was a minor outbreak of Madoc fever there.

The fever hit Wales after 1791 and at a singularly appropriate moment. Overnight the legendary prince became the most miraculous hero of them all, a Jacobin Madoc. There was an outbreak of Madoc and America fever, particularly in Dissenter and liberal circles. Christmas Evans raised his organ voice in protest against the Two Clever Talkers — *Mr Gwladaethwr a Mr Mynd i America*, Mr Politician and Mr Go-to-America who were unhinging the Godly in Wales, even some of the Methodists. Iolo appointed himself missionary to the Welsh Indians, reconstructed their 'history', presented a paper to the Royal Society in British imperial terms and to his Jacobin friends in terms of a Welsh Republic in the New World. Young John Evans, a Methodist from Waunfawr near Caernarfon, threw up career and family, moved to a circle of Welsh Jacobins in London, crossed to America in the steerage along the Baptist network and entered the service of Spain and Jacques Clamorgan. He set off alone up the Missouri, with one dollar and seventy-five cents in his pocket, on an abortive mission. Driven back, he enrolled as second-in-command to

the Scottish explorer James McKay in the greatest expedition Spain
ever sent up the river, to win the Mandans for Spain and to find the
Welsh Indians. He did indeed reach the Mandans, he lived through one
of the worst winters on earth; he did hold those Mandans for Spain
against the Canadian fur companies, helping indirectly to fix the future
Canada-US border; he drew excellent maps which Lewis and Clark
were to use on their classic first land crossing to the Pacific only nine
years later. Madoc and Jacobinism turned this Welsh Methodist (who
duly defected to the Baptists and the Freemasons) into a pioneer of
American exploration and the last of the Spanish conquistadors in the
north. A disillusioned hero, he died of drink in New Orleans at the age
of 29 and was forgotten for a century and a half.[28]

After him, two years later, went Morgan John Rhys the Jacobin
Baptist, giving up the unequal struggle at home as his *Journal*
succumbed to the reaction. After a horseback grand tour of the
American Republic, he launched the Welsh national home, the
gwladfa, at Beula in western Pennsylvania.[29] And after both of them,
particularly during the desperate years, 1795-6 and 1800-1, years of
famine prices, mass riots, political witch-hunts and redcoats marching
and counter-marching across north and west Wales, went Welsh
families by the hundred, braving hideous sea-crossings with their 50
per cent casualties, Algerian corsairs and hostile British warships.[30]

They went, as many of them told the clerk in Philadelphia as they
took out their American citizenship papers, to found *The Kingdom of
Wales*.[31]

Birth and Death of a Nation

For politics in Wales begin with the American Revolution. The first
purely political publication in the Welsh language was a translation of
an English pamphlet on the dispute with the American colonies. For a
few years even the homespun ballad-mongers were disturbed.
Temporarily unhinged by what they saw as a civil war, they were able to
relapse with relief into their customary John Bull jingoism only with
the entry of France and Spain into the conflict. So visible were Welsh-
Americans in the struggle that the people at home firmly believed that
most of the signatures to the Declaration of Independence were Welsh!
Five certainly were; David Jones, minister of Great Valley Baptist, had
a price put on his head by the British. John Rice Jones of Merioneth
migrated to fight alongside the Americans in 1776 itself.

The war turned most Welsh Dissenters and whole ranges of people who espoused the liberties being fought for into spiritual Americans within British society. From that point, politics thrust its enquiring snout into the book production of the Welsh-speaking Welsh. In the 1760s, there were some 230 publications in Welsh; by the 1790s the total had climbed to nearly 500 and among them the number of political texts multiplied six-fold. Over a hundred appeared, mostly in the 1790s, and their message echoed through the larger numbers of historical studies, biographies, verse, left its impress even on the serried ranks of volumes (600 and more out of a total of 1,300 printed between 1760 and 1799) devoted to theology, sermons and hymns.[32] David Williams, a celebrated Welsh Deist, dated the birth of Jacobinism from 1782 and located that birth not in France but in Britain. It was certainly during the 1780s that the Gwyneddigion in London acquired their distinctive character.

Out of that post-colonial crisis grew the first serious reform movements in Britain, calling for the political emancipation of Dissent, the end of British slavery, the creation of a representative parliament, and finally for political democracy, a thrust which, after the French Revolution, debouched into the first systematic popular politics. Welshmen, mostly Dissenters, who were enmeshed in this movement were relatively few in number but strategically placed. One striking centre was Glamorgan, which emerges as a nursery of the democratic intellect.[33] One of the wealthiest and most literate of the Welsh counties, its Vale nurtured, not the customary scattered Welsh hamlets, but nucleated villages, which could cultivate urban graces. Bristol, an intellectually lively and politically alert city, was the region's capital. Swansea was itself a cultivated little town, Cowbridge Book Society could disseminate seminal works and the new town of Merthyr Tydfil, nearly 8,000 strong and growing at breakneck speed, could boast a bookseller taking weekly consignments from London. The Vale, anglicised in early modern times, was experiencing a Welsh-language revival. Perhaps it was the very interaction and friction between Wales's two cultures which made it so open and lively a place. It has the feel of that Philadelphia which was the spiritual capital of so many of its village intellectuals. This society with its creative bilingual artisanry and its aspiring lower middle class, could produce men like John Bradford, a Deist dyer at ease in the literatures of France and England and passionate in the cause of Welsh revival, William Edward who built the lovely single-span bridge at Pontypridd, Lewis Hopkin a multi-purpose craftsman after Ben Franklin's heart who trained a coterie of Welsh poets, Edward Ifan, a poet who became the first Unitarian minister in the hill country. This was the society which produced not only Iolo Morganwg, but two of the best-known trans-Atlantic radicals of the age of revolution: Dr Richard Price, celebrated as a political Dissenter, alleged author of the Sinking Fund, defender of the American and French Revolutions and the occasion for Edmund Burke's *Reflections*, a man formally invited by Congress to serve as financial adviser to the American Republic; David Williams, author of a Deist religion which won praise from Voltaire, Rousseau and Frederick the Great, friend of Condorcet and the Girondins, a man formally invited over to France to advise on its new constitution. From the scarp edge of Vale and hill-country came Morgan John Rhys, mentor and Moses to the Welsh on their journey of hope.

There were pockets elsewhere, in Denbighshire where Jac Glan y Gors was born, among Independents in north Wales and the concentrations around Llanbrynmair; Merthyr village was said to be full of 'sturdy old Republicans'; Iolo Morganwg spent much time there, his son opened a school in the heart of its radical, Unitarian, Masonic, eisteddfodic quarter (later its Chartist heartland). There were contagious individuals like William Jones Llangadfan. A small and scattered minority at home, they were much more visible in the trans-Atlantic perspective proper to British Jacobinism.

Their journey of hope was brief. Their campaigns mounted to a climax in the celebration of the centenary of the Revolution of 1688 just at the point when Washington took the presidency of the new US Republic and the Bastille fell in France. There was a brief but brilliant explosion of Welsh Jacobinism, in the eisteddfodau, the *Gorsedd*, Morgan John Rhys's *Journal*, Jac Glan y Gors's pamphlets. Official Britain reacted violently from as early as 1791; its magistrates hounded Jacobins, its mobs wrecked their houses. In 1793 Britain went to war with France, in 1794 the leading English radicals were tried for treason, in 1795 English liberties were suspended for the duration. These, too, were the years of the first implantation of modern industry in south-east and north-east, the years of the first cloth factories on the Severn, the closure of Barmouth, the crisis running through rural Wales. They were years, no less, of a surging growth of Methodism, which turned a face of brass to this new Welsh 'nation', to be copied by the more conservative leaders of Dissent. Morgan Rhys's journal was snuffed out after five issues; two attempts to restart it failed. Jacobinism shrank from public view into private correspondence; men like William Jones Llangadfan were leaned on; his mail was opened, he was threatened by shadowy figures. In this corner of a Britain disciplined by the suspensions of Habeas Corpus, patrolled by the Volunteers, deafened by *God Save Great George Our King* sung five times over in the playhouses to drown *God Save The Rights Of Man*, where could Welsh patriots turn but to that Land of Liberty where kindred spirits were waiting and where the Lost Brothers were even now ranging the Missouri?

These were the years in which minority radical Britain succumbed to what Mrs Lindsay called 'the rage to go to America'; the emigrants' handbooks came pouring from the presses; during the treason trials of 1794 there was a minor stampede for the America boats. In Wales the migration assumed Utopian and dramatic form as Madoc suddenly returned, to give struggling Jacobins a point of contact with a people in travail.

Their frontier proved a frontier of illusion. The liberty settlement, Beula, after a heroic struggle, was cracked by the simultaneous opening of the easier Ohio lands and the abrupt acceleration of emigration in 1801. The people dispersed to found Welsh communities in Ohio at Paddy's Run and Welsh Hills, at Utica in New York State, but they shed their Cymric ambition. Back home, the Jacobin nation was extinguished as the wars of the French Revolution became the Napoleonic Wars. A new Wales being shaped by industry, Methodism and a measured Dissent had no place for such as Iolo and William Owen. By the first years of the new century, they were already beginning to look like creatures from another time. It was a hundred years before the new and reconstructed Welsh recaptured their memory by an act of will.

And yet, if political economy, evangelical religion, Methodism and a methodised Dissent — a novel form of respectability — were colonising many of the Welsh, the year before the 'sturdy old Republicans' of Merthyr formed their Unitarian Association, colliers and ironworkers of the town, after a massive grain action in 1800-1, made contact with insurrectionary and republican movements in England which debouched into the abortive Despard Conspiracy. The first trade unions in Wales came hard on the heels of the Cyfarthfa Philosophical Society. Jacobinism, however brief and illusory its moment of truth and fantasy, left a living and constantly renewed tradition which interacted with the new world of industry and so interacted in increasing and intensifying power.[34]

The ideology of democracy is pre-industrial: witness America, Britain, France, western Europe, even Russia. It was the new Welsh democracy of an old regime which came to inform and ultimately to shape an even newer Welsh working class.

There were two strongholds of radicalism in Wales during the 1790s, Merioneth-Montgomeryshire (with the south-west slithering into social malaise) and Merthyr-Monmouthshire. In the former, Jacobinism took wing towards the Ohio, in the latter, it could find a home at home.

The history of the first Welsh working class, in the industrial valleys of Gwent and Glamorgan, around the textile townships of mid-Wales, in the smouldering hinterland of *sans-culotte* Carmarthen, is largely the history of the interplay between Unitarian and Infidel heirs of the Jacobin tradition and the leaders and organic intellectuals of the newer plebeian and proletarian people.

When Wales produced its first working-class journal in the service of Owenite socialism, the *Gweithiwr/Workman* of 1834, its editors were two Unitarians straight out of the Jacobin tradition: *Ieuan Ddu*, John Thomas from Carmarthen town, the finest Welsh music scholar of his day, the man who introduced Handel's *Messiah* to Welsh choirs, a man of freethinking sympathy who started eisteddfodau of Free Enquirers (the Zetetics of Richard Carlile's *Republican*) in the Merthyr of the Reform crisis, and Morgan Williams, master weaver, son of one of the 'sturdy old Republicans' of the Merthyr of the 1790s, mathematician star of a family of harpists and destined to become the foremost Chartist leader in Wales. It was Taliesin Williams, schoolmaster of Merthyr and the son of Iolo Morganwg, who gave them a motto which in time became the motto of the town itself, a motto which Iolo had wished on a sixth-century Glamorgan saint and which appeared in the *Myvyrian Archaiology* of the London-Welsh: *nid cadarn ond brodyrdde,* no strength but brotherhood.[35]

The leadership of the first working-class movements in Wales represents a posthumous triumph for the European Enlightenment in its particular Welsh translation.

Notes

1. A *gorsedd*, originally meaning a mound, was a term applied to an open-air tribunal. Iolo Morganwg extended the term to embrace a guild of poets who were 'bards' because they exercised social functions (*beirdd* in Welsh, the root of 'bards', simply means 'poets'). Iolo charged this guild with mythical Druidic properties and located its origin in remote Celtic Britain (hence the 'Island of Britain'); he invented robes, ceremonies and ritual for it. A version of his *gorsedd* ultimately lodged in the National Eisteddfod of Wales (below) to entertain and bewilder TV audiences.

Basic sources on Iolo are his manuscripts in the National Library of Wales, Aberystwyth (henceforth NLW); G.J. Williams, *Iolo Morganwg* (University of Wales, Cardiff, 1956: in Welsh); his broadcast essay in English, *Iolo Morganwg* (BBC, Cardiff, 1963); and Prys Morgan, *Iolo Morganwg* (Welsh Arts Council and University of Wales, Cardiff, 1975: in English).

I provide a fuller portrait of Iolo and his work in my *Madoc: the making of a myth* (Eyre Methuen, London, 1980) and, in context, in my *The Search for Beulah Land: the Welsh and the Atlantic Revolution* (Croom Helm, London, 1980).

2. An *eisteddfod* is a competitive cultural festival, with poetry in the strict classical metres as the premier mystery, free poetry, prose and music as secondary themes. In modern times, it has acquired a strongly folkloric and quasi-nationalist character. Institutions of this type existed in the middle ages; those of the guild of poets were strict and exclusive and imposed rigorous standards in the manner of an academy; they can probably be traced back to the shadowy guilds of lawmen, remembrancers and poets of Celtic Britain; early Ireland provides the most developed models.

3. The address: 13 June 1791 in W. Jones-W. Owen, 6-7 August 1791, NLW 13221, fo. 341-2 342-339, 340-343; on William Jones, voluminous correspondence in William Owen papers particularly NLW 13221 and a schizophrenic obituary by Walter Davies, *Cambrian Register 1796*, ii (1799) 237-151; I provide a fuller portrait of this remarkable man in my *Madoc: the making of a myth*.

4. My *The Search for Beulah Land* focuses on Rhys and is based on American as well as Welsh material; see the references there. There is a memoir, J.T. Griffith, *Morgan John Rhys* (Philadelphia 1899 and W.M. Evans, Carmarthen, 1910) and a life and times in Welsh, J.J. Evans, *Morgan John Rhys a'i Amserau* (University of Wales, Cardiff, 1935).

5. *Albion's Fatal Tree* (Allen Lane, London, 1975) especially Douglas Hay, 'Property, Authority and the Criminal Law' and E.P. Thompson, *Whigs and Hunters* (Allen Lane, London, 1975).

6. B.R. Mitchell and Phyllis Deane, *Abstract of British Historical Statistics* (Cambridge, 1962) inadequate on iron, where I have been helped by my friend Brian Davies; S. Drescher, *Econocide* (University of Pittsburgh Press, Pittsburgh, 1977) a study of the abolition of the slave trade, very revealing on copper; A.H. John, *The Industrial Development of South Wales* (University of Wales, Cardiff, 1950); W. Minchinton (ed.), *Industrial South Wales* (Cass, London, 1969) and a host of local studies too numerous to mention.

7. A mass of material summarised in my *The Search for Beulah Land*; key texts: R.T. Jenkins, *Hanes Cymru yn y Ddeunawfed Ganrif* (University of Wales reprint 1972, a short and brilliant essay on 18th-century Wales); D.J.V. Jones, *Before Rebecca: popular protest in Wales 1793-1835* (Allen Lane, London, 1973); Geraint Jenkins, *The Welsh Woollen Industry* (National Museum of Wales, Cardiff, 1969); A.H. Dodd, *The Industrial Revolution in North Wales* (University of Wales, Cardiff, 3rd ed., 1971).

8. My *The Search for Beulah Land* and *Madoc: the making of a myth*.

9. A very useful summary of his own comprehensive work in Peter D.G. Thomas, 'Society, Government and Politics' in Donald Moore (ed.), *Wales in the Eighteenth Century* (Christopher Davies, Swansea, 1976).

10. This section of the chapter represents a reworking of material from multiple sources which I have deployed in several books, notably *The Search for Beulah Land, Madoc* and 'Locating a Welsh working class: the frontier years', in David Smith (ed.), *A People and a Proletariat: essays in the history of Wales 1780-1980* (Pluto Press and *Llafur*, Society for the Study of Welsh Labour History, London, 1980).

11. The Clarkson Diaries are in NLW.

12. A more detailed picture of the crisis and the migration movements in my *The Search for Beulah Land, Madoc,* and *The Merthyr Rising* (Croom Helm, London, 1978, paperback 1979). Critical sources: papers of Dr Samuel Jones, Pennepek in Mrs Irving H. McKesson Collection (Jones section) Historical Society of Pennsylvania (Philadelphia); the work of David Williams, see bibliography in special number of *Welsh*

History Review (1967) in his honour and especially his *The Rebecca Riots* (University of Wales, Cardiff, 1955); D.J.V. Jones, *Before Rebecca*; D. Thomas, *Agriculture in Wales during the Napoleonic Wars* (University of Wales, Cardiff, 1963). A good general survey of Welsh migration to the US is E.G. Hartmann, *Americans from Wales* (Christopher, Boston, 1967).

13. A vivid source are the letters of William Jones Llangadfan in William Owen collection, especially NLW 13221.

14. Essential here is D.J.V. Jones, *Before Rebecca*, with its brilliant essay on the Scotch Cattle.

15. I have covered this remarkable migration, made in the teeth of appalling difficulties, in *The Search for Beulah Land*.

16. My *The Merthyr Rising* and an essay in the twenty-first celebration number of the *Welsh History Review* in June 1981, 'The Merthyr Election of 1835'.

17. My *Artisans and Sans-culottes* (Edward Arnold, reprint, London, 1973) pp. 74-6.

18. On the London-Welsh, R.T. Jenkins and Helen T. Ramage, *A History of the Honourable Society of Cymmrodorion and of the Gwyneddigion and Cymreigyddion Societies* (Cymmrodorion, London, 1951); I present a picture of them in *Madoc*.

19. E. Williams-M. Williams, nd Iolo 822 (NLW); I try to cope with this wizard in *Madoc*.

20. G.J. Williams, *Iolo Morganwg* (in Welsh); unfortunately the incomparable Griffith John Williams, professor of Welsh in un-Welsh Cardiff, died before he could finish his second volume. The loss seems irreparable.

21. A version of the gorsedd was associated with the eisteddfod from the early 19th century; a version of it is today an integral part of the ritual of the National Eisteddfod of Wales (which has also become Royal). I doubt whether Iolo would have recognised it, until 1974 that is, when the late Dai Francis, Communist Secretary of the NUM South Wales Area and founder of the South Wales Miners' Eisteddfod (bilingual, in sharp contrast to the monoglot Welsh National) and a leading member of *Llafur*, the Welsh Labour History Society, was admitted under the bardic title of *Dai o'r Onllwyn* (Onllwyn is a mining village in the anthracite).

22. Benjamin Rush, mercilessly pilloried by William Cobbett, then a bilious Tory in Philadelphia, became a friend of M.J. Rhys and supplied the land for the Welsh liberty settlement, as he did for the New Caledonia attempted by the son of the Scottish social philosopher John Millar.

23. I deal with John Dee in a Welsh context in *Welsh Wizard and British Empire: Dr John Dee and a Welsh identity* (Gwyn Jones Lecture, University College Cardiff and Welsh Arts Council 1980) and in *Madoc*. Central is the remarkable scholarship of Dame Frances A. Yates in many hypnotic volumes, notably perhaps *The Occult Philosophy in the Elizabethan Age* (Routledge and Kegan Paul, London, 1979). See also, in the same stimulating tradition, Peter French, *John Dee: the world of an Elizabethan Magus* (Routledge and Kegan Paul, London, 1972).

24. I detail the Welsh-American connexion, the migrations and Morgan John Rhys's epic journey in *The Search for Beulah Land*.

25. I deal with Jacques Clamorgan and his enterprises in *Madoc*.

26. To supplement the Samuel Jones Pennepek papers, the Loxley Papers, Uselma Clark Smith Collection, Historical Society of Pennsylvania. M.J. Rhys married a daughter of Ben Loxley, a very striking figure of a revolutionary artisan, originally from Yorkshire. He, and all the others, put flesh on the notion of an 'Atlantic Revolution' in the late eighteenth century; I discuss him in *The Search for Beulah Land*.

27. I have discussed the Madoc myth at length, tried to locate its various forms in social and political context, and concentrated on the 1790s in my *Madoc*.

28. I have treated John Evans's remarkable career at length not only in *Madoc* but, with the precise references denied me in the book, in 'John Evans's mission to the Madogwys 1792-1799', *Bulletin of the Board of Celtic Studies*, xxvii (1978).

29. My *The Search for Beulah Land* comes to a focus on the Rhys mission.

30. For some hair-raising accounts — Rees Lloyd-Jonah Lloyd, 4 September 1837, Cambria Historical Society, Ebensburg, Pennsylvania; George Roberts-Samuel Roberts, 1 March 1850, *Y Cronicl*, printed in Alan Conway (ed.), *The Welsh in America: letters from the immigrants*, trans. Judith Lewis (University of Wales, Cardiff, 1961) and George Roberts-his parents, 13 October 1801, NLW 14094 and others, reprinted in A.H. Dodd, 'Letters from Cambria County 1800-1823', *Pennsylvania History*, xxii (1955).

31. Based on the naturalisation records of the federal district court, the county court of Philadelphia and of fifteen Pennsylvania counties: Veterans' Building Federal Record Centre and City Hall Philadelphia and local courthouses in the state.

32. Listed in J.J. Evans, *Morgan John Rhys a'i Amserau*, pp. 121-2, but no source given.

33. I derive my picture of Glamorgan and its organic intellectuals from G.J. Williams, *Traddodiad Llenyddol Morgannwg* (University of Wales, Cardiff, 1948: on Glamorgan's literary tradition), Ceri W. Lewis, 'The literary history of Glamorgan from 1550 to 1770' in Glanmor Williams (ed.), *Glamorgan County History* iv (Cardiff 1974) and from my own work.

34. On the Jacobin tradition and the Welsh working class, my *The Merthyr Rising*, 'Locating a Welsh working class: the frontier years' in *People and Proletariat*, 'The Merthyr Election of 1835' and 'South Wales radicalism: the first phase', in Stewart Williams (ed.), *Glamorgan Historian*, ii (1965).

35. My 'Dic Penderyn, the making of a Welsh working-class martyr', *Llafur*, 2 (1978).

3 LOCATING A WELSH WORKING CLASS: THE FRONTIER YEARS*

The chapel stands on the slope, square and uncompromising in the manner of Welsh Dissent, but with gracefully rounded windows and an unexpectedly Palladian aspect. Above it, on the tops, a big sky suddenly opens up on a breathtaking sweep of hill country running north to Mynydd Bach. There in the 1820s, men and women of Cardiganshire fought their *Rhyfel y Sais Bach* (War of the Little Englishman) with their Turf Act and their huntsman's horn, their *ceffyl pren* (wooden horse) secret society and their six hundred men in women's clothes, so many premature Children of Rebecca, under Dai Jones the blacksmith, to drive out an enclosing English gentleman, his soldiers and his hired goons, even as their cousins were similarly engaged, in similar style, as Children of the *Tarw Scotch, gelyn pob dychryndod* (Scotch Bull, enemy of all fear) among the Scotch Cattle of Monmouthshire's militant and ingenious colliers. North, too, lies Tregaron, a black gnarled knuckle of a drovers' town in a crook of the moors; Henry Richard's town, the Apostle of Peace, first Welsh Nonconformist radical MP to be elected on working-class votes and working-class issues, when the men of Merthyr got their vote in 1868.

Look east; across the river down there is Llanybyther, famous for its horse fairs. In the nineteenth century it specialised in pit ponies for the Valleys over across the Black Mountain. And to the south and west curves the Teifi, threading its way from bleak uplands to the summer lushness of a coracle-haunted mouth, peopled with gentry mansions and the craggy chapels of radicalism — and peopled in the nineteenth century with woollen mills churning out flannel shirts for the Valleys' miners. The whole region in the nineteenth century was locked into the industrial world of the south-east, in its migrant workers, its chapel fraternities and its kindred networks, as the gravestones in its churchyards testify.

Not far from this hill Daniel Rowland used to hurl thousands into those public ecstasies which earned Welsh Methodists the nickname of

---

*Written for *A People and a Proletariat: Essays in the History of Wales 1780-1980* ed. David Smith (Pluto Press and *Llafur*, the Welsh Labour History Society, London, 1980).

Holy Rollers and Jumpers. On this rock, however, he made no impression whatsoever. For this is *The Black Spot* of Calvinist demonology, the original Unitarian hub in Wales; this is Rhydowen, a mother church of Welsh Unitarianism, founded in 1726 in a heretic secession from the Carmarthen Academy. It was the Unitarians of Wales who were the motor force in the creation of the first Welsh democracy, the first Welsh populist nation, the first Welsh Jacobinism, the first Welsh working-class movement. It is a tradition which, in our own day, re-engaged its radicalism and experienced its most significant mutation.

For this chapel is Gwilym Marles's. It was built in 1834, the year in which two Unitarians over in Merthyr produced Wales's first working-class newspaper, *The Worker/Y Gweithiwr*, in the service of Robert Owen's syndicalist movement. Gwilym Marles took time off from becoming Dylan Thomas's great-uncle to fight a great battle against landlords. He was thrown out of his chapel and radical Wales built him a new one. This old one has become a museum. You'll see something familiar yet incongruous in one of the windows: a bust of Lenin.

A bust of Lenin alongside the pulpit is unusual, even for a chapel of Welsh radical Dissent. It was presented by a Unitarian from Aberystwyth who, rumour has it, is buried in the Kremlin Wall. For this was the final *persona* (to date) of Welsh Unitarianism's extraordinarily adaptable yet intransigent organic intelligentsia, personified in the Welsh-language poet, an Independent of 'unitarian' temper and Communist veteran T.E. Nicholas, (Niclas Glais); a dentist, he used to preach the Five Year Plan to his victims as he pulled their teeth: Suffering, like Freedom, is Indivisible.

The history of the Welsh working class in the frontier years seems familiar; the familiarity is false. Long neglected by a Welsh historiography created by the new 'nation' of a 'Nonconformist people' to which it was alien, it was marginal to the customarily ethnocentric historiography of the English, even the Labour English. The first recapture was by an act of will in the generation of militancy around the turn of the nineteenth and twentieth centuries, the enterprise of such as Ness Edwards. The work of academics in our own time has built a formidable structure, impressive in its scholarship and its sympathy, with David Williams and Edward Thompson as twin if opposite architectural supporters; recently there has been a shift into a deeper historical autonomy. We have our *Llafur*, our societies, our workshops, our miners' library. But we inch our way across continents of ignorance. And the people whom we try to serve as people's remembrancers, are a people without memory. Even 'traditions' have been manufactured late and imperfectly; not until the 1970s did Merthyr raise a plaque to its 1831 martyr Dic Penderyn (but not to the leader Lewsyn yr Heliwr) or Gwent celebrate the March on Newport of 1839.

We do not have many answers yet; indeed the first struggle is to find the right questions. The first need is to rid ourselves of the illusion that these frontier years from the 1780s to the 1850s are an historical region whose contours and parameters at least have been mapped. Maps we do not have; maps are what we need to draw.

Perspectives

Some truths remain truths even if they are familiar. If the nascent Welsh working class in the early nineteenth century had a vanguard, it was without doubt the colliers of Monmouthshire who staffed it, in the most consistent and most effective tradition of *proletarian* militancy in early industrial Wales. And it was Merthyr the iron town which produced the first working-class martyr, the first working-class press, the first serious political movement, the first red flag.

Other truths remain truths even if they are unfamiliar or perhaps ideologically awkward. The first revolt against capitalism in Wales broke out in Merioneth and Montgomeryshire, in rural west and north; the first Welsh trade union known to have affiliated to a national British movement was formed in Newtown; the first Working Men's Association in Wales emerged in Carmarthen. In the 1790s, it is possible to detect a species of 'radical triangle' in Wales, with its points in Montgomeryshire's Llanbrynmair-Llanidloes-Newtown (with southern Merioneth as a spiritual annexe until Britain blew its radical brains out across the Atlantic), the southern Valleys and that complex in south Cardiganshire/north Carmarthenshire/north Pembrokeshire which was the human matrix of so many working-class movements. That triangle appears and reappears in the years which follow, to find some kind of appropriate symbolic climax in Hugh Williams the Chartist leader *and* grey eminence of Rebecca, with his patriotic songs and his tricolour, linking in his person the textile workers of mid-Wales, the urban and rural *sans-culotterie* of Carmarthen and its hinterland and the ironworkers and miners of the Valleys.

The first obstacles to confront are the related notions of isolation, backwardness and 'primitive rebels'.

Running across mid-Wales in the late eighteenth century, from Machynlleth to the English border, was the flannel country, a scattered industry of farm-based weavers and spinners focused on the mini-factories of the fulling mills and dependent on the Shrewsbury Drapers. When industrial capitalism drove into the region on the backs of 'Welsh drapers' from Liverpool and Lancashire, the whole district was thrust into a crisis of 'modernisation'; the emergence of shoestring native entrepreneurs, the first factories in Llanidloes and Newtown, a massive growth in pauperisation as small commodity producers were turned into proletarians. The response was a distinctive and millenarian migration to the USA, highly Jacobin in temper, and the emergence of a rooted radicalism which was ultimately to debouch into Chartism. It would be ludicrous to talk of isolation, backwardness and primitive rebels in the Llanidloes-Newtown Montgomeryshire which was the stamping ground of Henry Hetherington, the *Poor Man's Guardian* himself, of Charles Jones and Thomas Powell and their kin. But it would be no less ludicrous to apply such terms to that rural Llanbrynmair to the west which became virtually a factory-parish in its own right, even if its inhabitants did speak Welsh. There, over the winter of 1795-6, great crowds assembled in defiance of the civil power, men made Jacobin speeches. Llanbrynmair, home of one of the most distinctive of Madoc migrations, was the home of the man who fathered the first native-born governor of the state of Ohio in the USA. Customary descriptions of the weavers of Montgomeryshire talk of 'part-time' work by farmers. In fact, the cloth trade was the vital margin between survival and desperate poverty; the first migrations in 1793 were stopped at Liverpool under the law against the migration of *artisans*; the leader, Ezekiel Hughes, had been apprenticed to a clock maker; their first concern in their Welsh liberty settlement of Beula in the USA was to create a rural industry, with which they had been familiar at home. This was a population of worker-peasants with its own breed of tough, literate and effective organic intellectuals. Desperate they may have been; isolated, backward and primitive rebels they were not.

Even more striking is the *web* cloth country of Merioneth, a belt of unremitting mountain poverty running along the Berwyn mountains to Corwen and north and west to the armpit of Llŷn. Over the winter whole families from this intensely poor and intensely Welsh people would meet to knit *en masse*, cheered on by the harpists, poets and singers who turned the district into a heartland of Welsh popular culture as it was later to be of popular preachers and craggy polemicists over Biblical texts. Peasants with primitive technique in a harsh environment, no doubt. But their production, which could sell 20,000 pairs of stockings at £18,000 a year in Bala and Llanrwst, was directed entirely at Charleston in the USA, the West Indies and the Gulf of Mexico, through the busy little port of Barmouth. There was a panic over American Independence in Dolgellau in 1775, and it was when Barmouth was closed in the French Wars, as the Welsh drapers moved in, that Merioneth suffered its crisis, with Jacobin toasts in the pubs of Bala, mass riots against the militia, calls for a 'government of the poor' and its own Madoc migration to the Land of the Free.

Much the same was true of the south-west, of the similar stocking trade concentration around Tregaron and Llandovery, of the hard-pressed artisans and smallholders of Cardiganshire encroaching without cease on the two-thirds of its stubborn soil owned by the Crown, of the deeply *American* temper of its southern district with its neighbours in upland Carmarthenshire and Pembrokeshire. This was the region most intimately in contact with America, the source of some of the earliest migrations. Here, the Baptist trans-Atlantic inter-national, focused on Pennsylvania and Rhode Island College, with its own small fleet of four or five favoured vessels, its endless flow of Jacobin letters between Wales's unofficial consul in the USA, Samuel Jones of Philadelphia, and his brethren back home, found a firm and fecund anchorage. The American dimension is central, of course; it turned relatively affluent and literate Glamorgan, for example, with its coteries of craftsmen, artisans, small merchants and workshop owners, patriots Welsh and universal and Jacobins, into one of the nurseries of the democratic ideology in an age of Atlantic Revolution. But, once more, to apply such terms as backwardness and primitivism to such a region would be ludicrous; Joseph Priestley could bring pious divines in deepest Cardiganshire to the point of fist fights; the Unitarian hub was here, 'buried' in Welsh Wales. It was the Baptist Association of the south-west which committed itself to produce French translations of the Puritan and millenarian Canne Bible and to produce them *en masse* to serve Morgan John Rhys's crusade for Protestant liberty among the *sans-culottes* of Paris.

Even in the more familiar world of the ironworkers and miners of Glamorgan and Gwent, the primitive-rebel approach has been grotesquely overworked. Certainly God never meant men and women to live at those valley heads, but from the 1790s, the whole area was ribbed with canals and tramways; along one of the latter the first steam locomotive in the world ran in 1804. Before 1789 the 'primitive'

frontier village of Merthyr could boast a bookseller taking weekly
consignments from London; I repeat, *weekly*. Lewsyn yr Heliwr
himself, charismatic hero of the Merthyr Rising of 1831, was the son of
a butcher in the marginal mountain parish of Penderyn; he was literate
in English, so literate in fact that on the convict ship *John* he was
employed in teaching his English fellow prisoners to read and write
their own language. The discourse of English radicalism, in its most
advanced form, was commonplace in Merthyr and Monmouthshire by
the 1790s; *Infidelity* was a periodic mushroom growth. It was not
ignorance or isolation or primitiveness or the Welsh language which
made the response of these men to sophisticated practice and ideology
so apparently sporadic and discontinuous; it was their predicament,
which was in fact that of American workers during their years of
frenetic and revolutionising industrialisation.

That much of Welsh hill farming was primitive and at subsistence
level, that communications were poor (at least before 1790 in the
south-east), that many Welshmen were 'traditional' (as many were
continuously mobile), that the Welsh language was an insulating
factor (which I do not believe for a moment, having lived with it and in
it through an English-speaking adolescence) have become truisms. A
triusm may be true, but it is necessary not to submit to useful
simplification, even in a good cause; it is necessary not to see modes of
production advance in a preordained column-of-route. One minor but
symptomatic fact: Volney's *Ruins of Empires* (1791) which became, as
an exercise in revolutionary fantasy or science-fiction, a standard text
of working-class intellectuals for three generations was available in
Welsh in 1793, just after the first English version and earlier than the
first popularly effective version in English.

Two factors need to register in the mind: firstly, the autonomy of the
'superstructural', to quote the vernacular — 'primitive' structures are
quite frequently exposed to quite unprimitive ideologies and secondly
the coexistence of modes of production.

The only way for a serious historian of the working class, for a
marxist historian, a people's remembrancer, to approach the early
history of a Welsh 'working class', is firstly for him/her to shed all
notions of backwardness-isolation-primitive rebels (however august
their apostolic descent), to shed all notions of a linear progression in
orthodoxy (and comprehensibility) and secondly, to accept, in its full
reality (and analytical horror) the idea that modes of production
coexist, that people can simultaneously live in different time-scales.
Time is not indivisible. At one moment in the early nineteenth century,

a man in Merthyr could be living within the world of a highly skilled worker in an integrated firm, probably the largest and most advanced of its kind on earth, while another man, tramping after sheep in some cloud-capped and barren valley, could be living in a world whose *mores* were fixed by the medieval, kindred and 'tribal' laws of Hywel Dda. More disconcerting is the thought that these men might well have been brothers.

Modes of Production

The industrialisation of Wales was imperial from birth and it hit a country which, almost uniquely in Britain, still had 'peasants'.

The Wales of the *Ancien Regime*, no less than the Wales of the Alternative Society, was a product of the creation of Great Britain with its Atlantic dimension. The historic British nation formed in the eighteenth century around the armature of Anglo-Scottish union, merchant capitalism and liberal oligarchy. Wales, subjected to the jurisprudence of capitalism from the days of the Tudors, was formed in the process. There was a massive shrinkage in the political nation, power in parliamentary terms shrivelling up into a handful of magnate families, often Scottish in origin and devoid of any Welsh content, just as the Church in Wales became the fief of broad-bottomed and Whig bishops *en route* to higher things (one of them was accused by his clergy of being an atheist); Wales's own judicial system, the Great Sessions, could be abolished in 1830 without a quiver. The multitudinous lesser gentry of Wales was decimated, lost its foothold in public life, dwindled into a merely local and poverty-stricken prestige; men of long pedigree and short purse, they cultivated an alternative system of values, lending some power to Dissent, the new Methodism and the Welsh cultural revival. Challenging them were the multiplying professional and artisan groups which gained power from the rapid sweep of British Atlantic and mercantile empire. A peasant society living on the edge of subsistence characterised most of upland and pastoral Wales, but it was a society which also lived by the drove-herds of cattle seasonally tramping into England, bringing back currency and breeding banks, accompanied by the great droves of equally skinny people tramping no less purposefully into England to be fattened. And into and through this 'peasant' society throbbed the thrusts of merchant capitalism. Before 1800, the copper and brass industries of Britain were located, 90 per cent of them, around Swansea with its dependent mines in Anglesey under that Thomas Williams who clawed out a world monopoly. Tin-plate differentiated itself in the same period, located in Monmouthshire and around Swansea, almost totally directed to export, once more a British monopoly. By 1800, no less, the new iron industry with its coal dependency was accounting for 40 per cent of British pig iron production and was also geared almost wholly to export. Even Merioneth fed the Gulf of Mexico; the production of Montgomeryshire, through Blackwell Hall in London, went out to Europe and the Americas. The great thrust of British capitalist breakthrough during the Revolutionary and Napoleonic Wars was pivoted on Atlantic slave power. The British export sector in copper, brass, iron, tin-plate, plebeian cloth, was in Wales; the new Welsh economy was built on the backs of the blacks.

In consequence a plurality of modes of production coexisted within a country measuring scarcely 200 miles from end to end, to generate a bewildering complexity of popular response. Each mode of production produced its own working population; each working population had to live with others and with a rural population of peasants and worker-peasants in complicated interaction. It was the thrust of the iron industry, above all, after the adoption of the vital puddling process, the 'Welsh method' from the 1790s, which most closely approximated to Marx's model of an endlessly innovative, revolutionising, expanding process of self-generated contradiction.

The overall consequences are familiar but no less staggering. Over little more than two generations, the population of Wales nearly tripled; from 1841, most of it was sucked into the frenetically industrialising and increasingly English-speaking south-east. The Welsh, by the thousand, broke away from Establishment. Dissent, with the novel Methodism, may have accounted for perhaps 15 per cent of the population by 1800; by 1851, Dissent's predominance was so overwhelming that Anglicanism became a kind of historical joke. Together with Methodism, driven into Nonconformity by official repression in 1811, Dissent outnumbered the Establishment by seven or even ten to one in some places and averaged a five-to-one hegemony. From mid-century onwards, only the Nonconformist Welsh (maybe about half the Welsh on the ground) are historically visible. The rest, before the 1890s, are un-persons.

It is in this context that one has to locate the emergence of a Welsh 'working class'. During the 1830s, its presence is *visible* and *audible*; from the conjuncture of 1829-34, the Monmouthshire colliers' strike of 1830 with its remarkably sophisticated system of control, the Merthyr

Rising of 1831, the penetration of the Lancashire colliers' union and the National Association for the Protection of Labour, the enrolment of the locked-out workers of Merthyr in the National Union of the Working Classes in November 1831; from that climacteric moment, through the revived but now quasi-political Scotch Cattle of the early 1830s, the upsurge of the Owenite movement with the first Welsh working-class journal in 1834, the massive and decisive intervention of the Merthyr working class in the election of 1835, the crystallisation in Chartism which united Carmarthen, Llanidloes and the Valleys, the abortive national uprising whose trigger was the march on Newport, the generation-long experience of Chartism which became virtually a sub-culture within British society, Welsh working-class consciousness, sometimes in revolutionary form, is an unavoidable *presence* in the history of Wales.

The 'disappearance' of that consciousness in the years after 1842, at least in the autonomous form which characterised it from 1829 onwards, no less than its formation in the preceding years, remain, in our virtually total ignorance of the things that matter, major priorities for the people's remembrancers of Wales.

Clearly the work situation was one determinant. A striking feature of the new working populations was, on the one hand, the high proportion of skilled men among them and on the other, their fluidity and class incoherence. Copper had the lowest proportion of skilled workers, maybe 15 per cent; tin-plate, however, with a skilled proportion of around 25 per cent was as stable as copper. The communities they created around the social and intellectual capital of Swansea had some of the worker-peasant characteristics of the northern slate quarries; there was no serious conflict in the copper industry throughout the period. To the east, however, the iron industry, 30-40 per cent of whose workers were skilled men, experienced continuous technical innovation and a roller-coaster growth; the colleries dependent on the ironworks shared some of their characteristics, while those of the sale-coal trade of Monmouthshire, run by under-capitalised Welsh entrepreneurs in cut-throat competition, witnessed some of the fiercest and most sophisticated struggles of the frontier years, led often by the skilled men who formed 20-25 per cent of the workforce.

Most works were a mosaic of sub-contractors, ranging from the master-craftsmen of tin-plate, through co-operative contracts with 'gentlemen puddlers' to the cutter commanding his team, with the *butty* or *doggy*, in effect a minor sub-capitalist of working-class origin, a distinctive figure — and an ambiguous one, now a staunch defender of the rights of property, now a spokesman for 'responsible' if militant protest. All over the coalfield, workers were mobile, flitting from job to job, following the shifts of an unpredictable iron-coal complex. The inflow from west Wales, at first seasonal, was continuous; the Irish started to flood in during the 1830s, when the huddled clusters of houses, chapels and pubs clinging to the valley sides went through their major ecological disaster; as many as 10,000 people could move through Merthyr in a year; men would tramp twenty miles to watch a foot-race; there were many Klondyke settlements alongside the model housing of the ironmasters and the indescribable tangles of cottages thrown up by middle-class speculators. The accident rate was high and, from the 1830s, became murderous; the infantile death rate was catastrophic; three-quarters of those who died were under five and average life expectancy at birth in the 1830s was about twenty. The 'natural' death rate, however, was lower than that of country towns and the housing was superior to that of the west. Friendly societies were as numerous as the pubs which housed them and the chapels which confronted them. Wages were high if fluctuating, though sectional unemployment was rife and, in the Monmouthshire sale-coal areas, general unemployment was epidemic. Some of the more skilled trades had regular training systems and most had some kind of rough and ready approximation to apprenticeship, but with the continuous inflow and permanent insecurity, with the townships collapsing under the challenges, with no-go areas like Merthyr's *China* coexisting with a black economy of penny capitalists and drifters, permanent organisation proved extraordinarily difficult.

In the process, distinctive communities with distinctive patterns of action and response mushroomed. Most striking were the sale-coal villages of the lower valleys of Monmouthshire. Bleak, barren places, lacking even the amenities of a Merthyr, they were largely one-class settlements. Considered only half-human by their employers and the middle class, often quasi-permanently trapped in debt by the truck system, racked by the merciless competition of shoestring firms and by periodic bouts of miserable unemployment, this people, distinguished from each other often only by the presence or absence of window-sashes in their houses, proved the most militant and also the most capable of sustained and sophisticated struggle. More mixed in origin than most coalfield townships, they developed out of a very Welsh and semi-rural popular culture, highly organised and effective resistance movements and unions. From these villages came the hard core of the physical force Chartists; it was at Blackwood that the Newport insurrection was planned. By the 1830s these embattled men and women had created a vivid, living working-class culture, at once intransigent and cultivated, and had made themselves into a proletarian vanguard.

The ironworks settlements to the north, clustering around their capital of Merthyr, were more varied and richer in texture, with resident masters and a fashionable 'society', with a more complex (and wealthy) middle class. Skilled men like the puddlers were organising themselves early and *ad hoc* combinations of ironstone miners and colliers were frequent, with marginal, semi-artisanal groups like the hauliers playing a distinctive role. Artisan crafts were themselves strong and, above all, there was a persistent tradition of multi-class Jacobin democracy, very visible in Merthyr, but present throughout northern Monmouthshire. It was from the late 1830s and the 1840s that the *mores* of the colliers began to rise within this iron-dominated complex, as the valleys of Aberdare and the lower Rhonddas were opened up and Monmouthshire men moved west.

In that same period, driven on by its technical development, iron and its related trades were also shifting west to disturb the more settled pattern of the anthracite coalfield and to impose a more uniform style on the whole region from Pontypool to Llanelli. Beyond the latter lay a south-west Wales in quasi-permanent crisis and in continuous adjustment into a catchment zone for the south-east. Hit harder by the population explosion than most regions, Cardiganshire was the most disturbed county in Wales, a county of land hunger, inching self-improvement, smallholder resistance movements and seasonal migration, the Galicia of Wales. The Dissent of the region, heavily colonised by the newer Methodism, was moving out of the defensive and negative withdrawal of the west into militancy as the whole region slithered into an occult malaise and a permanent disaffection from an Anglican magistracy. It was this which tipped the already and traditionally turbulent town of Carmarthen with its press, its myriad small trades in crisis, its tribes of bloody-minded artisans, its brisk Bristol Channel commerce, over the edge into a kind of secession from public order. The endless faction feuds of Blues and Reds in Carmarthen took on a sharper tone, as its hinterland was riven by that tension between Dissent and the Church in which a populist 'nation' was shaping itself behind a language and religious line which was also a class line. There was a rooted populist radicalism in Carmarthen, fed by its neighbour villages, which could make it a *sans-culotte* sort of place. In a sense, it served as a staging post between the south-west and the industrial complex; Chartism in Wales was appropriately born there.

Hugh Williams certainly found it a fairly easy jump from the textile towns of mid-Wales, with their small but alert and highly self-conscious factory population among a countryside scarcely less industrial in character. It was a tougher jump up into the north, where the relationships between the subculture of the quarry men of the north-west and the ironworks, collieries and mixed industry of north-eastern Denbighshire and Flintshire resembled those between Swansea and Merthyr at first. It was out of the Denbighshire of the 1790s, from 'remote' Cerrig-y-Drudion that Jac Glan y Gors, the Welsh Tom Paine, came; the north-eastern coalfield was the first seriously to respond to the millenarian unionism of 1830. The industrialisation of the north, however, ran into stasis, the population drain was continuous and Methodist-dominated Dissent a defensive reaction before the 1840s. With some brief exceptions, working-class radicalism in the north, before the great struggles of the late nineteenth century, was a matter of scattered groups and even individuals, though the quarrymen were already shaping that distinctive commonwealth of theirs which in later years would turn a lockout into a three-year civil war and a major crisis of community and tradition.

Each group, in its own particular environment, within its own pattern of authority and resistance, had to find its own way to cope with class incoherence and fluidity, to seek modes of thought and action within whatever traditions they brought with them from the sparse and bitter villages or artisan towns, whatever practices and skills they had learned from earlier struggles in industry, whatever they could marshal from their native cultures and the cultures to which they were continuously and often dramatically exposed.

What is clear, from a necessarily cursory and ill-informed survey of their actions from the 1790s to the 1840s is a pattern of episodic but frequent (sometimes annual) organisation to resist wage reductions and defend a traditional standard, occasional eruptions from what was, evidently, the familiar world of the 'moral economy' and a steady and ever richer elaboration of more permanent fellowship, whether in pub, craft, club, chapel or eisteddfod. There is quite evidently some qualitative change in the 1820s and at the critical conjuncture of 1830 a veritable 'explosion' of self-consciousness. Three factors seem general and influential: debt as the forcing-house and negative definition of a working class; a shift from consumer to producer awareness and, concurrent with the latter, a shift from protest to control as the objective. Indeed, control, of their workplace, their trade, their industry, their communities, moves centre-stage in working-class and popular action in the crisis of 1830. This drive for control, which was also a drive for dignity, found a more secure and a more permanent anchorage in a political outlook than earlier consumer protest had done. Indeed working-class consciousness in recognisable form emerges in the Valleys of South Wales with abrupt and explosive force around 1830 precisely because a popular thrust for control, in the teeth of a debt crisis among a population which had elaborated a dense network of partly occult institutions, essentially cultural in character, coincided with an equally sudden incursion of a political culture at the crisis of the Reform Bill.

Politics had been present, in some form or other, throughout; politics was in fact central. A radical and populist political culture, providing a possible frame of reference, already existed: it was there, to their hand.

For the birth of democracy had preceded their own.

Cultures and Ideologies

The ideology of democracy is pre-industrial (a truth whose implications we do not seem to have thought through). The Chartist programme was first published in 1780, in the reform campaign of the American crisis. The Anglo-American character of British Jacobinism, of which Thomas Paine is an appropriate symbol, was even more marked in Wales, one of the sectors of Britain in the most direct contact with America. In the last years of the eighteenth century, the first Welsh democracy and the first modern Welsh 'nation' were born of the conjuncture.

One of its strongholds was Glamorgan, with its big Vale villages full of a bilingual artisanry and a patriot lower-middle class, its Cowbridge Book Society, its Dissenting network linking it to the tough-minded chapels of the hill country, with its own Academy and its access to Bristol colleges. Such men as Lewis Hopkin, craftsman extraordinary, his house full of books, Welsh, English, Latin, French, grammars of the Welsh bards and the latest number of the *Spectator*; John Bradford of Betws near Bridgend, traditional nursery of Glamorgan's Welsh poets, a Deist fuller and dyer; William Edward who built the bridge at

Pontypridd; Edward Ifan of Aberdare, apprentice in wood and verse to Hopkin and on tramp like most of them before he settled as Unitarian minister, created a lively, open but frustrated society living in the interstices of gentry politics like some kind of diffused Philadelphia. They nurtured the political culture of Morgan John Rhys of Llanfabon, a Baptist Jacobin who travelled to France to preach Protestant liberty, brought out the first political periodical in the Welsh language in 1793 and founded a Welsh liberty settlement in America, and of Iolo Morganwg, Edward Williams, the tramping stonemason of the Vale, a fantastic and maimed genius who invented the Gorsedd of Bards as Jacobin, Unitarian and Masonic inheritors of a Druid tradition turned into something akin to Rousseau's Natural Religion, and gave the newly-awakening Welsh a half approximation to a national and radical ideology. Out of this world came two of the major British radicals of European and American reputation: Richard Price, the political Dissenter whose sermons on the French Revolution provoked Edmund Burke into his *Reflections* and who was invited by Congress to serve as financial adviser to the new USA and David Williams the Deist who may have supplied Robespierre with his Cult of the Supreme Being.

These people worked closely with the London-Welsh in their new and radical society of the Gwyneddigion, staffed largely from modernising Denbighshire, by such as Owen Jones, William Owen, David Samwell and the rest who tried to revive the eisteddfod as a kind of national academy and to re-engage an interrupted tradition. In alliance with Iolo Morganwg, these men, with some radicals of the Old Dissent, shuffled together into a loosely united organic intelligentsia in the 1790s with a journal and a campaign to create (in their own words, to 'revive') a Welsh nation conceived in liberty.

They made heavy weather of it, in the teeth of population explosion, wartime pressure-cooker industrialisation, government repression, loyalist witch-hunts, and Methodist advance. They used the revived Madoc myth to break through this wall and make contact with the disaffected working populations of west and north, whose migrations to the USA were charged with a millenarian passion, but their combative little 'nation' foundered on the rocks not only of the old regime but of the alternative society battling its way into existence.

For the real organic intelligentsia of the populist Welsh were the preacher-journalists of Dissent. It is from the 1790s that Methodism, closely followed by Dissent, surges forward in west and north, to disrupt Old Dissent itself. There was a profound difference in quality.

In 1823, when Thomas Clarkson went on an anti-slavery mission to Wales, he found Dissenters of west and north, there mainly Methodists, almost an underground of withdrawn, inward-looking and defensive dissidence; the gentry would not sit with them on committees, subjected them to endless petty persecution and exclusion. John Elias himself, the Methodist leader who towered over many Welsh minds like a pope, did not dare meet Clarkson at home; they had to slink off to Chester. In the more varied society of east and south, Dissenters, among whom Baptists and Independents were more prominent, moved with far greater ease and sharper radicalism.

This distinction between 'quietists' and 'politicians' which, under the drive of evangelicalism, with its sensuous hymns and mass participation, actually ran *through* the Old Dissent itself, persisted. The first major press of Welsh Dissent, from *Seren Gomer* onwards, moved in an Independent-Baptist milieu to generate the radical *Diwygiwr* of Llanelli in the 1830s and to supply Chartism with many of its spokesmen, but a great body of Nonconformist opinion, particularly the Methodist, was a dead weight of apolitical quietism, often indistinguishable from a bilious Toryism.

As the chapels moved to embrace more and more of the working population of the industrial areas, the consequences were complex. The sweeping advance of Methodism and a 'methodised' Dissent into north and west could perhaps be interpreted in terms of the currently fashionable 'psychic compensation'; I cannot say. It was clearly a response to the disruption of traditional society. For a couple of generations, it locked its people away in a defensive bunker, a passive self-definition against hegemonic society. But there was a trend, a minority but powerful trend running in the opposite direction driving men out with God's Sword to build a new Jerusalem. The Unitarian cause, minority but trenchant and highly influential, grew stronger right through into the 1830s; trends called 'unitarian' within Independency and Baptistry bucked the dominant evangelical drive. The Baptists were split wide open around 1800 as Independent chapels fell to Unitarians. There is a clear regional divergence; it is in Glamorgan-Monmouth and in mid-Wales that the minority Dissenting radicalism found some kind of permanent home, fed by the productive powerhouses on the Teifi and in Carmarthen. They produced a free-thinking, Deist, Infidel wing of outriders and ran into congruence with the patriot Jacobinism of bohemians and unbiblical radicals.

After the great storms of the revolutionary decade, the migrations, the repression, the rampant evangelicalism, a new political tradition was rooted in Wales, in clusters of Unitarians, radical Baptists and Independents, Deists, Welsh revivalists scattered over the face of the south-west, mid-Wales and, most visible of all, in Merthyr and Monmouthshire. Merthyr village became a stronghold of Jacobinism, its freeholders 'sturdy old Republicans', with their Cyfarthfa Philosophical Society, their radical and, in 1831, freethinking and Deist eisteddfodau, their *Patriot* pubs and political societies of Welsh-patriot *Cymreigyddion*; Zephaniah Williams over in Nant-y-Glo and Blaina, with his Humanist Society and political clubs, sprang from the same root and all across the Valleys, there was a scatter of such men, some flamboyant like William Price, many, earnest moles of democracy who were often the backbone of working-class movements and ended their lives as Liberal municipal reformers.

The relationship between these people and the nascent working-class movements was complex, as the single, unified tradition of democracy splintered in the early nineteenth century under the pulverising hammer of class formation which ground society apart like some clumsy cast-iron mechanism. Petty-bourgeois many without doubt were, in social status and outlook, but it is not in fact possible to draw a clear line; there were working-class and artisan Unitarians and free-thinkers. Much the same is true of the chapels, at least of the Old Dissent. Not until the mass Temperance movement of the late 1830s do the chapels in the Valleys play that unambiguously social-control role which English working-class historians unhesitatingly allot to them. It is quite possible that class structures and the ideologies which went with them created a quite different pattern in Wales; certainly the Welsh elementary schoolteacher of later generations did *not* play the role customarily assigned to him in England; very often he displaced the minister and challenged the miners' agent as a popular leader. Something of that *populist* order seems to have held good, at least in the Valleys, in the textile townships of mid-Wales and in parts of Cardiganshire, Carmarthenshire and Pembrokeshire. Many chapels were exclusive, battling for grace and respectability out of the sinful world of the 'roughs', but many were not and most chapels in the Valleys were strongly working-class from their foundation. It was the heavy commitment of Baptist and Independent spokesmen to the Welsh Chartist movement which was one of its distinguishing features. Certainly the cultural world of the chapels with their big and busy Sunday schools, their training in music and poetry, offered not only a home to the displaced but an arena for their talent. A rival to the pub world, the chapel world in the early generations in fact interacted with it. Not until the massive restabilisation of the middle years of the century and the impact of Temperance, does the more familiar dichotomy register clearly.

What is striking is that the radicalism of what one can call, loosely, the 'unitarian' connexion found an entry into working-class life through its popular culture. Ultimately derived from old Catholic Wales and settled by the eighteenth century into a form of 'folkloric' and customary adaptation to a hard life, this was rich and complex, with its *cwrw bach* (little beer; self-help mutual loan and community celebrations rather like the American 'shower') its *ceffyl pren* (cock-horse) extra-legal village discipline, its passion for games, for betting, for sometimes almost incredibly arduous foot-races, its admiration for physical prowess and pugilism, its folk-heroes like the red-haired giant Shoni Sguborfawr, champion of Wales (so he claimed), *Emperor* of China, army spy among the Scotch Cattle, mercenary hero of Rebecca and Australian convict dead of drink; or like Lewsyn yr Heliwr, the huntsman leader of the Merthyr Rising, a local Emiliano Zapata. Equally passionate, however, was the commitment of many of them to the standard-bearers of a culture ultimately derived from the old and dead bardic order, the harpists, the singers of the complex verse *penillion*, the ballad singers. Shoni Sguborfawr's boon companion in his Rebecca phase, after all, was Dai'r Cantwr, Dai the Singer, a hedge-poet. Dic Dywyll, Dic Dark, a blind ballad singer from north Wales, was the Voice of the People in the Merthyr of 1831; selling his song sheets on a Saturday night, he could make more money in a week than a furnace manager. It was in 1831 that Dic Dywyll won an eisteddfod prize — and the eisteddfod was that of the Merthyr Free Enquirers, the Zetetics who had been organised by Richard Carlile around his journal the *Republican.*

This amorphous and vivid world of the popular culture could find some organised outlet not only in eisteddfodau but in the choirs and verse festivals of the chapels, with their combative working-class conductors and teachers. Characteristically two of the recognised centres of this new kind of popular excellence in Wales were Merthyr and Llanidloes. It was the Unitarians who launched the secular eisteddfodau which blossomed from the 1820s in Merthyr and Monmouthshire to find a focus in Abergavenny, home of that dreaded figure in modern Welsh folklore, the eisteddfod adjudicator. And it is characteristic that it was out of this world that the first Chartist leaders in Wales came: Morgan Williams, a master-weaver of rooted local stock (there were harpists in his family), Unitarian like the brothers John, sons of a Unitarian minister. At the height of the rebellion of 1831, Matthew John walked alone up the fortress of Penydarren House to present the rebels' terms and to make clear his hourly expectation of national insurrection. Most striking of all was John Thomas (Ieuan Ddu), a Unitarian from Carmarthen who was the greatest music teacher in south Wales (he is said to have introduced Handel's Messiah into Wales); a Zetetic friend of Zephaniah Williams, he launched his Zetetic eisteddfodau in 1831 and with Morgan Williams, edited Wales's first working-class newspaper, *The Worker/Y Gweithiwr*; he was responsible for the Welsh section: a eulogy of the Tolpuddle Martyrs. Men like these were among the first generation of Chartist leaders; they served their apprenticeship in the crisis of 1830. Those of Merthyr are *visible* because they were concentrated and because their activities have been documented. But they were everywhere in the Valleys, around Llanidloes and Newtown, in Carmarthen and the south-west. Zephaniah Williams in Monmouthshire, William Price in Pontypridd were highly distinctive individuals, but it would be a fundamental error to consider them unrepresentative; they had hosts of brothers, far less visible, but identifiable from their actions and occasional side-comments.

It seems to have been through this cultural milieu, under the dramatic pressures of industrial capitalism (much as the Scotch Cattle grew out of the *ceffyl pren* world) that the new working class achieved an identity and committed itself to democracy.

Such an outcome, of course, was not inevitable.

Forms of Action

In considering working-class and popular action between the 1790s and 1840s it is difficult to avoid some sense of a linear and almost inevitable progression towards Chartism. Even if one tries to break free of this teleological prison and to analyse particular and concrete conjunctures, the end-product seems much the same.

The 1790s clearly belong to Edward Thompson's moral economy of the crowd, mass actions in north Wales against the militia, the Navy Acts, enclosures, grain prices; 'traditional' price actions all over Wales during the dreadful years of 1795-6 and 1800-1; and in those latter years a natural justice insurrection at Merthyr, with the troops in and two men hanged. Even then, however, a political thread of Jacobin democracy runs through everything, weaving in and out of the crowd actions. It is present in the slogans of Swansea colliers in 1793, in the speeches during the great Denbigh riot of 1795, in the crowd protests in Merioneth and Llanbrynmair; it is present above all in the emigrants who voted with their feet and in their free Wales in America drank toasts to the brave *sans-culottes* and voted for Thomas Jefferson. It finds some kind of institutional base in the Merthyr and Monmouthshire of the 1800s. Moreover, as an epilogue to the Merthyr grain action of 1800-1, a broadsheet found locally locks at least a militant minority into the nation-wide insurrectionary conspiracies of that year which were to debouch into the abortive Despard affair. How far this represents any interaction between Jacobin villagers and proletarian and populist rebels it is difficult to say; the Jacobins had re-emerged in the petitioning campaigns of 1800. By 1806 the local ones were organised into a Philosophical Society even as friendly societies, often the cover for trade unions and gun glubs, mushroomed in the pubs of that same radical quarter of Merthyr on the lip of what became *China.*

Even more mysterious is what was clearly a decisive conjuncture in 1810-13; in a country so heavily dependent on Atlantic trade, the crisis which precipitated the American War of 1812 in the middle of the Napoleonic blockade was bound to be severe. Yet we know practically nothing about it. What we do know seems significant. These were the years when puddlers formed trade unions and took a Luddite oath, in which tradition places the origin of the Scotch Cattle of Monmouthshire, certainly Luddite in their impenetrable secrecy. The garrison at Brecon was established at the same time. One senses a proletarian rebellion in virtually total autonomy, made manifest by the remarkable south Wales strike of 1816, perhaps the most massive movement on the coalfield throughout the nineteenth century (and trenchantly reconstructed by David Jones). That strike, against the vicious wage reductions of the post-war slump, was an intensely active and sustained movement, ranging back and forth across Monmouthshire and the Merthyr complex, using traditional forms like the marching gangs and attacks on works and masters' houses but also evidently characterised by a high degree of organisation and an apparent independence of any other social grouping. In the aftermath, once more, a leaflet unmistakably linking at least some militants to national insurrectionary movements, such as the Pentrich Rising hints at. How far was this totally independent? Speeches by Hunt and Cobbett came down in Welsh translation immediately afterwards and from 1811 there had been a harsh government crackdown on itinerant preachers (driving Welsh Methodism to seek the protection of the Toleration Act) which radicalised Dissent. The anti-war campaign of the Ricardo-influenced bourgeoisie certainly mobilised radicals and the Merthyr Jacobins made their first organised entry into parliamentary reform in 1815. We just do not know. What *is* clear, however, is that working-class and popular protest on the whole seems to have taken a familiar form, essentially a defensive protest, expressing a consumer mentality, including that of wage-earners as consumers.

There is a qualitative change in the 1820s, mysterious in Merthyr — which nevertheless seems to have shared in the 'silent insurrection' of those years, to judge from responses after 1829 and suggestions of a leftward lurch in the eisteddfod world (there was also a Mechanics Institute at Dowlais by 1829) — most vivid in Monmouthshire. It is at this point that the Monmouthshire colliers take the initiative, wrest it from the skilled iron-men. The colliers' strike of 1822 was a highly sophisticated exercise and running alongside the mass actions, often violent, always highly intelligent, of the troubles of the 1820s are the Scotch Cattle. A highly effective underground movement, with its own Scotch Law and code of honour, its regular rhythmic practice of warning notes, summons by horn, midnight meetings, intimidatory visits by a Herd (from a different valley) under its Bull to blacklegs, profiteers, aliens, offenders against community, this was rooted in the colliery villages which were to be strongholds of the physical force Chartists, but subjected much of the ironworks belt to its moral authority. The 'primitiveness' of this movement (again brilliantly analysed by David Jones) has been grossly overstated. It was in fact a sophisticated, well ordered exercise in solidarity (necessarily terrorist in the circumstances of Monmouthshire). It looks like a wholly proletarian exercise moreover and noticeable is the stress on *control.* This, however, is no less apparent, strikingly so, in the great strikes of 1830s when the colliers, trying to impose production quotas on shifty and arrogant employers, were in fact elaborating a complicated mechanism in defence of their trades, their communities and their standard of living, and moreover did not hesitate to call in a local surgeon to help them. By 1832 the Bull's warning notes were carrying the slogan *Reform.*

This rising significance of ideas of workers' control, running into congruence with the explosion of self-consciously *working-class* politics in the early stages of the crucial Reform crisis, is also visible in Merthyr, where of course the outcome was dramatic. The slump of

1829 generated a severe debt crisis. The new stipendiary's court together with the local debtors' court co-operated to hold the working class together during the slump. Inevitably this imprisoned much of the working class in debt (Merthyr at one time ran out of funds for poor relief) and thrust the shopocracy into crisis. Distraints for debt and a campaign against petty criminals subjected a whole sector of the population to misery and repression, began to mark off a 'working class' negatively defined *against* the rest of the population at the very moment when the great tide of radical and working-class propaganda of 1830 came flooding into a Merthyr, whose Unitarian radicals were organising political unions, preaching them to workers, striking for local power in alliance with William Crawshay, a radical ironmaster who did not hesitate to deploy his own men in the cause.

The trigger was the arrival of delegates from the new colliers' union affiliated to the National Association for the Protection of Labour. The latter had made its first penetration into Wales at Newtown; the colliers' union swept north-eastern Wales over the winter of 1830/1, provoking riots and a millenarian response. The coming of the delegates to the great working-class Reform meeting in Merthyr at the annual Waun Fair (last of three such held by independent working-class initiative) precipitated an explosion, in which Owenite unions were engulfed in a classical (but highly organised) natural justice action against the shopocracy, led by Lewsyn yr Heliwr; a direct attack on soldiers marched in from Brecon, again led by Lewsyn, with the loss of two dozen dead and seventy wounded, was itself followed by a communal insurrection which held the town for four days, defeated regulars and yeomanry twice, mobilised (too late) a force of 12,000-20,000 from Monmouthshire and was beaten only after anything from 800 to 1,000 troops had converged on the town and after sustained efforts by masters, using some of the town radicals, to divide and disorganise the rebels. Melbourne played the whole incident cool; a dozen or so scapegoats were punished; Lewsyn was reprieved and only Richard Lewis went to the gallows, as Dic Penderyn, to become (and to remain) the first martyr of the Welsh working class.

More significant in many ways than the Rising itself (and generally ignored by historians) was the massive union campaign and the ghastly, hard-fought lockout which followed, as dour and grim as anything in the black history of the coalfield. In this lockout, the men of Dowlais and Plymouth works acted as a conscious vanguard for the whole working class of south Wales. Support came from as far away as Maesteg; at the last moment, as the Plymouth men were caving in, men marched to try to stiffen them, not only from Cyfarthfa but from Nant-y-Glo. In this struggle, when the men were left isolated, even by Unitarian Jacobins and radical Baptists, the emphasis was wholly on working-class independence and, as among the Monmouthshire colliers, on *control*. By the November when the men were finally beaten, they were rallying to the simultaneous meetings called for by the National Union of the Working Classes (NUWC) in London and committing themselves to the radical, self-consciously working-class wing of the movement at the crisis point — the people Francis Place and the Birmingham crew were organising to defeat. In this cause moreover, the Merthyr men sent delegates to Carmarthen.

The movement was patchy. Of course it was. Dowlais was often out of step with Cyfarthfa; there was great difficulty in co-ordinating with Monmouthshire and such difficulties often led to recrimination and disunity. The men of the Swansea and Neath valleys acted independently. This kind of phenomenon is normal and customary in working-class action; it reflects some rooted realities; Merthyr was never a stronghold of the Scotch Cattle, for example, probably because of its more complex mix of trades and much more visible democratic organisations. But what is really significant is that in both Merthyr and Monmouthshire, as men's minds concentrated on the idea of control (central to the new colliers' union) in a context of almost millenarian political crisis, what can only be called a working-class consciousness emerged. It was defeated, as the NUWC and their kin were defeated in the nation. It had to live in a south Wales where there were garrisons in the five major towns and in which the middle class had been armed against them. This consciousness could not immediately act in independence; it had to operate under other people's hegemony.

But its existence was real enough. Patchy and incompletely autonomous though it was (the Merthyr men of 1831 were committed to Free Trade, for example), it persisted and billowed up in strong waves of feeling and action through the 1830s; in the massive Owenite union movement of 1834, when its first newspaper appeared; in the last great movement of the Scotch Cattle in support, in the intervention in the Merthyr election of 1835 and the power which buttressed the Unitarians as they took over Merthyr from 1835, above all, of course in the unforgettable experience of Chartism, that Chartism which yoked Scotch Cattle and Unitarians, the eisteddfod world and *China*, which united the Valleys with the not-so-very-different world of Llanidloes, Newtown and their villages (where the differences are really those of scale and concentration) and the distinctly more *sans-culotte* milieux of Carmarthen and its villages; that Chartism which was so much more than the march on Newport, significant though *that* is, the Chartism with its coveys of girls in white dresses and green flags, its men marching blue uniformed into the churches, its ritual and colour and ceremony, its endless debating clubs and hidden arms clubs, its Chartist caves and Chartist churches, its massive and all-pervading working-class culture, which lived on in south Wales long after the climacteric moment of 1838-42 and the upsurge of 1848, which so registered on the minds of Marx and Engels and which indulged in its last ghost campaign as it former militants moved on to councils and library committees and sat on the platforms of Nonconformist radicals (including Henry Richard).

The strength and reality of working-class consciousness in the 1830s and early 1840s is best measured by the response of its enemies. Official and respectable reaction to the Merthyr Rising, at the height of the Reform Bill crisis of course, had been hesitant, unsure, careful. Ironmasters were divided over the unions; the Home Secretary of an alarmed government, recognising it eight years later as 'the nearest thing to a fight' they had ever had, trod very carefully indeed. As soon as the Act passed and the great wave of anti-working class legislation began to surge through the Commons, as soon as necessary if rather rowdy allies had become Destructives, all that changes. In 1834 the masters presented a uniform face of brass to the unions and broke them without mercy; troops, police, spies, propaganda, the pulpits were turned massively against the Scotch Cattle to stamp them into the ground. After the Newport march, the Cabinet were hell-bent on hanging Frost, Williams and Jones and were stopped only by a liberal Chief Justice, while the working-class people of the Valleys were drenched in the respectable spittle of ferocious class hatred. Not until the later 1840s, with the education commissions and others coming down to 'solve' the problems of Wales, did that virulent tone slacken.

But by that time, of course, Chartist militants were already on their long march into the radical wing of Liberalism.

Memory

The realignment and the absorption of much working-class enterprise into a liberal consensus, the 'disappearance' of militancy, of autonomy, are, of course, as familiar in Wales as in Britain as a whole. They remain unexplained, peculiarly so in Wales.

Some of the central features are symptoms rather than causes. There is the creation of county constabularies and the battle for *China*; the Temperance movement with its great choirs which wrenched the eisteddfod out of the pub; the preoccupation with education and the renewed Nonconformist drive against the Anglican counter-attack, the increasing mobilisation of working-class leadership by Dissent. Can there be a more structural explanation along the lines advocated, in varying terms, by Lenin, Eric Hobsbawm and John Foster, the articulation of a labour aristocracy in a new imperialism? Certainly, from the 1850s, there was another pulse of growth which made south Wales into yet more of an Atlantic economy, in the world-wide and massive railway empire of its iron industry; coal begins its thrust into world power. Sub-contracting dies out rapidly. But, to put it bluntly, we do not yet know enough to be able to give even a tentative answer.

What is clear is that with the rise of south Wales into an imperial metropolis of British world hegemony, the Dissent of rural Wales moves over to the offensive. From 1843 dates the first aggressive Nonconformist press of rural west and north; reaction against resurgent Anglicanism and the bilious anti-Welsh racism of an education report of 1847 whipped a species of Welsh nationalism to life. Since it took the form of a 'Nonconformist people', there were here the makings of a powerful synthesis, as the leadership of working-class self-help movements in the industrial areas also moved into the orbit of Dissenting populism. Such a synthesis in fact occurred. It is visible as early as the 1840s in the Aberdare Valley to which initiative in the south had been shifting; it registers dramatically in the shock election of Henry Richard at Merthyr in 1868. The seeds had been germinating earlier of course. Popular and working-class radicalism through the frontier years had been a dialectic between attitudes and actions which later commentators could and did label 'middle class' and 'working class'; in its later phases the Chartist movement itself seems to have acted as a force for integration. By the late nineteenth century, the Nonconformist people had become the hegemonic power in Welsh popular life; the un-persons were not to acquire historical existence, and then a Socialist one, until the 1890s.

The most striking consequence for a historian is that, in this process, the Welsh working class lost its memory.

Industrial capitalism seems to destroy the popular memory; perhaps it needs to. The circumstances of its rise in Wales, its cultural expression in the pseudo-nation of Welsh Dissent, were even more inimical to working-class memory and therefore of identity. When the history of Wales came to be written, it was the new organic intellectuals of that pseudo-nation who wrote it, spitting the Anglican gentry out of it. Within it, the Welsh working class figured as 'hearers' in a Nonconformist service or as incomprehensible hooligans outside. On no people do the corpses of the dead generations weigh with quite so peculiar and particular a heaviness as on the working class of Wales. It is time to remove them.

We have one, rather melancholy, consolation. There is evidence that *some* memory of the frontier years *did* survive into the later years of the century. Characteristically it was a martyr, not a leader they chose to remember. My great-grandmother, Sarah Herbert, came from a Tredegar family of long radical tradition. A pillar of the chapel in Dowlais, she was the sister of a Chartist. She was an indefatigable worker for Henry Richard and on behalf of the 'working classes' of the Nonconformist people. But she was prepared to spend the not inconsiderable sum of 4d to see what was alleged to be Dic Penderyn's ear on display in Dowlais market. Some kind of Dic Penderyn was alive, then, in people's memory. What those people chose to remember from the frontier years was the condition which Dic himself had denounced in his last cry from the scaffold: *injustice.*

Bibliographical Note

I assume that you've just read the essay to which this note is an appendage. If you want to follow up this early period and you're a newcomer to the history of Wales, the first thing to do is to read the essays in this volume. [i.e. *People and Proletariat*]. Then get back to the 1920s and the organic intellectuals of the Welsh working class. Read Ness Edwards, *The Industrial Revolution in South Wales*, brought out by the Labour Publishing Company in 1924 complete with foreword by A.J. Cook and a bibliography which includes *The Times (Bloody Old)*.

The first serious history of Wales, serious in the sense that it (a) took cognisance of the Welsh as they actually existed on the ground, rather than in an instrumental ideology which bordered on theology, i.e. took cognisance of a 'proletariat' as well as a 'people' and (b) was theoretically aware at a high level of intensity, worked to a 'problematic' without losing its grip on the essential *human* character of its discipline, employed the empirical method without succumbing to empiricism, was produced in the 1920s *by* organic intellectuals of the

Welsh working class. Classic examples themselves of that Gramscian Hero, they dedicated themselves to the no less Gramscian objective of achieving the *historical autonomy* of their class.

Inevitably at that stage they were obsessed with their own experience, in industrial south Wales; only recently, of course, have 'peasants' ceased to be 'sacks of potatoes' in Marxist thinking. Their enterprise did not outlast the 1920s. Nearly two generations later, however, it has been re-engaged, characteristically by a generation of academics whose family roots lie deep in the same seam (soil sounds too folkish). It was such people as these who launched *Llafur*, the Welsh Labour History Society, which now has some 1,600 subscribers, which successfully assimilates academics and workers and whose journal, published annually, were it more charged with theoretical awareness, could be identified, albeit through the refraction of two generations' dark-glass experience, as the (or perhaps an) inheritor in apostolic succession of those maimed but creative militants of the Central Labour College and the Plebs League.

In between lies Dagon's Country, black as night, peopled by one ambivalent giant and a clutch of industrious and unduly defensive apprentices. But this is no place for an essay in historiography. Begin with our onlie true begetters in the twenties.

You can savour something of their calibre (and their sweat) in the *Position Paper* which the Ruskin History Workshop Students Collective presented to History Workshop 13 (Oxford, 1979). They raided the archives of Hywel Francis and the South Wales Miners Library (50 Sketty Road, Swansea) to print the syllabuses, notes and other material of D.J. Williams, Glyn Evans and George Thomas from the CLC of the 1920s. Their project was stunning in its sweep, its rigour, its ambition, with a literally ferocious concentration on *totality*, conceptual precision, theory of knowledge and *process*. Not until our own day, as our bookshelves and journals have slithered into that acid-bath of clinical scholasticism which leaves the consumer feeling he has just got drunk on vinegar, have we met people quite so obsessed with 'epistemology' and 'conceptual rupture'. The 1920s brew is more accessible and congenial. Admittedly, their syllabus left little scope for *particularity*; this was *inserted* by an act of will or tribal loyalty. Their enterprise bore all the stigmata of its time and place. We are uncomfortably aware that some of these militants were to tread that road, so faithfully followed by the labour movement from its birth, onward and upward into the huge absorbent sponge of the bourgeois hegemony in its peculiarly succubus-like and voracious

British form. Nevertheless, 'The point was', said George Thomas (and he had *and has* a point):

> we had the bourgeois textbooks of course but we knew how to handle them . . . It was this drilling in Marxism really that put us on our feet, also Marxist philosophy, they did a lot with Dietzgen in those days, Joseph Dietzgen, *The Science of Understanding*, as an introduction to dialectical materialism. So when I left the Labour College I was equipped, I knew what I was doing and why I was doing it . . .'

And, nevertheless, after a syllabus almost blinding in its totality and its methodological and epistemological obsessions, George went on to focus on the history of Dic Penderyn, the first Welsh working-class martyr. And D.J. Williams, in a course of lectures in 1926, after a Long March from the General Strike and Modern Capitalism through a breathtaking vista of medieval heresies, Marxism, Problems of Knowledge, the British Working Class Movement, and Economics, closes with: 'No. 11. Early Industrial Development in Gwaun-cae-Gurwen'.

Out of this world comes Ness Edwards's *Industrial Revolution in South Wales* (sample his own histories of the Miners, too and Mark Starr's *A Worker looks at History*). Faults it has in plenty and conceptual ruptures by the dozen, no doubt, but there had been nothing like it before and there was to be nothing like it for more than a generation. It is a remarkable achievement, not least in his pioneer use not only of Blue Books and the press but of what became the celebrated Home Office 52 series. We should dig it up like the Republicans of 1830 dug up Tom Paine.

We have no political economy yet in Wales but there are some very useful 'economic-history' introductions, notably A.H. John, *The Industrial Development of South Wales* (University of Wales, Cardiff, 1950) A.H. Dodd, *The Industrial Revolution in North Wales* (University of Wales, Cardiff, reprint 1971) and J. Geraint Jenkins, *The Welsh Woollen Industry* (National Museum of Wales, Cardiff, 1969). If you have, or can learn, Welsh, there are brilliant essays by the man who taught David Williams how to walk a country like an historian and was himself the 'organic intellectual' of a whole people, R.T. Jenkins, *Hanes Cymru yn y Ddeunawfed Ganrif* and *yn y Bedwaredd Ganrif ar Bymtheg* (Wales in the eighteenth and first half of nineteenth centuries) (University of Wales, Cardiff, reprints, 1972).

But the only real place to 'begin' is David J.V. Jones, *Before Rebecca: Popular Protest in Wales 1793-1835* (Allen Lane, London, 1973). David Williams, of course, is stepfather to the lot of us. He is a small universe in himself. But if we are to boldly go where no man has gone before, it's necessary to get our parameters right. David Williams did an almost incredible job in mapping out the territory; his list of writings is longer than de Gaulle's nose. You can find it in the special number of the *Welsh History Review* (1967) devoted to his work. His master-piece, of course, is his *Rebecca Riots* (University of Wales, Cardiff, 1955) which is a *total* achievement (Art Schoyen, Harney's biographer, exploded into ecstasy over it: — 'a gem . . . a gem . . . a gem' and rightly so). David Williams came from Narberth, of course, where they demolished the workhouse. On industrial Wales his work is technically strong, informative and a starting point. *John Frost* (University of Wales, Cardiff, 1939; reprint, Evelyn, Adams and Mackay London 1969) was written *in a single year* and he followed up with his essay on Chartism in Wales in *Chartist Studies*, ed. Asa Briggs (Macmillan, London, 1959). These badly need to be corrected and followed through in David J.V. Jones, *Chartism and the Chartists* (Allen Lane, London, 1975), his article in the special Welsh Labour History number of the *Welsh History Review*, vi (1973), the work of Angela John, 'The Chartist Endurance: Industrial South Wales 1840-68', *Morgannwg* (journal of Glamorgan History Society) xv (1971) and her MA (Wales) thesis on the theme, and the work in progress of Brian Davies.

On industrial militants, David Williams's sympathy faltered; his favourite adjective for them was 'unsavoury'; his comments on two of them in Gwent Chartism, *Jones the Watchmaker* and *Mad Edwards the Baker* would fill an anthology of feline malice. But his heart was in the right place and he tolerated the vagaries of the young. So David Jones managed to break through to his thesis and his fine book *Before Rebecca*. This has quite literally opened up a world. Particularly effective are the essays on the South Wales strike of 1816, on riotous Carmarthen and on the Scotch Cattle. This last is quite brilliant — compare it with the 1920s essay of E.J. Jones reprinted in *Industrial South Wales 1750-1914*, ed. W. Minchinton (Cass, London, 1969) and even more revealing, with the section on the Cattle in Eric Wyn Evans's technically sound *The Miners of South Wales* (University of Wales, Cardiff, 1961).

So, as a quick (well, relatively quick but essentially painless) initiation into the half-explored years of the emergence of a 'working class' in Wales, start with this book, go back to Ness Edwards, brief yourselves in A.H. John and A.H. Dodd and Geraint Jenkins and then get down seriously to David Jones, *Before Rebecca*. Read his Chapters 1 and 2 first, together with Chapter 5 on Carmarthen. Then switch to my *The Search for Beulah Land: the Welsh and the Atlantic Revolution* (Croom Helm, London, 1980); for further human material, Chapter 5, 6 and 7 of my *Madoc, the Making of a Myth* (Eyre Methuen, London, 1980). Go back to David Jones, *Before Rebecca*, for his Chapters 3, 4 and 6 and follow up with my *The Merthyr Rising* (Croom Helm, London, 1978). Then go for David Williams, *The Rebecca Riots*. Stop for breath before you tackle Chartism as I've suggested above. To look ahead, read Ieuan Gwynedd Jones's essay in this book and trace his many articles in Welsh journals. To get some sense of movement over time in one, quite important area, sample *Merthyr politics: the Making of a Working-Class Tradition,* ed. Glanmor Williams (WEA, Cardiff, 1966) — a series of lectures organised by the WEA.

Keep your eyes on the *Welsh History Review,* of course, and see if you can work through the Byzantine labyrinth of the *Bibliography of the History of Wales* (University of Wales, Cardiff, 1962, supplements in the *Bulletin of the Board of Celtic Studies*). After 18 years, I still can't.

Above all, of course, after a reassimilation of Ness Edwards and Mark Starr and the History Workshop Position Paper of 1979, read *Llafur*. Read it constantly. In fact, you'd better subscribe to it; you don't know what you're missing.

4 THE MERTHYR ELECTION OF 1835*

'It is with feelings of unspeakable delight that we announce to our readers by far the most auspicious event that could have befallen the country — 'THE DISMISSAL OF THE WHIG MINISTERS BY HIS MAJESTY!' On 22 November 1834 the *Merthyr Guardian* blew its blast on a Tory trumpet to herald the first disputed election in the new parliamentary constituency of Merthyr, Aberdare and Vaynor created by the Reform Act. It proved to be the most ferocious election Josiah John Guest ever had to fight and it represents a critical moment in the formation of radicalism in south Wales.

In the spring of 1831 when the Reform Bill had been introduced into the Commons, Croker, the leading Tory spokesman, had summarily dismissed the government's embarrassed plea that the multitudinous petitions in its support did not in fact come from the dangerous classes ...

> Of the many hundreds that I have read, there were only two or three which did not demand infinitely more than the bill conceded. I will select one, because it is well and moderately worded and affords the best specimen of the sort of demands made by the people. It is the petition from Merthyr Tydfil, a large manufacturing place with a numerous and intelligent population.[1]

Croker's dangerous classes in Merthyr were the elite of its commercial and professional families who, from 1828, moved to take over its Select Vestry and during the crisis years of 1829-30, in conjunction with William Crawshay, the greatest ironmaster in the kingdom and at that date a fire-eating democrat, riveted on the parish a radical caucus dominated by the small but influential Unitarian connection.[2] Central to that connection were the James family: Christopher the patriarch, a merchant from Whitchurch who built the Bush Hotel, ran a flourishing business in grocery, drapery and wine, led the carriers on the Glamorgan canal, made a fortune from turnpikes and his Treforest estate and was elected mayor of Swansea

---

*Published in *The Welsh History Review*, x, no. 3 (1981).

on his retirement; his brothers William, landowner of substance, proprietor of the Globe and the Swan, who married into the radical Herberts of Abergavenny, and Job, a former naval surgeon and bookseller-admirer of William Cobbett. Around this populous and thrusting cousinhood with its Bristol affiliations and wide-ranging interests grew a powerful and wealthy fraternity which sent its sons to the gentry schools in Swansea or Unitarian establishments around Bristol as preparation for Glasgow University or the Inns of Court. There were the cousins William Jones, a draper who owned the town meat market and could offer loans of £800 a time at 4 per cent, and Henry Jones, 'gentleman' with a gift for appalling verse and a pillar of the eisteddfodau of the patriot Cymreigyddion and of Taliesin Williams, the schoolmaster son of Iolo Morganwg. William Howell, keeper of the radical and eisteddfodic inn, the *Patriot*, hard by the no-man's-land of *China*, was connected by marriage, kinship and political outlook, as were Richard Jenkins, the auctioneer from Aberfan, the highly respected William Williams of Heolgerrig, the managerial families of Joseph and Kirkhouse, and the solicitor William Perkins, tall, lazy and amiable, who specialised in those debts called small which could blight a working family and who was the inveterate rival of the portly and potent lawyer William Meyrick, solicitor to Crawshay and the Canal, purchaser of Gwaelod-y-Garth House at £2,500 when the ironmaster moved out to Cyfarthfa Castle, presenter of bills for £20,000 at a time and, with his 'cold grey eye', prosecutor of Dic Penderyn, Lewsyn yr Heliwr and the rebels of 1831 and a shadowy eminence of Glamorgan Toryism, distrusted by the marquess of Bute but strong in the London clubs.[3]

These men were no hucksters. Christopher James's second son, William Milburne James, became a QC, a justice and married the daughter of the Bishop of Chichester. The son of the Penydarren agent, John Petherick, served as consul to the Sudan; the son of the highly successful grocer, W.D. Jenkins, ended as an ecclesiastical historian in Oxford and 'apostle to the railwaymen'. Edward Lewis Richards, son of the keeper of the Greyhound, was a geologist and barrister, became an FRS who chaired Flintshire Quarter Sessions. Walter Morgan, Georgetown solicitor, brewer and land-speculator and an abrasive radical of the small-town bruiser variety, produced a barrister son who moved to Calcutta and was made secretary to the Legislative Council of India by Dalhousie. It was, after all, a time when 'money was absolute trash', to quote a contemporary.[4]

During the economic depression which ran from 1829 and through the chain sequence of crises over the Test Act, Catholic emancipation and the Reform Bill, such men as these moved to the leadership of the hundred or so tradesmen who regularly staffed the Vestry and town meetings. The Jameses and their friends started to colonise the Vestry in 1828, when the curate was ejected, in a community of some 30,000 people where, among the organised religious, Dissent outnumbered the Church by at least ten to one. In 1829 the ironmasters secured the appointment of a stipendiary magistrate, the Tory J.B. Bruce of Aberdare, and from that point, through a succession of bitterly disputed Vestries in a parish driven into bankruptcy by the depression, the Unitarian radicals and their supporters in alliance with William Crawshay moved to a dual power in Merthyr, symbolised by a radical restructuring of the parish and the creation of a standing reform committee in March 1831. In March 1831, of the effective governors of Merthyr, from a third to a half were either Unitarians themselves or their kinsfolk and close associates; among the representatives of the Village, as opposed to the Ironworks, the proportion was nearly two-thirds. On the standing committee, the real force in parish life, every man, apart from the ironmasters or their agents and William Thomas of the Court estate, a bluff and popular Tory surgeon who was 'squire' to the place through a fortunate marriage, was a Unitarian or a Unitarian's kinsman. Three were members of the James family.[5]

Concurrently with the local struggle ran the national. The Merthyr radicals served their political apprenticeship in a great battle against truck, ignited by the presentation of an anti-truck bill in the Commons by E.J. Littleton, a Staffordshire member. The quarrel in the Commons rapidly acquired a Merthyr focus. W.M. James and E.L. Richards, then at Lincoln's Inn and Gray's, lent Littleton their professional assistance while Job James fed him medical material. Joseph Hume, the leading parliamentary radical, who bitterly opposed the bill in terms of classical political economy, marshalled the Dowlais company in support with the active assistance of its master Josiah John Guest, then MP for Honiton in Devon. From September 1830 there was a violent polemic in the Swansea *Cambrian* against the 'truck doctors' of Merthyr. The prime target was Guest. Young Christopher Herbert James, William's son and articled to Perkins, went about denouncing the Dowlais master as an enemy of the working man; Crawshay and Anthony Hill of the Plymouth works lent their support. Guest's poll of Dowlais workmen favourable to truck was unavailing. When the bill ultimately passed, it was Christopher James senior who headed a Merthyr committee promptly established, with occult Crawshay backing, to enforce it.[6]

From November 1830, the advance of the radicals who had organised themselves around the truck campaign abruptly accelerated, as the Wellington ministry fell and Whigs, excluded for a generation, moved into power with a promise of Reform. Through November and December 1830, the Merthyr radicals called meeting after meeting, to denounce the Corn Laws, to demand the abolition of the Assessed Taxes, to sustain radical beershop keepers in their kiddlewinks or *cwrw bachs* against a Tory magistrate and his corrupt police, finally to hold the great meeting for parliamentary reform whose petition so struck Croker.[7]

It was in the autumn of 1830 that they formed their Political Union. An affronted William Thomas, the Court, locked in battle with Job James over 'truck-doctoring', denounced the 'diction and frothy declamation of a spouting club' in the November. By that time, it had become an accepted truism that Merthyr people were great readers of Paine, Hunt and Cobbett — evidence, said E.L. Richards as he lambasted William Thomas, of their 'well-known liberality of sentiment, talent, information ... quickness of thought, soundness of judgement and superior cultivation of general principle'. Military men and magistrates after the Merthyr Rising of the following year singled out this Union as the mother of the mischief; certainly Morgan Williams, the future Chartist leader who entered political life in December 1830, could in 1837 address a letter to workmen singling out 'those of you who were members of the late Political Union'.[8] For it was about this time that the great tide of radical and working-class political propaganda unleashed by the fall of Wellington came flooding into a distressed and excited town. The streets were inundated in a poster war asserting the claims of the poor against the rich; subversive sheets and newspapers circulated; there were delegates from Birmingham and Wigan. Early in 1831 John Thomas, Ieuan Ddu, a Unitarian schoolmaster from Carmarthen and a music scholar, the future teacher of Joseph Parry and the man alleged to have introduced Handel's Messiah into Wales, started a new sequence of political eisteddfodau organised by the Merthyr Free Enquirers — or Zetetics, the *Infidels* who had been grouped around Richard Carlile's journal, the *Republican*, probably in conjunction with the Humanists/*Dynolwyr* of Nant-y-Glo where Zephaniah Williams, the free-thinking leader of the future Chartist march on Newport, was active, founding a political union in Tredegar to supplement the short-lived organisation which fought its way into existence in Aberdare in the teeth of an aggressive church and a strong membership of the Orange Order.[9]

Commissions of inquiry after the Merthyr Rising denounced the town's Union for trying to energise working people, already in the throes of a debt crisis and a crisis of identity, already experiencing abrupt politicisation. By May 1831, certainly, working men were organising their own political unions to drive straight into the insurrection of June. When the dust had settled, the Merthyr Political Union emerged as a fully fledged organisation with its own 'interrogatories' for parliamentary candidates, locating itself firmly on the tougher wing of the radical movement, trying to impose pledges and mandates on Members of a reformed Parliament. From the beginning, though there is no evidence of any direct affiliation, the Merthyr Union had operated fully in the spirit of those classic institutions of 1831 of which Francis Place was the moving force, the Parliamentary Candidates' Society and the militant National Political Union.

Their attitude, however, was not uniform. How could it be? The single democratic tradition of the Jacobin 1790s had splintered under the pulverising hammer of class formation. The most direct heirs of the Jacobin tradition, their populism transmuted into a 'working-class' sympathy, formed a left wing of Merthyr radicalism, in the fiery Unitarian minister David John and his even more incendiary sons David and Matthew (who during the Rising went up alone to the fortress of Penydarren House to present the rebels' terms),[10] perhaps in William Perkins, the only villager to defend the trade unions of the autumn of 1831, certainly in Morgan Williams who was shortly to edit Wales's first working-class newspaper. More central were those who had adapted their 'republicanism' to the hour, personified in the leading local radical David William James, Christopher's eldest son. He and his kin advocated universal male suffrage, but were prepared to settle for something less, annual parliaments (but were prepared to compromise on triennial) and the ballot; they fought for free trade, the end of the Corn Laws and strict retrenchment in public expenditure. Hostile to trade unions and the old poor law, they cultivated a distinctly political populism. To their right were a range of 'moderates' (a newfangled idea, cried Richard Carlile, like the word radical, coined in 1819, and liberal, coined in 1820; a 'moderate reform' was a contradiction in terms) perhaps characterised by the idiosyncratic but in some senses representative Taliesin Williams. The son of Iolo Morganwg advocated the abolition of primogeniture in favour of the *cyfran* (gavelkind) of Hywel Dda, a Reformer before his time, but he thought the franchise extension of 1832 sufficient and cultivated a very measured outlook on most issues of the moment. He was to recollect, in 1835, with a wry smile, that when he had first come to Merthyr, Napoleon had been the hero of the Cyfarthfa Philosophical Society, manhood suffrage and the ballot the rage, issues, he thought, which in 1835 'had had their day'.[11]

The division comes out vividly in the great meeting of 23 December 1830 to petition for parliamentary reform. The demands were radical enough: the expulsion of placemen from the Commons, the representation of large towns, annual parliaments (or at the least triennial), vote by ballot and the franchise for all who contributed directly or indirectly to local or national taxation. But David John, the Unitarian minister, was so revolutionary and republican in his utterance that Walter Morgan, William Jones and Perkins's partner stalked out.[12]

The publication of the Reform Bill in March 1831, however, on the eve of their assumption of a local power shared with Crawshay, concentrated their minds wonderfully. On 9 March, the James brothers, Taliesin, E.L. Richards and Guest's nephew, E.J. Hutchins, called a meeting to rally support even though the Bill fell short of their demands. They organised a census to press Merthyr's claims, and sent up a petition to the House. On 8 April they called a more general meeting, which several of the more radical democrats shunned but which was attended by the Tories Bruce and William Thomas as well as the ironmasters. The sweeping drive of the previous autumn was narrowing into a campaign to get the town an MP and on 19 April, after a fruitless deputation to the chancellor, Althorp, Alderman Thompson, part-owner of Penydarren works and MP for the City of London, sent William Crawshay an ominous letter. Be on the alert, he said, Guest is on the move. The long shadow of Dowlais House fell across the perspiring brows of the Merthyr radicals.[13]

Josiah John Guest was a Canningite and, like several such, had entered the Commons by the patronage of one of the most notorious of the aristocratic borough-mongers.[14] Setting himself to serious public business from the 1800s, he had built Dowlais works into the second largest iron plant in the country, which by 1830 was rapidly overtaking Cyfarthfa. Its dependent and distinctive community, recruited largely from south-west Wales, he turned into a strongly paternalist society with his school, his church, his housing, his support for chapels, Sunday schools, savings banks and friendly societies; there was a mechanics' institute at Dowlais by 1829. His commitment to truck and his fanatical hatred of trade unions (he once summoned a Dowlais minister to his presence for merely attending a workers' meeting) were complementary facets of his paternalism. He became an Anglican though the family tradition was Wesleyan and his entry into Merthyr public life was characterised by endless bickering, particularly with the Unitarians, whom he once threatened with the ecclesiastical courts. During the 1820s he was enmeshed, tenurially and socially, with the lord lieutenant, the Marquess of Bute and the Tory landed oligarchy of Glamorgan, partly in dependence for supply, partly in rivalry. He served as sheriff of the county. Such conduct rendered him suspect to his fellow ironmasters who tended to consider him a fifth columnist from the Cardiff Castle set. He quite evidently shared the instincts of the liberal Tories who followed Canning and Huskisson, wary of a parliamentary reform which would enfranchise the illiberal and ignorant, but anxious to move in a liberal direction in matters of trade, pragmatic reform, the currency, above all Catholic Emancipation. 'Measures not men', he told David William James on his election for Honiton, and from his pragmatism in the 1820s one can filter out as permanencies a firm commitment to cutting public expenditure, to free trade and educational liberalism, a hostility to monopoly and any form of parliamentary corruption and privilege.

Through his Tory connections and above all through the operations of William Meyrick, he found a seat at Honiton in Devon, a borough in the gift of the Earl of Falmouth who, at the bitter election of 1830 with its Tory split, became a by-word for his manhandling of his boroughs. Characteristically his fellow Honiton MP was Harry Baines Lott, a die-hard. He followed the trajectory of most Canningites after the death of their hero in August 1827, moving into opposition to Wellington and Peel; when the aristocratic 'ultras' rebelled at Catholic Emancipation, and like so many French 'aristos' of 1787, launched the campaign for parliamentary reform, Guest was given his head and took it.

There is no record of his having spoken in the parliament of 1826-30, but his votes form a recognisable pattern.[15] During Canning's spell as premier in 1827, Guest voted for a reduction in the corn duties, and an inquiry into electoral corruption and supported Burdett's motion in favour of Catholics. He opposed Hume's motion to repeal one of the Six Acts against seditious and blasphemous publications. After the succession of Wellington in 1828, as the Canningites began to move into dissidence, he voted for a pension to Canning's family while supporting Hume's general assault on the Civil List. He voted against the Navy Estimates and for a reduction in corn duties. He supported the repeal of the Test Act, buttressed by a phalanx of petitions from the town he invariably described as 'the place of my nativity': from Ynysgau chapel, Cefn Unitarian, Zion, Bethel, Ebenezer, Aberdare, Hirwaun and Dowlais. Most striking was his support for Burdett's celebrated motion in favour of the Catholics which, together with O'Connell's Clare election, initiated the disruption of the old Tory party.

For the crux came in 1829. Though he did not speak, Guest voted consistently for Catholic Emancipation and as the rage of the 'ultras' broke over the party and drove them into action against the representation, he supported the Marquess of Blandford's motion for parliamentary reform. He did this in the teeth of virulent anti-Catholic feeling in the south-west and of a Merthyr where the Orange Order acquired notable momentum in reaction and where among Dissenters only the Unitarians proved consistent in their liberalism. As his patron, the Earl of Falmouth, moved into opposition to the 'traitors' Wellington and Peel, Guest voted repeatedly against the government. At the general election of 1830 which crippled the administration, he got his reward. Lott, who remained loyal to Wellington, was turned out, to be replaced by the celebrated Sir George Warrender, Falmouth's brother-in-law and a committed Canningite, while Guest sailed through.

By this time, of course, the conflict over Littleton's anti-truck bill had brought Guest into unwonted contact with Hume and the parliamentary radicals and his trajectory carried him further than Warrender. After the fall of Wellington, in an atmosphere electric with rumours of Reform, war against the French and Belgian revolutions and even of a military coup in Polignac style, Guest began at last to speak in the Commons. His first act, on 21 December 1830, was to contradict his fellow Warrender who had said that people were apathetic over Reform. On the contrary, asserted Guest, nineteen-twentieths of the 'thinking part of the country' were in favour of reform 'though they might not all be prepared to go to the same length'.[16] It was on 23 December, however, that he made his personal declaration of independence and a sensational affair it was. He moved for an inquiry into pensions granted on the Civil List, 'as an independent MP'. He raked them all, Lady Hill, the Earl of Minto, the families of Greville and Cockburn. The main target of his attack, however, was none other than Mrs Harriet Arbuthnot, intimate confidante of the Duke of Wellington himself. This was independence with a vengeance and the press responded eagerly.[17]

On that very same day, back in Merthyr, the radicals were holding their meeting on parliamentary reform which was so crowded that it had to be moved to the parish church; present was Guest's own nephew, E.J. Hutchins. A little earlier, E.L. Richards's scarcely veiled attacks on Guest as a truckmaster in the *Cambrian* came to an end with hints of a 'reformation of character' on the part of hitherto misguided individuals (when he was ultimately chosen as Merthyr's MP Guest gave up his truck shop). Clearly something of a détente was in the making here. There is no evidence however that the ironmaster had his eye on a possible Merthyr seat. In February 1831 he presented joint petitions against slavery from both Dowlais and the Unitarians of Honiton and one from Merthyr demanding parliamentary representation, but when he spoke, it was of Glamorgan county. After he lost his seat at Honiton in 1831, he offered himself as candidate for the second Glamorgan seat, an offer he renewed in June when a reform bill was re-presented.[18] He evidently accepted the government's refusal to accord Merthyr anything except the status of contributory borough to Cardiff, a position they adamantly maintained until March 1832. Alderman Thompson, however, who led the Merthyr deputation to Althorp, convinced himself, against all the evidence, that a seat for Merthyr was in the offing. He warned Crawshay on 19 April:

Guest is upon the alert, and I have no doubt he will *start* for the *County*. He has consulted me upon the subject and I declined for the present to commit myself, for I clearly perceive there is an understanding between him and Lord Bute to act conjointly in electioneering matters in Glamorganshire . . .

Thompson, despite Guest's shift, was still steeped in an older suspicion and, ominous foretaste of the future, wanted the other ironmasters of Merthyr to combine against 'that paltry fellow,' as Crawshay called his Dowlais rival.[19] All manoeuvres were thrown into confusion when the Reform Bill was stopped in its tracks and the country went to a disturbed and excited poll. Guest duly voted for the Bill — 'gloried to be in the majority of one' as he was wont to recall — and the 492 pot-wallopers of Honiton duly replaced him with Harry Baines Lott.[20] In Merthyr, it was Crawshay's hour.[21] At a meeting on 27 April, the reunited radicals pledged themselves to a mass intervention in the Brecon election. Crawshay spoke 'with his customary piquancy' of universal suffrage and the ballot, denounced tithes and offered to die in the streets fighting for the Bill. *Martyr*

Crawshay mobilised his working men, helped them draft a petition of their own, permitted them to demonstrate in the streets of Brecon and Merthyr. From 2 May, they began to break away, to form their own unions and call their own meetings, to devise plans for direct action in the cause of natural justice, a process which reached its climax in the assembly at the Waun Fair at the end of May where the arrival of delegates from the colliers' union affiliated to John Doherty's National Association for the Protection of Labour, which was advancing rapidly in the north, the midlands and north Wales, acted as a trigger. Bands of men like Thomas Llewellyn moved around Merthyr, Ebbw Vale, Nant-y-Glo and Tredegar trying to form trade unions, which were as political as economic. At NAPL union meetings, proceedings often began with a raising of the tricolour and a ritual invocation of Tom Paine, whom the French Revolution of 1830 'had proved right after all'. While larger numbers rallied around 'Lewsyn yr Heliwr' in the popular rebellion in the name of Reform against the shopocracy which led inexorably on to the confrontation with the soldiers, with its two dozen dead and seventy wounded, to the communal insurrection of the early days of June, the execution of Dic Penderyn, the mass mobilisation in trade unions across the entire coalfield and the grim, losing battle for union recognition in the autumn which meshed into the national crisis after the Lords' rejection of the Reform Bill and the rupture in the working class, as radicals were torn apart by the confused battle for their loyalties between the National Union of the Working Classes and its kin and the many local organisations which rallied around the National Political Union, created by Francis Place and his friends expressly to neuter the violent upsurge of root-and-branch populist democracy. In Merthyr, Anglicans and Unitarians, Tories, Canningites, radicals moderate, centrist and extreme, were alike engulfed in the Merthyr Rising as the inhabitants of the ironworks entered their politics as dramatically as Josiah John Guest had left his.[22]

'Chartism, my Lord, began in 1830 and 1831', wrote Henry Scale of Aberdare to the Marquess of Bute a few days after the Chartist march on Newport in November 1839.

Although it was then called by *another name* the populace understood it in the same sense as they do now — a *Re*-forming of society. 'The *thumb* has stood over the *fingers* long enough' said an orator in June 1831 — 'we will turn the hand upside down' — suiting the action to his words ... The words 'Remember Paris' and 'Think of the Poles' were on the mouths of many of the so called ignorant men of the mountains in June 1831 and the distress (hunger that will break through stone walls) *then* existing soon induced the mass of the population to lend a ready ear to the Demagogues whose ultimate views went far beyond a mere riot for increased wages...[23]

Scale was correct: the European revolutions were central to British working-class radicalism in these years, above all of course the French example, which struck a deep chord (all misfortunes were traced back to 'Pitt's war against liberty'). It was among the popular movements that the 'Glorious Days' of July in Paris registered; tricolours began to fly in England from the summer of 1830; the massive mobilisation in London against Wellington was triggered precisely by fear of a Tory war against the French and Belgian revolutions. The Poles moved into the revolutionary pantheon with the revolt of 1831. The Whig attitude to the French, Belgian and Polish revolutions was repeatedly used as a yardstick to measure their sincerity in Reform.[24] Wales was no exception. A Jacobin tradition, offering an alternative political culture, had been present since the 1790s, in the slogans of Swansea colliers and Merioneth and Denbigh rioters, in the Despard pamphlet in Merthyr in 1801, the insurrectionary summons of 1817 during the general strike in south Wales, in the translations of Hunt and Cobbett which came down after every conflict. It was during the 1820s that this political culture seems to have become a structural element in working-class formation, penetrating characteristically through the dense web of partly occult and essentially cultural institutions which working people had created.[25] John Thomas's Zetetic eisteddfodau of 1831 were exemplary; it was there that 'Dic Dywyll', the blind ballad singer who was the voice of the people in the south Wales of the early 1830s (and who was present at the Waun Fair assembly), won his prize; John Thomas went on to co-edit Wales's first working-class paper, *The Workman/ Y Gweithiwr* of 1834.

In the English language section of that paper, young Morgan Williams, politically blooded during the crisis of 1831, had no hesitation in deploying French example in a style as casual as it was central:

When the 'heaven-born minister' [Pitt the Younger] got them [the Jolterheads of the Landocracy] to vote such famous loans (in paper) to put down jacobinical principles, noble was their chaunt . . . But the Day of Reckoning was yet to come and it is now most legibly seen, as Cobbett has so often written . . . This proceeding of our Government against the Trades Unions, this attempt to prevent the working people to combine has more than its parallel in France. . . . Again have the starving weavers of Lyons risen in insurrection and seven days fighting and the slaughter of six thousands of its inhabitants have been the answer to their demands for food . . . Oh these Kingly Governments! Hell upon earth seems to be embodied within them . . . But retribution will come and Louis Phillippe has not taken warning by the fate of Louis 16th or Charles 10th . . . It will come, it will come, the unwashed artizans of the Days of July will not, cannot submit to such a despotism . . . If the French Government can succeed even for a short time in this effort at the destruction of the starving workmen, we may rest assured of seeing a similar effort tried in England. The movement of the workmen of Lyons was nothing more or less than the Trades Unions of England . . . The crisis is coming. What then? Why, the warm sun will shine as bright and the green earth be as beautiful for Painter's pencil or Poet's song as they were after the French Revolution of 1789 which crushed with one blow a tyrannical Aristocracy and destroyed at an effort a licentious and fanatical Priesthood. But labour cannot be destroyed, for it will produce, it will create, it will fashion into every shape the rude ores of Nature, and whether untaxed Bread or a social revolution be Britain's destiny, after all labour will be the source of Wealth.[26]

Talk like this, if perhaps a trifle less literary, was commonplace in Merthyr and Monmouthshire in the late 1820s and early 1830s. Many of these men after all were more than instrumentally literate. The leaders of the justice raids in Merthyr carefully made out their 'receipts'; Lewsyn yr Heliwr, son of a Penderyn butcher, was so literate in English that on the convict ship, *John*, he was employed in teaching his English fellow convicts their own language.[27] The visible rise of workers' participation in the leftward lurching eisteddfod world and in the verse and music festivals of the chapels is striking; what was discussed at the Dowlais Mechanics' Institute? Morgan Williams was quick to press on 'my fellow-workmen' the example of Rowland Detrosier, the working-class Deist who formed the breakaway Manchester New Mechanics' Institute as an organ of working-class self-education (though he omitted to mention that Place made him secretary of the NPU in the desperate November of 1831).[28] The flood of popular journalism into south Wales proved to be permanent. By

1837 the proto-Chartist *Merthyr Chronicle* could talk of 'dozens' of benefit societies and 'the great number of London newspapers and cheap periodicals that find their way into this place' (though Merthyr Village could boast a bookseller taking weekly consignments from London even before 1789).[29] So did the political commitment of many a workman. In 1831, young Abednego Jones or Johns carried a banner during the Merthyr Rising, a mark of distinction among the people and one recollected by authority, to his loss, during a dispute over a coal level in 1833. As late as 1843, then a miner in Nant-y-Glo, he could say to 250 Chartists in the Three Horse Shoes, Georgetown, 'I am very glad to see so many present of that principle which we have been holding out so many years . . .'[30]

While it was the debt crisis in Merthyr, an intensified version of the standard predicament of the colliery villages of the lower valleys of Monmouthshire, which afforded the radical political culture its point of entry, the resonance and permanence of that culture had their roots in the distinctive shift in working-class action which occurred in the 1820s — the shift from consumer protest to producer awareness and workers' control as modes of thinking and acting; these found a more permanent anchorage in a political consciousness. First visible in the Monmouthshire colliers' strike of 1822, it is very striking in the renewed Gwent strikes of 1830 and the Scotch Cattle actions of the spring of 1832 in support; it is central to the Merthyr rising and to the terrible struggle to create unions in the autumn of 1831; it yokes the Merthyr district and Monmouthshire once more in the ephemeral but extraordinary trade union mobilisation of the spring and summer of 1834 in the cause of Robert Owen's Grand National Consolidated Trades Union, when Morgan Williams and John Thomas produced *The Workman* in its service.[31]

It is customary to stress the disunity and localism of popular action in south Wales. It is correct so to do. Dowlais was out of step with Cyfarthfa during the Merthyr Rising; the responses of Monmouthshire and Swansea-Neath workers were out of phase and unco-ordinated; magistrates reported that the Scotch Cattle, the terrorist guerilla characteristic of lower Monmouthshire, failed to establish itself in Merthyr; this dislocation is visible as late as the Chartist march on Newport of 1839, which in some ways was the last kick of the Scotch Cattle. This emphasis, however, excludes as much of reality as it embraces. On the last day of the Merthyr rising, some 12,000-20,000 Monmouthshire men and women were marching to join the armed insurrection; the breaking of their will by 450 soldiers levelling muskets was probably the most critical moment of the entire struggle. Merthyr militants regularly mobilised the ironworks settlements of northern Monmouthshire and vice versa (though rarely the coal villages of the Cattle who were sometimes reluctant to act on behalf of even ironstone miners). The movement of men and women to and fro between Merthyr and Monmouthshire was continuous. Edward Morgan, the Dic Penderyn of the Cattle who was hanged in 1835, had a brother who lived in Merthyr and effected a celebrated citizen's arrest in *China* during the notorious Tamar murder case.[32] The lock-out of 1831 brought support for the two chosen and vanguard Merthyr plants of Dowlais and Plymouth from Monmouthshire as well as Maesteg and when the Plymouth men were finally caving in, men marched to try to stiffen them not only from Cyfarthfa but from Nant-y-Glo. Most striking of all, the Scotch Cattle outbreaks of the spring of 1832, which were heavily politicised, the Bull's warning notes carrying the slogan *Reform*, and those of 1834, which were both directed primarily at ironworks settlements in northern Gwent and Breconshire and which overflowed into the Merthyr district, characteristically among the colliers' villages of Gelligaer and Aberdare, were treated by authority as a particular sector of a single movement embracing the Merthyr complex. There is hard evidence that during the Owenite movement of 1834, violent Scotch Cattle operations in Monmouthshire and non-violent underground organisation in Merthyr were in fact co-ordinated.[33] There appears to be a contradiction between a visible *pays légal* (the *Monmouthshire Merlin*, for example, rarely reported events in Glamorgan, though admittedly the latter was already sewn up by its own press) and a scarcely visible *pays réel*, whose contours can be dimly perceived only through an exercise akin to Althusser's 'listening to the silences'. Nevertheless, although the Scotch Cattle may represent a difference in style rather than purpose, differences in style can become differences in content. The ironmasters, before 1834, found it equally as difficult to concert joint action, and the working-class consciousness which without doubt emerged with explosive force throughout the south Wales coalfield in 1830-31, found difficult expression in a tense dialectic between unity and disparity.

One central factor is that the expression of any such consciousness had to struggle into existence in the face of massive and quite brutal physical coercion. The Merthyr rising brought something of the order of 1,000 troops into the district; barracks were raised at Dowlais, quasi-permanent garrisons established in Merthyr, Abergavenny, Cardiff, Swansea and Newport to supplement that at Brecon. The real climax of the movement was the bitterly fought lock-out of the autumn, in which Josiah John Guest took the lead in organising the smashing of the unions, strongly supported by the Home Secretary Lord Melbourne, who connived at the Merthyr magistrates' breach of the law to break the insubordinate.[34] The paroxysm of that struggle was the November of the rejection of the Reform Bill, the hideous riots at Bristol, the rebellions in Nottingham and Derby, the sudden surge of radical democratic ambition and the agonised response of the National Political Union. Merthyr followed the national pattern with almost comic fidelity. The men's leaders rallied to the mobilisation call of the National Union of the Working Classes for simultaneous meetings (prelude to a general strike and a People's Convention) on 7 November; in the cause they sent delegates to turbulent Carmarthen, later birthplace of Welsh Chartism.

Throughout that harsh summer and autumn, the Merthyr radicals had been absentees except for a faint protest from William Perkins in support of the men. In November 1831, when authority called a tight emergency committee to organise resistance to the 7 November threat, it was the radicals it relied on. David William James, E.L. Richards, William James, William Perkins, Joseph Coffin and Thomas Darker joined Meyrick and William Thomas to organise the defence. Their response precisely mirrored that of the NPU to the NUWC in London.[35]

The collapse of the 7 November enterprise and of the whole crisis with the emergency recall of Parliament and the reaffirmation of Reform, was followed by the collapse of the south Wales movement, followed in its turn by the clobbering of the Scotch Cattle who went into action in the same cause in the early months of 1832. The Marquess of Bute caught the predicament of the defeated and demoralised Merthyr men in the shadow of that Scotch Cattle campaign in April 1832 when, transmitting to the Home Office a Cattle warning carrying the slogan *Reform*, he reported,

> I will not pretend to say that if any general rising should take place in the neighbouring districts that the Merthyr Men might not be drawn in to join them, but I will say that I believe they would be among the last to do so. I believe that the Baptist Ministers are anxious to prevent any violent proceedings, which is very important, and although there can be little doubt that much of the mischief in June last may be attributed to the construction put by the workmen upon the political instructions of their Spiritual advisors, yet it must be

remembered that these ministers made themselves very useful in the suppression of the Union clubs last Winter . . .[36]

Given the astigmatism of the commanding heights — by Baptist, Bute probably meant Dissenters generally (the gentry tended to be vague and patronising about such matters: Bruce reported a Cefn man talking about 'something he calls his chapel') — this is a High Tory view of reality but a reality all the same. It was a single movement with divergent styles which went down to piecemeal defeat, consummated no doubt by the cholera and completed by scores of south Wales shopkeepers, many of them good radicals, 200 in Abergavenny, 200 in Merthyr, 150 in Cardiff, 200 in Newport, 300 in Swansea, patrolling the streets and hills armed with cutlasses, and buttressed by the 11th Foot, the 93rd Foot, the 98th Foot, the 14th Dragoons, the 52nd Foot and two artillery detachments. Between January and March 1832 the Horse Guards revived the old Severn Military District, dismantled in 1814, to handle the 1,300 soldiers who, relative to population, turned eastern Glamorgan and north-western Monmouthshire into one of the most intensely militarised districts in Britain.[37] It was in these circumstances that Merthyr got a parliamentary seat and promptly installed Josiah John Guest in it.

After the defeat of the unions and the Scotch Cattle; ironmasters and radicals resumed their campaign. Already in August 1831, with the insurrection fresh in their minds, Tories had, in opposition to the enfranchisement of Russell's Gateshead, paraded Merthyr as a victim of Whiggery. From February 1832, a whole sequence of linked petitions from Cardiff and Merthyr tried to prise the two apart, with the active support of Croker. Guest, having managed to mobilise thousands of workmen behind a petition for Free Trade, even as he gave up his truck shop, moved to the forefront. On 9 March 1832, when Merthyr petitioned for a separate member or else to be included in Monmouthshire, not only Croker but Peel himself rallied: 'On what principle was Whitby to have a member? How did that agree with Merthyr Tydfil?' Government was unmoved; the new member for Monmouthshire, directed at the manufacturing districts, would 'virtually represent' Merthyr. By 14 March Merthyr was petitioning to be removed from the Reform Bill altogether, but over the intervening five days, Lord John Russell had changed his mind; he informed a stupefied House that Merthyr was to be treated 'as an English town not a Welsh contributory borough' and to get its member after all at the expense of Gwent.[38]

Within two days a meeting at Merthyr had chosen Josiah John Guest.[39] Such a choice, by no means inevitable in 1831, had perhaps become so. Guest had behaved well during the rising; he was credited with having prevented a massacre at Dowlais Top on the last day; his stand against the unions would please many among the new 500-strong ten-pounder electorate. Crawshay was widely blamed for the rising, for having instigated it by his radicalism and provoked it by his temper; he had to make tortuous speeches in his defence even as he was wrestling with the War Office for compensation for the town, finding a dowry for his daughter and quarrelling with his father; he praised the troops in Merthyr for being trigger-happy and at the same time gave money for the defence of the rebels at the assizes; he periodically withdrew into angry sulks.[40] Guest had a clear run.

The Tories shuddered into an appalled response. In a south Wales apparently slithering into the grip of unions, Scotch Cattle and pretentious radical shopkeepers, a pillar had crumbled. William Meyrick, who must have felt peculiarly affronted, offered to stand against Dowlais House, but the Tories lacked the local clout. They turned to the moulding of opinion. Bute, Bruce and the Glamorgan Conservatives, with the support of the Carlton Club, launched the *Merthyr Guardian* in the autumn, specifically to fight against radicalism in any shape or form.[41] For a few months it enjoyed a honeymoon; first an MP, and now a newspaper! What next?

Gleams through the lowering prospect one bright ray,
My native place, to chase thy gloom away?

enthused Henry Jones in a welcoming ode. Yes,

We'll hail thee Guardian of the Rights of Man.
The Rights of Man! the Rights of Paine? no, no —
Of Whig? or Tory? neither — both? — not so —
The rights of all that breathe the breath of life,
All human rights, the balm of human strife.

The *Guardian* survived even this inauguration, but not for long.[42] Its editor, the London journalist William Mallalieu, commanded prose which was lively and tough and certainly had a nice line in vituperation, but his attitude proved somewhat colonial, oscillating between hearty patronage, lofty contempt and virulent class and sectarian hatred. 'It has been the misfortune of Merthyr', he informed his readers, 'that in the kingdom at large it was known only by the riotous conduct and the supposed intractable ignorance of its inhabitants prior to the establishment of the *Merthyr Guardian* . . .'[43]

The radicals had their answer. Dissatisfied with the *Cambrian* which despite its shift into support for Reform, remained a rather pallid sheet, suppressing or playing down any news which might mar the image of south Wales as a progressive and developing community ripe for investment, they found their salvation in the new *Hereford Times* launched at the end of June 1832 by Charles Anthony. Locked in battle with the church and the corporation, it became the very voice of that country-town radicalism of which Carmarthen was an exemplar in Wales. Written in a lively, battling style with a penchant for flamboyant radical hyperbole, it tended in fact to follow the line of the NPU. From the start it set itself to win a south Wales and border public, had agents in twelve towns in Glamorgan, Brecon, Monmouthshire and Cardigan as well as strong connections with the Manchester radical press: the headmaster of Lewis's School Pengam was a devoted reader.[44] The Merthyr agent was at first Howell's the bookseller, but in October Thomas Darker began to advertise in the paper. He was one of the town's leading radical tradesmen with a grocery and drapery opposite the Castle Inn and a house stocked with very superior mahogany, a superior piano and an elegant organ 'big enough for a chapel'. A select vestryman from the start in 1822, he had served as churchwarden and overseer of the poor, sleeping with two pistols loaded with swanshot at his pillow 'Merthyr fashion'. The first man to use gas in the town ('It fizzed and bounced and frothed like as many tailors at a political meeting', said the *Guardian*), he remained the *Hereford Times* agent until his removal to Dowlais in November 1833 and was probably the local correspondent for its Merthyr news.[45]

In the *Hereford Times* several of the Merthyr radicals served their apprenticeship as writers. John Jones, the new Unitarian minister of Aberdare and worthy successor to Tomos Glyn Cothi (who got a good Jacobin obituary in the paper), a social democrat before the concept had been invented and a tough fighter against an oppressive establishment in his locality, sent letters to the *Times* which neither the *Guardian* nor the *Cambrian* would print. Morgan Williams began to write for it in January 1833, very high-toned stuff arguing for the abolition of the 'taxes on knowledge' and calling for the strictest constituency supervision over the new Reformed MPs.[46]

The Merthyr Political Union certainly followed up; they printed their questionnaire with a list of pledges to be demanded of all

candidates. Anyone they supported would have to promise to vote for
the repeal of the Septennial Act, the Corn Laws, the malt tax and the
assessed taxes. He would vote for the abolition of both tithes and
slavery, promote education and relieve the taxes on labour by
instituting a property tax. They gave Lewis W. Dillwyn of Swansea,
liberal candidate for the county, a severe grilling when he came
canvassing in the November, irritating his sponsors Guest and
Crawshay beyond words.

> **Walter Morgan** Are you prepared to answer yes to these questions?
> If he be not, I tell the worthy candidate, though I may stand alone in
> my determination, that he shall not have my vote (cheers).
> **Dillwyn** I will not pledge myself to any thing. I will not be a slave. I
> am determined.
> **Morgan** Then, sir, you shall never have my vote.

Guest intervened to calm them down, but got embroiled with
Crawshay over free trade. When the latter urged a cautious approach
to the abolition of slavery he was greeted with cries of 'No property in
man!' while Guest was heckled over his opposition to the ballot.
Although they finally agreed to support Dillwyn as a lesser evil to an
'acknowledged conservative', the meeting broke up in some disorder
with the gentlemen at the bar of the Bush toasting Walter Morgan for
his 'manly independence'.[47]

Very different was their attitude towards Guest. 'His integrity', said
D.W. James, 'was a satisfactory substitute for any pledges that might
otherwise have been desired.' Of course, with a new electorate only 500
in number and overwhelmingly shopkeeper-publican-professional in
character, they could expect their opinion to carry weight.
Nevertheless the relationship was uneasy. The key seems to have been
Guest's conduct during the last crisis of the Reform Bill, the incredibly
tense Days of May when Birmingham and Francis Place were
organising massive civil disobedience and Britain teetered on the brink
of civil conflict. David William James, at the unopposed election in
December, reported that he had several conversations with Guest at
that critical moment and had been convinced that the ironmaster
would 'stand in the breach', which must mean that Guest had
committed himself to support very radical action, in the event of a Tory
coup.[48]

He was, however, far less radical than his caucus. He shared their
views on the Corn Laws, slavery, tithes, the church, the currency and

the taxes on knowledge (though advocating cautious progress on them all), but was hostile to manhood suffrage and distinctly uneasy over the ballot which, like many others, he considered unmanly, un-English and the vehicle for American corruption. The much more radical Crawshay was able to chivvy him on such issues at the election dinner and while the election itself was simply a celebration of newfound civic pride, with a procession of 10,000, gifts of £500 in clothing to the poor, a general illumination (and a boy carried through the town in parody by his friends, making speeches with hand on heart and throwing bits of paper at the crowd), Walter Morgan continued to ask awkward questions:

> I am a Guest man and it has all been pleasant sailing today, as there is no opposition. But suppose Mr Crawshay, who as well as Mr Guest, is a wealthy ironmaster, had thought proper to offer a candidate, how could the electors who were many of them in their employ with safety have voted publicly in the manner the law now called on them to vote? We must have the ballot. Mr Guest must not only vote for the ballot but exert himself to get it.

Crawshay cheerfully retorted, 'If I ever do bring forward another candidate, depend upon it, that candidate will be myself!' while Guest havered over the ballot: 'if nothing else will do, let us have it'.[49] But the exchange was chillingly prophetic. Guest and the town radicals, shuffling into a cordial but tentative liaison in December 1832, were within two years clinging desperately together for sheer survival.

For in the autumn of 1833, the *Guardian* opened a press war on the *Cambrian* and launched a vindictive campaign against Guest and the James family. It inaugurated a sustained Tory effort to roll back radicalism, unseat Guest and recover Merthyr.

After an uneasy winter with heavy unemployment, wage cuts and an abortive mass meeting of workmen on Aberdare Mountain (an event now becoming traditional which broke up in conflict over objectives and methods), there had been a temporary easing of the depression during 1833, a major withdrawal of troops and some relaxation of tension.[50] Merthyr hummed with scheme after scheme for institutions proper to its new status, gas light, a direct railway to London, factories, a new branch mail, and the publication of the Municipal Corporations Bill was acclaimed by the radicals. A town meeting in November 1833 loudly endorsed Guest's promise to work for incorporation. The Tories recoiled from the prospect; the *Guardian* exploded in sarcasm at the expense of *Lord Mayor* James and his *Poet Laureate* ab Iolo. Every meeting to discuss incorporation was disrupted by party conflict and as soon as the bill was suspended in 1834, William Thomas and Meyrick came forward with a scheme for building a town hall and a market on their lands, evidently as a counter. The town hall came to nothing, but a company was formed to launch the market and schemes for a savings bank and a gasworks were mooted. The *Guardian* was severely jolted, however, by Guest's reiterated assertion during these meetings that Merthyr would be incorporated 'within a year whether we like it or not'. Fear of a municipal corporation with a Unitarian radical hegemony riveted in permanence on the town became a permanent Tory nightmare.[51]

Even more devastating was the fierce quarrel over rating which split the town in two during 1833.[52] The Standing Reform Committee of 1831 had launched a major re-organisation; but during the depression it ran into a quagmire. By 1832, the parish was £1,675 in debt; it dismissed the police officer it had secured from Whitehall during the lock-out, but an effort to increase the rates on the ironworks ran into head-on collision with the masters. Throughout 1833, there were endless and fruitless parish meetings, repeated and wholesale dismissals of parish officers, as the poor rate soared to an unprecedented 10 shillings to cover a quarterly expenditure of over £1,200. In the end, both sides agreed to submit to a valuation prepared by an outside agency. Messrs Bayledon and Fosbrook presented their new valuation in November 1833. It more than quadrupled the yield of the rates but had two controversial features. It proposed, a novel device, to rate the coal, limestone and equipment of the ironworks, which drove Crawshay into a fury and brought the threat of a test case before the King's Bench. More startling still, it brought cottages worth less than £6 a year under the rates. This touched an old nerve. For what debt was to a working-class consciousness, rates were to a middle class.

The £6 cottages were the workmen's homes; under the new scheme they comprised £13,900 of a total housing valuation of £25,000. They were largely the preserve of the town's middle class; rents and rates were prohibitively expensive or physically impossible to collect, claimed their owners; Walter Morgan complained that he could not get 2 per cent on his investment. They had been a target for irritated ironmasters. As long ago as 1817, Guest and Meyrick had proposed to bring them under the rates, to be defeated by a parish meeting rallied by Taliesin Williams and Walter Morgan who enforced a heavier rate on the ironworks instead. In 1833 the ironmasters, with Guest dithering in discomfort, pressed the attack harder; they proposed a bill to rate the owners of the cottages rather than their occupiers; without this, they claimed, the masters would be paying two-thirds of the levy. The response was a blank negative.

Enraged, Crawshay called a meeting to petition for a bill in February 1834. Walter Morgan, roaring that ironmasters had never paid their fair share, and supported by Henry Jones, had it postponed until March. A petition nevertheless went up to the Commons, to be followed by a counter-petition within a week. At the March meeting, the James family and their supporters turned up *en masse* and crushed the scheme amid scenes of total confusion, with the factions withdrawing to separate rooms to avoid physical conflict. The next month, in riposte, D.W. James, Joseph Coffin and their friends voted to rate the machinery of the Canal Company, despite opposition from Meyrick as parish solicitor and a report that £677 of the small cottage rates could not be collected. By October, the ironworks were taking their appeal against the rating of coal before the King's Bench and the quarrels over the rates bill and the Canal company went thundering on into the Commons through 1835 and beyond.

At about the same time, Crawshay and his allies launched a campaign against the Court of Requests, target of the rebels in 1831 which was abolished in 1834, amid showers of contradictory petitions. In response, opinion splintered. Many radicals thought this another case of ironmasters bullying the shopkeepers. Morgan Williams urged Merthyr workers to support the Court because of its cheapness (and it had indeed served as the occasion rather than the cause of the rebellion in 1831; there had been no popular complaints against it since). Some Tories however, including the *Guardian*, took it as a prime example of the 'hard law' the middle class would give the workers if they were untrammelled.[53] The net effect of all the squabbles was to fragment opinion in Merthyr and to range Crawshay in fierce opposition to the James connection.

In these circumstances, the conduct of Guest in the Commons assumed an ominous significance.[54] In a House where the cluster of radicals, riding the popular tide of anti-clericalism during the Reform crisis, made the church a prime target to affront many patriots, Guest, except for a few brief interventions, did not speak until he introduced a bill of his own in the spring of 1834. The *Guardian* maliciously observed that he had been absent from 38 out of 58 important questions during 1833, from 41 out of 58 in 1834. The source it used, Richard Gooch's *Book of the Reformed Parliament* of 1834, in fact lists positive votes by

Guest on twenty occasions during 1833, fifteen positive and two negative votes in 1834. He was hardly a blood-and-thunder radical; he voted consistently against Daniel O'Connell and William Cobbett, though his vote coincided with Hume's on 31 occasions out of the 37. What riveted the attention of his enemies was that he voted in favour of the Irish Church reform with its parliamentary disposition of church property — the 'spoliation of the Irish church' — in favour of the expulsion of the bishops from political functions in the Lords and in opposition to Church rates. This was guaranteed to inflame men of conservative temper back in Merthyr, particularly since it was an Anglican who was voting. It would have done him no harm at all among much of the Merthyr shopocracy; his votes in favour of a property tax to replace those which pressed on industry, of any measures which reduced public expenditure and the corn duties and, more surprisingly of Grote's motion in support of the ballot, would have pleased his caucus.

Other votes of his were more divisive of the radical ranks. He was absent from key divisions on the new Poor Law, but he supported it. William Meyrick and the *Guardian* were running a campaign against it — every case of bastardy, infanticide and child abandonment the latter reported under the heading 'Another Triumph for Lord Brougham'. It was lucky for Guest that working-class opinion in Merthyr had not yet fully taken the bill in, though a Vestry had come out strongly in favour of a workhouse. At the election of 1837 he had to face a mass workers' rebellion over the Poor Law. In 1834 there were no petitions from Merthyr against it and its import had not fully registered even on Morgan Williams. Guest however came out strongly for an amendment to the Beer Act, deploring its effects in industrial areas and arguing for a ban on drinking on the premises of the kiddlewinks. This ran head-on into a petition from Merthyr with 4,000 signatures against any change; the *cwrw bachs* were strongholds of popular radicals.

Altogether this was a course of conduct, along with other minor votes, designed to mobilise his enemies, rally a majority but not all of his friends and to offend many potential supporters. His own bill, which was ultimately taken up by the government and received the king's assent in August 1834, was one to reduce the salaries of Commons officials (whenever Guest spoke at length in the House, someone lost money). This certainly pleased D.W. James, who cited it as proof of Guest's courage and integrity, but it seems unlikely to have set the Taff on fire.

Such matters assumed a significance Guest was not fully to realise until the New Year when, in the spring of 1834, the inhabitants of the ironworks once more intruded their unwelcome political presence.

'WORKMEN OF ENGLAND STAND BY YOUR ORDER!', shouted the posters from half the walls of the North and the Midlands during that embattled spring and summer as the members of the Grand National Consolidated Trades Union were summoned to the defence of the Tolpuddle Martyrs.[55] The response at Merthyr was almost instantaneous; as early as February 1834 the town, in the Owenite cause, brought out Wales's first working-class journal. Morgan Williams, the Unitarian master-weaver from Heolgerrig, son of a highly respected father and leading light of a family of harpists, known as the Young Mountain Solomon for his mathematics, and John Thomas, the Unitarian schoolteacher and musician, Ieuan Ddu of the Zetetic eisteddfodau and Handel's Messiah, published *The Workman/Y Gweithiwr*, printed by a former Merthyr man at Brecon. Morgan, fresh from haranguing Dissenters at a mass meeting at Bethesda where he quoted Fox and the Jacobin martyr Muir,[56] was in the English section squarely in the old tradition, hammering the Jolterheads of the aristocracy and denouncing the Corn Laws, but he elaborated a comparison between the Unions and the French weavers and called on workers to defend the Court of Requests, while John Thomas wrote a long essay in Welsh justifying unions and drawing comparisons with the Freemasons and the Oddfellows.

This was the organ of a movement.[57] By March, all the works in the Merthyr area were unionised. Magistrates were paralysed. An attempted trial of one militant for intimidation was halted as delegates from all the works crowded around the Lamb Inn and threatened a rescue riot. They were working closely with the men of Monmouthshire and in the same essential cause — control of admission into the trade, the exclusion of blacklegs and what Colonel Love, the military commander, called 'the securing of a regular and constant demand for labour'. By May, the Scotch Cattle were breaking loose against any who were 'learning men to be miners', concentrating their efforts on the Glamorgan-Monmouth border, Bute, Tredegar, Rhymney, Gelligaer; the Welsh at the Varteg drove out the Irish. The Owenite union, from its base among the miners, swept the whole coalfield, managerial authority was eclipsed, government authority frozen. By June every man of substance was shouting about 'the intolerable tyranny of the trades unions'; in May an angry Bruce sent Melbourne a copy of *The Workman*, heavily underscored, and demanded a prosecution for sedition.

Memories of 1831 were in everyone's minds. Anthony Hill of the Plymouth works, denouncing the men's 'extreme bad feelings . . . and the high notion they entertain of their power', reported that 'in all the threatenings since the last riots, it has been declared "we will take care and be *before* the soldiers the next time" . . .' Col. Love was certain — 'From what has already been seen of the principles of the Trade Unions, more system and combination may be expected than when the Disturbances took place in 1831.'[58] In Newport, where all the trades had been organised in unions 'on the same regulations as the large towns of the North', the funeral of one member in April, a bemused observer reported, was attended by marching men from all the crafts, 'dressed in the prescribed costume of the lodges of which they were members, wearing a kind of white surplice. The Bible was carried on a black velvet cushion open before the corpse.'[59] The GNCTU was committed to ritual, ceremony, hymns; south Wales, though marginal to the movement as a whole, was fully a member and by June had forced matters to breaking point.

For memories of 1831 were alive in the minds of their enemies, too. This time, government threw its full power behind a campaign to break the unions at all costs, and for the first time the employers of the region achieved total unanimity. The Merthyr masters offered to raise a barracks at Quaker's Yard to house 500 men, as the 75th Foot disembarked at Cardiff and the troops came flooding back.[60] They dug up Major Digby Mackworth's plan for a Mountain Police drafted in 1832 and put it into operation. Every ex-serviceman on pension in the three counties of Glamorgan, Brecon and Monmouth was registered — there were over 450 of them — and 100 were mobilised for a month on pay as a Mountain Police. The depot was the Tredegar works and they were spaced out among six stations from Pontypool to Aberdare. The magistrates clamoured for firearms at the depot, but Melbourne would allow them only cutlasses. But under Capt. Howells of the Glamorgan militia, they were activated for a month with infantry and dragoons in support as the employers went over to the attack.[61] On 13 June, the masters and magistrates of the three counties met at the Rhymney Inn; nineteen industrialists, every ironmaster and the leading coalowners, with eleven magistrates. They set the Mountain Police in operation and issued a public Declaration:

That it is the determination of this meeting not to employ hereafter any man who is engaged in any Trade Union Society or in other association not sanctioned by Law and that every Proprietor of

Works will issue notice on Saturday, 21 June at their respective establishments to that effect and further that they will not at any time hereafter employ any person who may be found to assist in or give countenance to the outrages committed against the Persons or Property of their workmen by miscreants who assemble at night under the denomination of Scotch Cattle.[62]

This dramatic declaration, with its cool assimilation of illegal Cattle and legal unions and itself of dubious legality, was no bluff. On 16 June, Bruce massed Specials at Merthyr and the notices went out. Many lodges cracked at once as troops and Police quartered the region, though the Cattle fought on sporadically till Christmas. The toughest resistance was at Blaenavon and at Hirwaun where the masters blew out the furnaces to intimidate the men. In July Crawshay was threatening to blow out all his furnaces. By mid-August it was over, when Hirwaun (storm-centre of the Rising of 1831) finally surrendered.[63] The *Workman* was driven out of existence. Only one copy survives, the fourth number from May, and we do not know when it folded. Comments during the election in December suggest that it was still operative then or had only recently died. Certainly it was still very much alive in the minds of the Tories and the *Guardian*.

It was once again in the aftermath of a workers' bitter defeat that Josiah John Guest achieved a personal ambition; on the day Hirwaun surrendered, his bill got the royal assent. He had little time to enjoy it, for in November the king abruptly dismissed the Whig ministers and summoned Wellington and Peel instead. This was, in fact, an arrangement to get Melbourne out of his difficulties but it hit Reformers like a kick in the teeth. After barely two years and with a very patchy record, the liberators of the Reform Act were confronted with the full force of reaction. The Dissenters' national committee were sitting and, optimistically claiming that the government had been about to initiate a major reform of the church, published a dramatic call to arms. It was in fact on the tide of Anglican revival that the electorate mauled the Whigs and beat back the radicals.

In Merthyr, the Tories acted with unhinging speed.[64] As soon as the coach brought the news, William Meyrick was out and about on 17 November with a loyal address he had drafted. A hundred people signed it at the Angel and he and William Thomas had collected two hundred more and sent a copy to Brecon by the time the London coach left. The Merthyr and Brecon addresses were the first to reach the king. They pledged undying determination to support the king in his choice of ministers and in his refusal to 'consent to any such measures as shall place in danger the integrity of the constitution of this country as now by law established both in Church and State'. Guest, caught on the hop in Lincolnshire, raced back to the Commons. 'You're going to be turned out at Merthyr, Guest', he was told. 'Wait a little', he replied, 'there is no hurry, all in due season. I have a better opinion of the electors.' He himself, however, did not wait. He dashed back to his consistuency, to find placards up: *To the liberal Churchman and the well-informed Dissenter.* Several of the most influential gentlemen of Merthyr had not yet pledged themselves, the poster asserted. Hundreds of electors would join any candidate who would uphold the constitution, particularly the Church Establishment, without which atheism and infidelity would stalk the land . . . 'Should neither of these gentlemen be prevailed upon to stand in the gap, I yet implore you not to pledge yourselves, for another will be found to support the cause of his God, his King and his Country . . .'

'It appears', thundered the *Guardian* a few days later, 'that Merthyr is neither more nor less than a rotten borough appertaining to Schedule A, the patronage of which is vested in the Jameses.' At a private meeting chaired by Mr James senior, 'Mr James jnr proposed sundry resolutions for which all the Jameses present held up both hands with most delightful unanimity'. The aldermen-elect of the new corporation had then moved from the family party to a big meeting. With Christopher James in the chair, 'our cousins, the Joneses were allowed to make a debut and our dearly-beloved son the Prince Royal to rebuke those who should dare interfere with the prerogative of the Jameses . . .' As for Guest, 'if the people of Honiton really prefer him, in God's name let them have him'; he was the candidate not of the town but of a clique; his public conduct seriously compromised his electors' reputation as good citizens and subjects: 'a more miserable and discreditable farrago of intrigue and trickery has never before been exhibited in any of the most contemptible of the rotten boroughs of the three kingdoms'.

It was, in fact, Christopher James who chaired a meeting at the Bush late in November which mobilised Guest's caucus. Forty-five men were there, all the Jameses of two generations, William Jones, Darker, Walter Morgan, Benjamin Havard (who was to lead a Poor Law revolt against Guest two years later), Henry Jones, Taliesin and other stalwarts. David Saunders *yr Ail*, Baptist minister of democratic temper, was present, so was David Jones, the watchmaker and chief organiser of the pub eisteddfodau. Most striking was the presence, despite the bitter struggle of the summer, of Morgan Williams and John Thomas, the editors of the *Workman*. At the public meeting, attended by 200 on 2 December, the stress was on unity. 'To some Guest had appeared to be going too far, to others, not far enough', said David William James. All 'minor differences' had to be merged; Taliesin was more specific: 'they had had party feeling, but let them at a crisis like this prove that union is strength'. E.L. Richards and D.W. James lavished praise on Guest in the vaguest terms, stressing his independence: 'I have opposed the men who carried the Reform Bill because I perceived them truckling ... gentlemen, I can hold up this hand unsullied'.

It was Walter Morgan, as usual, who abruptly voiced the real fears of the meeting. Any man who fomented discord in a place like Merthyr, he warned, would have a lot to answer for:

What! were they who had battled with such energy and so successfully for Reform, to have the feather plucked ingloriously by Tories from their caps? Were they to be prevented from returning the man of their hearts by men who would crush them if they could and who scarcely knew them at other times, who passed by them unnoticed in the streets but were now seeking to obtain their suffrage?

He, too, ended with a desperate appeal for unity.

At the prompting of John Jones, Aberdare, they chose an election committee, of whom Jones himself and Morgan Williams were to be the most active, and Guest held an immediate and rushed canvass during which he apparently told the voters there would be no opposition. They soon learned differently. A week later, *Brother Elector*, denied the *Guardian*, called from the pages of the *Hereford Times* — 'Electors! We live in fearful times! The corrupt days of Walpole, of Pitt and of Castlereagh are about again to debase the wavering member of parliament. The dark corruption of those times is about to assume a much darker colour for wealth and power are stalking the constituencies'. For on 8 December William Meyrick came forward as a Conservative defender of the Establishment and the *Guardian* took pains to circulate by denying it a charge that 'three of the principal ironworks of Merthyr have coalesced against a candidate connected with the other principal ironworks'. After Guest's canvass came Crawshay's. The master of Cyfarthfa, utterly alienated from the town radicals, had been approached by Tory agents — 'the Political

Itinerant who HAWKED the Borough over the country', snarled *An Elector* in the *Hereford Times*; he could not bring himself nor could his brother, nor Alderman Thompson. So 'you thrust it upon the shoulders of your Country Solicitor'. *Martyr Crawshay* of the Reform Crisis, with Thompson and Hill trailing behind, turned the mighty Cyfarthfa machine on a tiny electorate already largely pledged to Guest. Walter Morgan's nightmare came true; that electorate promptly splintered.

The *Guardian* hurled itself with ruthless zest on the enemy. Its central argument was that Destructives were creeping into power in the shadow of Dowlais House, with Guest as their unwitting tool 'The Duke of Orleans had domains worth even Dowlais twenty times told...' It linked Guest with Essex, Pym, Hampden and Cromwell, 'weak, well-intentioned men, popularity hunters'. Unitarianism was a conspicuous omission from its periodic listings of the creeds worthy of respect and it kept up a merciless hunt of the Jameses. It carefully exploited every chink in the enemy armour, printing letters from alleged Unitarians, signed the 'Ghost' of the Rev. Thomas Evans (Tomos Glyn Cothi), reminding Dissenters repeatedly of Guest's earlier political persona. Some of Guest's men tried to mobilise the beershop keepers in their cause. Thirty new ones had been licensed in October alone (one carrying the placard KING WILLIAM IV, licensed to be drunk on the premises);[65] their proliferation had brought the rent of pubs down. The radicals called a meeting to support Guest and to protest against oppression by the Tory magistrate J.B. Bruce. The *Guardian* was in like a flash, driving home the contrast (Christopher James and many of his kin were licensed victuallers) and exposing Guest's anti-kiddlewink flank; the attempted rally floundered into disunity and recrimination. It was no less assiduous in its attention to the beershops' clientele. It publicised the new Poor Law and stressed Meyrick's opposition to it. 'We have not written down the Corn Laws in order to afford a pretext to lower wages. We have not advocated the bastardy clause of the new Poor Law'. If the ballot were achieved, 'the labouring classes will be trampled into dust by that portion of the ten-pounders infected with liberalism, as soon as they can pull down all above them and give the law — hard law it will be — to all below them. The Court of Requests law has been a foretaste of it...' The *Guardian* addressed itself in particular, now in rebuke, now in appeal, to 'the readers of the *Workman* newspaper'. These shrewd strokes it supplemented with straightforward skullduggery, suppressing retorts, delaying Taliesin Williams's reply to attacks on him until it was too late to matter, imputing corruption to Christopher James, to withdraw the charge after the election was over, repeatedly reporting successful Meyrick canvasses.

Despite Merthyr's reputation for liberalism, it had something on which to build. At the routine and far less dramatic election of 1837, a third of the electorate proved itself ready to vote for a conservative. Even at the popular level, there was the Orange Order, specifically anti-radical, colourful, anti-Irish and distinctly chaotic in organisation, with lodges or 'warrants' as they were called, constantly forming, re-forming and lapsing into variant heresies. The central bases appear to have been Carmarthen which had six lodges in dependency and Tredegar which had eight around 1828. Catholic emancipation was a fillip. By 1830 there were central lodges with lesser warrants clustered around them in Nant-y-Glo, Merthyr, Tredegar, Pontypool, Brecon and Monmouth. Two years later four new ones formed around Tredegar and another at the Bell in Merthyr where a hundred men marched behind the coffin of a brother in 1833. On the eve of the election itself there had been a monster rally in Aberdare, where an 'immense number' from Aberdare, Merthyr, Pontypridd, and Cardiff marched in 'gowns, scarfs, banners, beautiful arch, a grand flag and band' to be harangued by combative clergymen and to make a circuit of the town's leading pubs, the Black Lion, New Inn, Cross Keys and Butchers' Arms, all of which were run by Orangemen.[66]

The major thrust behind the Tories, however, was the sheer power of the ironmasters and of Crawshay in particular. The *Hereford Times* hurled charge after charge at him that he had told shopkeepers, 'If you vote for Guest my men will not deal with you.' Crawshay vehemently denied it; he had never said such a thing. He did not, of course, need to. Behind him came the landowners with their pressure on tenants; E.J. Hutchins rode all the way to Ludlow to get a letter from the Hon. Robert Clive permitting his people to vote as they liked.

Guest's men saw themselves as battling against fearful odds. They had their base in Dowlais of course; Darker promptly resumed his *Hereford Times* agency there to keep the place immaculate. They had the Oddfellows to deploy against the Orangemen. During the Owenite upsurge a few months earlier, Anthony Hill had singled them out as the main sources of the infection. They were active against the Scotch Cattle at the same time (just as many of them were to be active against Chartism later).[67] It is possible to detect here a commitment to a respectable liberalism; certainly Morgan Williams was to praise their loyalty to Guest. The reformers' chief weapon, apart from an appeal to old loyalties and pledges, was ideological argument and an attack on Crawshay, whose volte-face of course laid him wide open. A torrent of vituperative, often well written, often savage letters poured into the *Cambrian* (until it wilted) and the *Hereford Times*. The master of Cyfarthfa was hounded without mercy. 'Is there a man among you who is not proud of the plebeian origin of Mr Crawshay?' with his well known 'calm temper, well regulated mind, discriminating judgement...'. Had he not stood for manhood suffrage and the ballot? Did he not remember his famous words of 1832? 'Surely he cannot have changed his mind? Otherwise you would have his image cast in iron and fixed as a weathercock upon the dome of your new Market House?'

Letter after letter cogently argued Guest's case and raked Meyrick. 'What manner of men are ye that this presumptuous lawyer can thus fling insult in your teeth? This British Constitution of his, destroyed over and over according to Meyrick and his party, can exist only by the perpetuation of unequal taxation... its toleration consists in tolerating the inviolability of an oligarchy'. Long analyses of Guest's performance grew more and more Dissenter and populist in tone as the campaign grew more desperate. 'Guest's pyramid has its base in integrity and uncompromising reform ... Meyrick's, whose apex is corruption in church and state, whose base (O what a base!) is the toadyism of the Merthyr Guardian'.

But as the Tory machine went on grinding into Guest's support, the vehemence of such attacks could backfire. The *Guardian* drove radicals into a frenzy: 'this worshipper of Aristocracy and abominator of the Democracy ... toadyism ... illiterate, illogical writer ... insults men, though they be but Merthyr tradesmen, whose shoe-latchets he is unworthy to untie ... counselling the middle classes to become slaves', but it was Crawshay's bland confidence which maddened them.

> Why 99 of 100 of your own men are averse to your proceedings and would betray their feelings were your notion of public virtue to permit their free expression ... It is known also that you are in open hostility to the Trade of Merthyr ... you have endeavoured to crush them by the abrogation of the Court of Requests; it is notorious that you are bent upon a *system of retaliation* from their having honestly opposed you in their detestation of parochial tyranny ...

This was highly dangerous ground. It brought a prompt and anguished affirmation of faith in Crawshay from 89 tradesmen of the town, including several of Guest's supporters. Crawshay in his reply avoided the crux of the charge of inconsistency (he could hardly have done otherwise) but laid about him with a will, to reach a climax in his request to readers to compare the quality of the supporters of Meyrick with those of 'the editors of the *Workman* newspaper and its readers'.

References to the *Workman* grew more frequent as the battle wore on; the radicals took the fight to the population at large, hammered a populist line, plastered the walls with posters until people began to talk of 1831. It was Morgan Williams who emerged as the most active of Guest's canvassers, working with a demonic energy and bringing floods of Tory sneers on the head of the Young Mountain Solomon. But nothing seemed to be able to stop the rot. On 3 January, the *Guardian* effectively argued that any previous pledges to Guest were invalid because of his early assurance that there would be no opposition. Coming five days before the poll, this seems to have unhinged his grip. Adam Newell, declared a bankrupt in 1830, a grocer friend of James Abbott the barber whose evidence hanged Dic Penderyn, organised a group which started to offer their votes for sale at £10–£50. An emergency meeting of Guest's caucus, according to the historian Charles Wilkins who was a personal friend of some of them, calculated that his projected majority had shrunk to ten.[68] There was nothing left but the ultimate deterrent, if it could be deployed.

On 6 January 1835, ten thousand working men assembled at what had become their traditional meeting-place on Aberdare Mountain, above Heolgerrig. They had been brought there through the efforts of Morgan Williams and John Jones, Unitarian minister of Aberdare, an achievement which, in the circumstances, must be called remarkable. For hours they listened to and argued with relays of Nonconformist ministers 'from the Deist to the Baptist', according to the *Guardian*. For hours they listened to people from their own ranks, as Morgan Williams was to recollect, in that ritual of motions and amendments, points of order and appeals to Mr Chairman which the British working man made peculiarly his own, and at the end of the day, they published their Declaration:

THE MECHANICS AND WORKMEN OF THE BOROUGH OF MERTHYR TYDFIL, VAYNOR AND ABERDARE at a meeting held on Tuesday 6 January have resolved unanimously to conduct themselves decently and to behave peaceably on the day of the election, Thursday 8 January.

To give every encouragement to those Tradesmen, Artists etc. that intend to vote (regardless of the threatenings and intimidations of some great men) for the candidate who, with regard to his political principles, as well as his private character, is most agreeable with the views of the public generally, considering that a Member of Parliament is a representative, not of the wealthy nor of those that have a right of voting alone, but also of all that inhabit the place, however unprivileged and low in circumstances and consequently that one should be elected that will advocate their cause and defend their rights.

TO WITHHOLD THEIR CUSTOM (the only way they have of showing their sentiments) from those Tradesmen, Artists etc. that will be so backward in the fulfilment of their duty as to be intimidated and threatened to vote against their own principles and contrary to the opinions and benefit of the multitude and the welfare of the people.[69]

This remarkable declaration, which embodies a plebeian version of the theory of virtual representation, with its open deployment of exclusive dealing, was in many ways the mirror image of that of masters and magistrates at Rhymney the previous June, anti-pope to its pope. It was no less ambiguous in law, no less an exercise of economic power in a political cause. Above all it was effective. Two days before the poll, the Merthyr Chapter of the Order of Workmen had spoken.

The declaration from Aberdare Mountain punched through the raddled fabric of Merthyr politics like a fist through papier-mâché. Meyrick in the morning organised a frantic canvass. He found that Tory pledges were flaking away like autumn leaves in a gale. There was a hurried evening consultation at Cyfarthfa Castle; Crawshay had promised not to push things to the limit if he found the support was lacking. He kept his word and told his lawyer to withdraw.

'One of the most remarkable struggles ever witnessed', cried the *Hereford Times* in understandable hyperbole. 'The cause of Toryism finding a champion in this gentleman (Crawshay) always supposed to be on the ultra-liberal side roused the whole population and nobly have the workmen of Merthyr sustained their independence. The moral strength which a united body of 10,000 workmen afforded will not be forgotten.' At Guest's orgiastic election, when he toasted his people from the Masonic goblet of the Bush and Mallalieu's windows splintered, D.W. James publicly acknowledged that they owed their victory to the unenfranchised and pledged a campaign for manhood suffrage. At the dinner, when the toast to the committee was proposed, it was Morgan Williams, appropriately who responded. He gave two toasts, one to the Oddfellows and the other 'to *The Working Classes* (tremendous cheering) . . . They are a class of people who have been foully calumniated and I stand forward as their humble representative to throw back the calumny. Their political rights long and unjustly withheld from them, thanks to the irresistible diffusion of knowledge must soon be within their grasp.' On this point, at least, the *Guardian* was in agreement. Calling for Guest to be struck from the commission of the peace on account of the Aberdare Mountain assembly, it said that mob law had won the election. All would end eventually 'in grape-shot sweeping the streets of Merthyr and dictating to a deluded people the most fitting representative of barbarism and riot . . . We tell Mr Guest openly that he is not fairly chosen as Member for Merthyr but of the SCOTCH CATTLE.'

The immediate consequence of the 1835 election, which propelled Guest bodily leftward along the liberal spectrum, was a sharp polarisation in Merthyr between Anglican and Dissenter. Henceforth, at every meeting called to levy a church rate, one of the Jameses or a friend would rally a majority to vote it down. Twelve attempts in three years were utter failures. The Vestry hounded Meyrick and William Thomas for their rate arrears. When in March 1835 the ironmasters advertised a parish bill to rate the owners of small cottages, a Vestry crushed it and compelled the parish officers to withdraw their names. In the autumn, the masters returned to the attack and retained Meyrick as their attorney. The parish sacked Meyrick and organised against the masters. William Perkins took Meyrick's place as the townsmen tried to repeal the Stipendiary Magistrate's Act and to eject J.B. Bruce; the *Merthyr Reporter* and the *Chronicle* were launched against the *Guardian*, which was soon driven out to Cardiff. In November 1836, when the Board of Guardians of the Poor Law virtually replaced the parish as the organ of local government, the elections in Merthyr were conducted with partisan ferocity. Guest's men and the radicals swept the board. The largest town in Wales fell to Dissenter radicalism.[70]

Equally significant was the organised weight of a self-conscious working class which first registered in conventional politics in 1835. That drive which had repeatedly hammered through the insurrection and the lock-out of 1831, the movements of 1832 and 1834, penetrated political life. The assembly of the Order on Aberdare Mountain entered the political equation. In 1835 it was deployed within and buttressed the coalition of interests and ideologies which was shaping a liberalism. But evidently that election was a political education. At the assembly during the election of 1837, Benjamin Havard led a mass revolt against the Poor Law and the ubiquitous Adam Newell (perhaps he was broke again) took some of the rebels to call upon Meyrick to stand again. Morgan Williams, in speech after speech and in appeals in the *Chronicle*, had to fight for his political life. The line just held in 1837 (and Guest duly became a sharp critic of the Poor Law which he had supported) but Morgan was no longer central to the election campaign; that role was taken, appropriately, by a vote-cruncher from Dowlais.[71] Within weeks, Morgan Williams was calling upon working men (in excellent Welsh) to take over the new Literary and Scientific Institution and turn it into an instrument for workers' self-education, in the manner of Rowland Detrosier.[72] Within months the assembly of the Order on Aberdare Mountain was adopting the six points of the People's Charter, electing Hugh Williams of Carmarthen to the convention and erecting Morgan Williams into its spokesman.

Back in the 1790s, when the 'sturdy old republicans' of Merthyr village made it a stronghold of Jacobinism, the old post-woman from Brecon used to bring two copies of a newspaper from the other end of the country, Benjamin Flower's Jacobinical *Cambridge Intelligencer*. Little Anne Nicholas, daughter of a Pant blacksmith, used to deliver them, one to John Guest, the manager of Dowlais furnace, who gave her a penny and a few grave words in the Welsh he had taken the trouble to learn before leaning on a rock opposite the furnace to read; the other went down to the republicans of Georgetown, Vaynor, and Cefn, among them the William Williams whom Anne was eventually to marry.[73] These men, however different they were, were members of a single fraternity. A generation later, as the descendant of John Guest entered the Commons as a Canningite on the backs of the ultras and started on his long march into liberalism and as the offspring of the republicans spaced themselves out along a spectrum of Reform, Anne's son Morgan Williams entered political life as a Jacobin during the Merthyr Rising, sharpened his pen in the *Hereford Times* and edited an Owenite journal. He and the forces he represented and could mobilise saved the Merthyr seat for Josiah John Guest in 1835. Within six years, it was the architect of that famous victory himself who would go down to the Glebeland hustings, to stand for the People's Charter against a liberal ironmaster and to be 'elected' by a forest of unenfranchised hands as what one of his intellectual mentors had once called, 'the unfee'd advocate of the disinherited sons of Adam'.[74]

Notes

1. *Annual Register 1831*, p. 60; *Cambrian*, 12 March 1831.
2. See my 'The making of radical Merthyr, 1800-1836', *ante*, vol. 1, no. 1 (1961), 161-92, for a fuller account.
3. James connection: *Dictionary of Welsh Biography* (London, 1959), sub Charles Herbert James and Sir William Milburne James, and *D.N.B.* for the latter; Charles Wilkins, *The History of Merthyr Tydfil* (Merthyr, 1867), pp. 251-2 and *passim*; C.H. James, *What I remember about Myself and Old Merthyr* (Merthyr, 1892); T. Lewis, *Hen Dy Cwrdd Cefn Coed y Cymmer* (Llandysul, 1947); Crawshay Papers (National Library of Wales): W. Crawshay II — George Thomas, 2 April 1831, to D. James, 15, 16 July 1831, to C. James, 1 November, and W.M. James, 15 November, 1833, vol. 3, fo. 97, 116, 123, 334 and C. James — W. Crawshay II, 19 July, Job James to the same, 30 December 1830, Box 2. 521, 544; general references in Merthyr Tydfil parish minute-book (Central Library, Merthyr Tydfil: henceforth M.T. Minutes), 1799-1833 and 1833-96; *Merthyr Guardian*, 1832 onwards, *passim*, and especially December 1834-January 1835 and November-December 1836; Meyrick: W. Crawshay II-W. Crawshay I, 26 February 1828, Crawshay Papers, Box 2, 404; W. Crawshay I-W. Crawshay II, 10 December 1824, 3 March, 22 August, 18 September 1825, Box 1, 278, 302, 324, 330, W. Crawshay II-T. Pierce, 29 June 1832 and to Jane Tyler, 26 July 1833, vol. 3, fo. 218, 298; Wilkins *History of Merthyr*, pp. 163, 333-6.
4. Wilkins, *History of Merthyr*, pp. 252, 253, 260-65, 294.
5. The essential sources are M.T. Minutes for 1830 and 1831, the entry for 25 March 1831 in particular; *House of Commons Journals*, vol. 83 (1828), pp. 173-4, 184, 188, 203; vol. 84 (1829), pp. 64, 107, 111, 130, 280, 304; my 'The making of radical Merthyr', pp. 169-70, and tables, pp. 188-9.
6. *Parliamentary Debates*, n.s. XXII (1830), 1010-11, 6064-65; XXIII (1830), 377, 461-74; XXIV (1830), 327; XXV (1830), 428, 595-612, 872-882, 954-988, 1130; 3rd ser., I (1830), 1043-1046, 1133-1174; *Commons Journals*, 85 (1830) and 86 (1830-31) *passim;* *Cambrian*, 20, 27 March, 1 May, 19 June, 18, 25 September, 2, 6, 9, 16, 23, 30 October, 20, 27 November, 4, 18, 25 December 1830, 1, 22, 29, January, 5, 12, 19 February, 15 October, 1831; *Merthyr Guardian*, 24 January 1835 (reference back).
7. *Cambrian*, 20, 27 November, 4, 25 December, 1830, 1 January 1831; Llandaff Records (NLW), LL/CC/G 2050 a-n; *Seren Gomer*, Chwefror 1831; Parl. Deb., 3rd ser. II, 206.
8. Colonel Brotherton-Lord Fitzroy Somerset, 14 June, Brotherton and Major Digby Mackworth — the same, 14, 20 June, Evan Thomas-Melbourne, 18 June 1831, H.O. 52/16; *Merthyr Chronicle*, 15 July 1837.
9. I have discussed the crisis in *The Merthyr Rising* (London, 1978), Ch. 3; the major sources are H.O. 52/16 and David Morgans, *Music and Musicians of Merthyr District* (Merthyr Tydfil, 1922), especially pp. 210-11 and the annotated list of eisteddfodau in Ch. xliii. The references to the *Dynolwyr* of Nant-y-Glo I owe to my friend and colleague, Jenkyn Beverley Smith, Aberystwyth.
10. J.B. Bruce — Marquess of Bute, 5 June, and Evan Thomas — Melbourne 18 June 1831, H.O. 52/16; Crawshay in *Cambrian*, 11 June 1831, for the deputation; the solitary man is identified as Matthew John in Henry Scale — Bute, 7 December 1839, Bute MSS (Cardiff Central Library) XX, 114. My attention to some relevant material here and elsewhere was first directed by my friend and colleague, Brian Davies of the National Museum of Wales, whom I thank for his kindness.
11. Evidence in speeches recorded in *Cambrian and Merthyr Guardian*, December 1832 and December 1834; performances in Vestry in M.T. Minutes; Taliesin's statement in a letter, *Merthyr Guardian*, 3 January 1835.
12. Llandaff Records (NLW), LL/CC/G 2050 a-n; *Cambrian*, 1 January 1831.
13. *Cambrian*, 12, 19 March, 23 April 1831; *Monmouthshire Merlin*, 26 March, 2 April

1831; W. Thompson-W. Crawshay II, 19 April 1831, Crawshay Papers (NLW) Box 2, 569.

14. On Guest, Wilkins, *History of Merthyr*, pp. 178-85 and *passim; DWB*; M. Elsas (ed.), *Iron in the Making: Dowlais Iron Company Letters, 1782-1860* (Cardiff, 1960); Samuel Lewis, *Topographical Dictionary of Wales* (1843), and 'The making of radical Merthyr, *ante*, vol. 1, no. 1 (1961), 161-92. My identification of him as a Canningite is based on my reading of his parliamentary record and on M. Brock, *The Great Reform Act* (London, 1973), Chs 1-3.

15. This section is based on a close analysis of his performance in the Commons. *Parl. Deb., n.s.* XVI-XXV, 3rd ser., I-III, covering 1826-31, together with *Commons Journals*, vol. 83-86 and the evidence from *Parl. Papers* (1878), ixii, Index. See M. Brock, *The Great Reform Act*, for context.

16. *Parl. Deb.*, 3rd ser., II, 10.

17. Ibid, II, 90-3, 170, 212, 376, 912.

18. Ibid., II, 206; *Cambrian*, 14 May, 25 June, 22 October 1831.

19. W. Thompson-W. Crawshay II, 19 April 1831, Crawshay Papers (NLW) Box 2, 569.

20. For Honiton electors, a return of 31 December 1831 in *Parl. Papers* (1831-32), XXXVI, 534.

21. *Cambrian*, 30 April 1831; W. Crawshay, *The Late Riots at Merthyr Tydfil* (Merthyr, 1831), and copious comment during the election of 1834-35 in *Merthyr Guardian, Hereford Times* and *Cambrian,* December 1834-January 1835.

22. I have covered this crisis in considerable detail in *The Merthyr Rising*: see especially Chs. 3, 4, 5, 6 and 9.

23. Henry Scale-Bute, 19 November 1839, Bute MSS (CCL) XX, 75; a critical reference I owe to Brian Davies.

24. The evidence is everywhere during the crisis; one of the best sources is the H.O. 64 series, police and secret service, with a myriad confiscated posters, pamphlets, broadsheets, etc.

25. Much evidence in D.J.V. Jones, *Before Rebecca: popular protest in Wales, 1793-1835* (London, 1973). I have discussed some of the problems in 'Locating a Welsh Working Class: the Frontier Years' in David Smith (ed.), *A People and a Proletariat: Essays in Welsh history, 1780-1980* (London, 1980).

26. *Y Gweithiwr/The Workman,* 1 May 1834, in Bruce-Melbourne, 5 May 1834, H.O. 52/25.

27. George Rudé, *Protest and Punishment* (Oxford, 1978), p. 162.

28. *Merthyr Chronicle*, 14 October 1837; and my *Rowland Detrosier, a working-class infidel, 1800-1834* (York, 1965).

29. *Merthyr Chronicle*, 26 August 1837; for the bookseller before 1789, see *The Cambrian Travellers' Guide* (London, 1813), p. 893; this is a greatly enlarged version of an 1809 edition which originated from a private publication of 1789. There was a printing office in the town at the same date.

30. *Merthyr Guardian*, 21 December 1833; report of Chartist meeting to Home Office, 6 August 1843 in H.O. 45/453, a reference I owe to Brian Davies.

31. This is my interpretation of evidence I have collected to supplement that provided in abundance in D.J.V. Jones, *Before Rebecca*. I sketch an argument in 'Locating a Welsh working class: the frontier years'.

32. Scrapbook No. 1, Glamorgan Police Museum, Bridgend, a reference I owe to the kindness of Mr E.R. Baker.

33. Magistrates' and military correspondence in H.O. 52/19, 52/25, 40/30, 41/11, 52/21 and Home Office correspondence with War Office, H.O. 50/445.

34. Bruce-Melbourne, 5 October 1831, H.O. 52/16; Home Office — Law Officers, 10 October 1831, H.O. 49/7; Law Officers — Home Office, 10, 11 October 1831, H.O. 48/28; Melbourne-Bruce, 7 October H.O. 41/10; *Cambrian*, 15 October 1831; I have discussed the operation in *Llafur*, I (May 1972) 3-15.

35. A. Hill-Melbourne, 31 October, 2, 3 November 1831, H.O. 52/16; W. Powell-Melbourne 7 November 1831, H.O. 52/14; Home Office — A. Hill, 3, 5 November 1831, H.O. 41/10; *Cambrian*, 22 October, 12 November 1831; *Monmouthshire Merlin*, 12 November 1831; D.J.V. Jones, *Before Rebecca*, p. 129; on the national and London scene, the excellent Iorwerth Prothero, *Artisans and Politics in early nineteenth-century London* (Folkestone, 1979), especially Chs. 13, 14, 15 (this absolutely essential book covers much more than its title implies).

36. Bute-Melbourne, 28 April 1832, H.O. 52/21.

37. The essential sources are the War Office papers, all three sections, but especially the Monthly Returns of the Army; for this period, W.O. 17/2800. I am preparing a full statistical analysis of the military presence in Wales from 1793 to 1851; the heaviest concentration of the whole period was during the winter of 1831-2.

38. *Parl. Deb.*, 3rd ser., V, 840-872; 3rd ser. XI, 60-73, 206-233; *Commons Journals*, 86, pt 2, pp. 730, 738; 87, pp. 126, 133, 189, 191, 193.

39. *Cambrian*, 24, 31 March 1832.

40. W. Crawshay, *The Late Riots at Merthyr Tydfil* (Merthyr, 1831), and my *The Merthyr Rising*, Ch. 7.

41. *Times*, 2 July 1832; M. Elsas (ed.), *Iron in the Making*, p. 227; R.D. Rees, 'Glamorgan Newspapers under the Stamp Act', *Morganwg*, III (1959), 72-6.

42. *Merthyr Guardian*, 24 November 1832.

43. *Merthyr Guardian*, 17 January 1835.

44. Based on a study of the *Hereford Times* in 1832, 1833, 1834 and 1835; for the Pengam head, *Hereford Times*, 31 May 1834.

45. For Darker, M.T. Minutes, 10 April 1822, 4 April, 30 October 1823; 15 April 1824, 1 April 1825, 23 November, 22 December 1826, 5 April 1827, 27 March 1828, 8 December 1830, 2 May, 23 November 1831, 23 March 1837; *Merthyr Guardian*, 3 August 1833, 5 March 1834, 23 January 1836; *Hereford Times*, 29 September, 6 October 1832, 2, 9 November 1833.

46. *Hereford Times*, 5, 26 January 1833 and *passim*.

47. *Cambrian*, 31 November 1832; *Hereford Times*, 1, 15 December 1832.

48. *Cambrian*, 22 December 1832; *Hereford Times*, 15 December 1832; M. Brock, *The Great Reform Act;* I. Prothero, *Artisans and Politics.*

49. *Cambrian*, 22 December 1832; *Hereford Times*, 15 December 1832.

50. Magistrates' correspondence in H.O. 52/22, 52/23; military movements in W.O. 17/2800.

51. *Merthyr Guardian*, 17, 24 August, 7 September, 9 November 1833, 25 October, 1, 8, 15 November 1834.

52. This problem fills M.T. Minutes for 1832 and 1833; I have printed the parish budget for 1833 as an appendix to 'The making of radical Merthyr', p. 190. For the key moments in the conflict, see M.T. Minutes, 21 November 1833, 3 March and April-October 1834 *passim; Merthyr Guardian*, 23 November 1833; *Commons Journals*, 89, pp. 34, 61; 90, pp. 124, 227, 228, 240, 260, 322, 326, 353; 91, pp. 43, 91, 217, 222, 229.

53. *Commons Journals*, 89, pp. 58, 153, 159, 186, 207, 221, 300, 324, 328-29, 333, 360, 399; *The Workman*, 1 May 1834; *Merthyr Guardian*, 20 December 1834; *Cambrian*, 27 December 1834; *Hereford Times*, 27 December 1834.

54. I have based what follows on the initial guide of Richard Gooch, *The Book of the Reformed Parliament* (London, 2nd edn, 1834; lists of votes), and on a thorough search of *Parl. Deb.*, 3rd ser., XV-XXV, and the related *Commons Journals*; for Guest's own bill, *Commons Journals*, 1834, pp. 142, 195, 253, 522, 545-6, 551, 558, 594; *Parl. Deb.*, 3rd ser., XXV, 458-9.

55. A wealth of posters and other material in H.O. 64/15 and 64/19.

56. *Cambrian*, 22 February 1834.

57. *The Workman* was a monthly; the May number was the fourth and J.B. Bruce, sending it up to the Home Office, referred to it as 'this month's Workman': Bruce — Melbourne, 5 May 1834, H.O. 52/25; on this Owenite crisis, see magistrates' and military

correspondence in H.O. 52/25; H.O. 50/445; W.O. 17/2800; H.O. 41/11, H.O. 41/12 and the *Cambrian, Merthyr Guardian* and *Monmouthshire Merlin* for 1834, especially March-August.

58. A. Hill-Bruce, 30 March 1834; Col. Love — Lord Fitzroy Somerset, 8 April 1834, H.O. 52/25.

59. *Cambrian*, 5 April 1834.

60. Col. Love — Fitzroy Somerset, 8 April 1834; Bute — Melbourne, 16 June 1834, H.O. 52/25; troop movements in W.O. 17/2800.

61. The Mountain Police in Bruce — Melbourne, 7, 16 June, Bute — Melbourne 16 June, Bruce — Melbourne, 20 June, Bute — Melbourne 23 June, Capt. Howells — Bute, 21 June, Chelsea Hospital — Home Office, 2 July 1834, H.O. 52/25; pensioners lists in H.O. 50/445; the original plan for a police, drafted by Maj. Digby Mackworth, is in W. Powell (Abergavenny) — Melbourne, 31 March 1832; it was sent to Bruce at Merthyr on 9 June 1834; H.O. 52/19.

62. Fullest account in Bute — Melbourne, 16 June 1834, H.O. 52/25; *Cambrian*, 21 June 1834, reports the meeting but does not give the resolutions.

63. *Cambrian*, 26 July, 2, 16 August, 27 September 1834; *Hereford Times*, 23 August 1834; in the week of the men's surrender, the *Hereford Times* lost its agency at Nant-y-Glo.

64. It would be tedious to list individual references for the election campaign, since my account is based almost wholly on newspaper coverage. Unless otherwise stated, the sources are the *Merthyr Guardian, Hereford Times, Cambrian* and *Monmouthshire Merlin* for December 1834 and January 1835.

65. *Cambrian*, 1 November 1834.

66. The major source on the Orange Order is the report of the Commons Select Committee on the Orange Institution, 1835; *Parl. Papers* (1835) XVII, especially pp. 71, 89, 200, 202, 203, 226, 246, 254, 274-5, 280, 314, 337-41; *Merthyr Guardian*, 19 October 1833; *Cambrian*, 18 October 1834.

67. A. Hill — Bruce, 30 March 1834, H.O. 52/25; D.J.V. Jones, *Before Rebecca*, pp. 100, 111.

68. Wilkins, *History of Merthyr*, p. 334.

69. *Hereford Times* and *Cambrian*, 10 January 1835. I think now that I misinterpreted this meeting in earlier writings, my 'The Making of Radical Merthyr' and *The Merthyr Rising*, where I spoke of the meeting as securing a massive defection of Cyfarthfa men to Guest. This is certainly how it struck many shopkeepers clearly and, indeed, how Charles Wilkins saw it (*History of Merthyr*, p. 334) when he mistakenly calls it a meeting of Crawshay workers. The *Merthyr Guardian* tried at first to take the opposite tack and to claim that only Dowlais workmen were present, but rapidly abandoned the argument because of its obvious absurdity. If the assembly had been merely sectional, it would never have worked. There is no evidence that Crawshay men would have obeyed him if he had ordered a boycott. In fact, I tend to agree with the *Hereford Times* correspondent who asserted that nine-tenths of Crawshay's men disagreed with his action. The really intriguing question about the meeting is how and why Morgan Williams and John Jones could have secured it at all, in view of the men's experiences of the summer.

70. M.T. Minutes, 9, 19 March, 9 April, 28 May, 10, 24 December 1835 and *passim*, 1835-8; see, e.g., the meeting of 30 June 1837; *Merthyr Guardian*, 5, 12, 19, 26 November, 3 December 1836; Wilkins, *History of Merthyr*, p. 357; R.D. Rees, 'Glamorgan Newspapers', pp. 76-8.

71. *Merthyr Chronicle*, July and August 1837.

72. *Merthyr Chronicle*, 14 October 1837.

73. Wilkins, *History of Merthyr*, pp. 142-3.

74. This article is a product of a research programme made possible by a generous grant from the British Academy, which I gratefully acknowledge.

5 DIC PENDERYN: MYTH, MARTYR AND MEMORY IN THE WELSH WORKING CLASS*

To Dic Penderyn, born 1808 at Aberavon.
Hanged 13 August 1831 at Cardiff.
Martyr of the Welsh Working Class.

So runs a bilingual memorial plaque on the wall of the Central Library, Merthyr Tydfil. The plaque was unveiled by Len Murray, General Secretary of the TUC, during a ceremony in 1977 graced by readings from Alexander Cordell, author of the novel *The Fire People*, whose efforts have led to the discovery of many of the missing records of Dic's trial.

Hard by the Library stands a Town Hall which looks as if it had been designed by an illustrator of Tolkien. The first in Wales to fall, briefly, to Plaid Cymru, it displays, as in a shrine, the bust of James Keir Hardie, whom Merthyr elected as the first Labour MP in Wales.

Merthyr Tydfil, mother town of iron and steel in south Wales and of much else beside, was in terms of numbers the first 'town' in Welsh history. For three generations it was the strongest single concentration of Welsh people on earth. It had been the first and proved to be the most persistent stronghold of Jacobinism in Wales in the time of the French Revolution. It produced Wales's first working-class martyr and its first working-class press. It was the first Welsh town to fall to radical Dissent. It was a heartland of Chartism and the home of the Welsh Chartist press in both languages. In 1868, it became the first Welsh constituency to elect a Nonconformist Radical MP on working-class votes and on a specifically working-class thrust of grievance and aspiration: Henry Richard, the 'apostle of peace'. Even in 1900, in the days of its relative decline, it elected Keir Hardie, though as a second member and on a minority vote.

I am no longer sure I know what a tradition is, but if such a

---

*The original of this chapter was written in haste, as a kind of running commentary on a whole chunk bodily lifted from my *The Merthyr Rising* (Croom Helm, London, 1978) which had just been published, at the urgent request of *History Workshop* which was apparently in crisis. Fortunately the crisis proved transient and they did not need the piece. *Llafur* (Journal of the Welsh Labour History Society)2 (1978) was kind enough to find a place for this section under the title 'Dic Penderyn, the making of a Welsh working-class martyr'. Re-reading it in 1981, I see every reason to reprint it and none not to.

phenomenon exists, Merthyr Tydfil must surely exemplify it. It is as I write those words that I experience what Aneurin Bevan once called, in capital letters, the Invasion of Doubt. My uneasiness, I think, is not simply personal, it is historical. It is the fear that, in our ceremony outside Merthyr Central Library, we were sanctifying an historical untruth.

This is certainly not a question of historical inaccuracy. That Dic Penderyn, Richard Lewis, was unjustly hanged in 1831, that he *was* a martyr of the Welsh working class, is now, I think, proven.[1] It is not even a question of the wealth of evidence which ordinary, professional, dry-as-dust history can marshal, year by year, from Merthyr's experience, to set against the tradition. From my own family, I can summon up a veritable roll-call of dissidents from the communal identity suggested by Dic Penderyn's plaque and Keir Hardie's bust. My paternal grandfather, known as Alf Gordon because of his alleged resemblance to the hero of Khartoum, was a 'ronk Liberal' to quote his son's Dowlais English, who was cordially hated by the Labour Party. During elections, Labour pioneers would congregate around his house. If they had won a local election, they contented themselves with the Red Flag; if they had lost, they tried to break the door in, against my grandfather and his sons standing armed with pick-axe handles in the passage. When one of those sons started to court my mother, whose sister married a Socialist pioneer who was victimised by the coal companies and driven into exile in Canada, something of a minor Montague-Capulet atmosphere developed. My mother's own father, however, a red-cheeked countryman from Cil-y-Cwm in Carmarthen-shire, resolutely refused to vote for Keir Hardie, 'Foxe-Davies a Rector Bach i mi' (the Conservative candidate and the Rector) 'Tory I am, me firrrst firrrst, you firrrst after' (which even today seems a fairly accurate portrait of the new Toryism).

Every native of Merthyr will have his own register of such dissidents. But dissidents they were. For many years I was known in Merthyr not by my own name or even by my father's; I was 'Alf Gordon's grandson'. I suspect that, if I had been a schoolteacher in Merthyr, I would never have got a headship.

The kind of argument which focuses on such contrary examples, however, misses the point. Those historians who see day-by-day empirical history, itself derived from a limited, slewed and inadequate range of evidence, as the only reality seem to me to be profoundly mistaken, indeed essentially anti-historical.

A myth is not necessarily a lie; on the contrary a myth often expresses an historical truth. A tradition of the kind I have been describing can in sober reality become 'consciousness transformed into a material force'. This has certainly been true of Merthyr. Voltaire was describing a 'climate of opinion' or a Gramscian hegemony when he once said that, whereas few people had actually read Isaac Newton, 'everybody' believed in Newtonian science. Not so much the tradition itself, but the whole historical experience of Merthyr which its tradition in a sense encapsulated and made usable, created a climate of opinion in the community which spirits who were not attuned to it could find stifling.

It is quite literally true that, as a youth, I had met a fascist before I ever met anyone who was shameless enough, indeed anarchically undisciplined enough, publicly to proclaim that he or she was a Conservative. Aneurin Bevan once said that Tories did not have horns growing out of their heads; politics would be simpler if they did. To a whole generation of Merthyr adolescents like myself, in all sober truth, this needed to be said. This may be triviality, but it reflects an historical reality.

No, what is worrying is the precise nature of this tradition: what it chooses to exclude, what it chooses to stress. Antonio Gramsci was working in the mainstream of the marxist tradition when he conducted those analyses of the way in which rebellious, dissident popular traditions can in fact serve the very hegemony they are ostensibly in revolt against. You may recollect Eric Hobsbawm's striking account of those seventeenth-century German bandits who, to distance themselves from the society of the straight, took up Devil Worship. They simply stood Christianity on its head. This in no way disturbed the hegemony of Christianity; it merely confirmed its primacy.

The Ford Motor Company, you will remember, found the South Wales Working Class (capital letters seem in order) the most intelligent and sensible in Europe (they brought a substantial government dowry with them of course). The Hoover Washing Machine Company of Ohio, which presides over Merthyr as potently as the ironmasters Guest and Crawshay ever did, has found little cause for complaint in the conduct of Labour militants who shed a manly tear over Dic Penderyn as they sweep away the relics of a past of capitalist oppression and regroup their people around supermarkets much as they were once regrouped around Norman castles and for a similar range of reasons.

Some forms of a tradition do not merely encapsulate a past, they sterilise it; they remove it from the historical equation of the present. This is not to cultivate an historical consciousness, it is to get rid of it.

The past, in this process, is in fact abolished, in much the same way as the physical fabric of a town.

The fear that gnawed at me as I wrote on the Merthyr Rising of 1831 was the fear that I might succumb to that celebratory style which seems to be gripping the industrial south Wales which is articulate. We are living through a somewhat desperate hunt after our own past, a time of miners' libraries rescued from institute collections sold off without compunction and at knock-down rates to hungry hucksters, of old militants religiously recorded on tape, of quarries turned into tourist museums. What is alarming is that this kind of recovered tradition is increasingly operating in terms of a Celebration of a Heroic Past which seems rarely to be brought to bear on vulgarly contemporary problems except in terms of a merely rhetorical style which absolves its fortunate possessor from the necessity of thought and choice.

Consider the tradition of Dic Penderyn. In the first place, it is very late. Feelings ran high in 1831; their expression may be traced at moments in the late nineteenth century, but it was not until 1945 that a tradition effectively broke into print, even on the margins. It was only then, too, that trade union banners of a formal nature appeared in south Wales. We have been a singularly unhistorical people, a people without memory.

Consider the Dic Penderyn ceremony. It was official in the sense that a Labour Establishment (I use the term in a neutral not polemical sense) has become official. The first generally official recognition of Dic Penderyn preceded the Merthyr ceremony by a few years, was based on the work of historians not populist novelists, and was conducted by no less an institution than the Church in Wales (and all honour to it), which for generations had been familiarly known as *yr hen fradwres*, the old traitress.

Consider the content of the celebration. We celebrate a martyr, a victim, a past of sacrifice and suffering. After the hideous disaster of the Depression of the inter-war years, this is difficult to avoid in Merthyr. The Town of Tydfil the Martyr, the novelist Jack Jones used to call it, rolling the sonorous title around his tongue. To be pedantic, this is inaccurate: *Merthyr* in place-names generally means tomb or a burial-place, not a martyr. This is no great matter, people call their own town what they like. It is, however, curiously symptomatic. The tradition of Martyr's Town is distinctly lachrymose. It is martyrs we remember, the victim we honour.

There are other figures from our past who were rather less lugubrious: Ifor Bach, a successful twelfth-century practitioner of the impudent political kidnap; Llywelyn Bren, who knew his French authors as well as his Welsh and could rock fourteenth-century Glamorgan. There are many others.

More important, there were people and there were qualities in the Merthyr Rising of 1831 itself, central to it in fact, who are eliminated from history and from present consciousness by this particular celebration of Dick Penderyn the martyr. This, not any academicism, is the reason why that tradition has to be confronted with events 'as they actually happened' in so far as we can reconstruct them.

This process of the elimination of awkward actuality finds an exemplar in the very act of association of the Merthyr community with Dic Penderyn. The plaque which commemorates him bears the St Tydfil coat of arms of Merthyr Tydfil with its motto: *nid cadarn ond brodyrdde*. This motto is universally translated as 'Not force but fellowship'. This translation is inaccurate. Again, in itself, this means little; people can do what they like with their own mottoes. The inaccuracy, however, reflects a decisive *shift in meaning* over time. This shift is central to the manner in which Dic Penderyn is celebrated. It is therefore central to the present state of mind of working people in south Wales who consider themselves inheritors of a tradition. And it generates an historical untruth.

Merthyr became a County Borough after 1906 during that Liberal high noon when not a single Tory MP was returned from Wales. The local historian Frank Treharne James, who had consulted Goscombe John, RA, on the coat of arms, presented several mottoes to the Armorial Bearings Committee. The translation actually adopted for the final choice was: There is nothing so strong as combination. However clumsy, and in these degenerate days potentially comic, this version was authentic. It used the very words of Taliesin Williams, a schoolmaster in Merthyr during the 1820s, a leader in the eisteddfod and the Welsh revival and a shaper of Merthyr's rich, popular, Welsh and bilingual culture. It was also apt, because the motto had in fact been devised by Taliesin's celebrated father, Iolo Morganwg.

Iolo Morganwg, Edward Williams, was the Bard of Liberty of the 1790s, moving spirit of an embryonic national ideology and a national intelligentsia, inventor of a *gorsedd* (order) of Druidic, Masonic and Jacobin 'bards' who were to serve, in succession to the old bardic 'people's remembrancers' as the radical and directive elite of a new Welsh nation (I am tempted to say *une nation*) which Iolo himself served as fabricator-in-chief and revolutionary Merlin. In this enterprise, Iolo, who spent much of his later life among the 'sturdy old

Republicans' of Merthyr village, composed 41 proverbs in suitably archaic style on the theme of *brodyrdde* and attributed them to a suitably Silurian sage of the sixth century, St Cadog. The motto first appeared in print in the third volume of the *Myvyrian Archaiology* of 1807, the major achievement of those genial London-Welsh intellectuals and their allies, Jacobins most of them, who 'revived' the eisteddfod as an instrument of Enlightenment and Revolution and who had their prize medals struck by the engraver to the new French National Assembly.

The word *brodydde* itself first appears in a dictionary composed by the leading figure of this movement, Iolo's colleague William Owen, an acquaintance of William Blake and a follower of Joanna Southcott the millenarian; it was Owen who edited the *Archaiology*. His dictionary came out in 1793, the very year when another Jacobin, Morgan John Rhys, a Baptist minister in Monmouthshire who had been born in Llanfabon nearby and who was to launch a Free Cambria in America, published the *Cylchgrawn Cymraeg* (Welsh Journal) which became the first political periodical in the Welsh language. Originally the word (which today suggests brotherhood) meant 'friendship, social ties' with the adjectival meaning of 'fraternal, brotherly'. Silvan Evans, in a later dictionary, talked of 'fraternal union'.

A Jacobin slogan was singularly appropriate for that Merthyr which was a stronghold of the new democratic ideology as it had been of Cromwellian Independency. In the hands of Iolo's son Taliesin, however, it acquired an additional dimension of meaning. Taliesin lived through the Merthyr Rising of 1831 which killed Dic Penderyn and also produced the first trade union lodges in south Wales which were branches of a national organisation. He lived through the Owenite socialist movement of 1834 when Merthyr, in that cause, produced Wales's first working-class newspaper *Y Gweithiwr/The Workman*. Taliesin lived through Chartism when the editor of the *Gweithiwr* published Wales's Chartist press.

Taliesin translated brodyrdde as 'combination'. He used the word precisely in the sense of the Combination Acts which declared trade unions illegal. Taliesin's translation captured the particular flavour imparted to the notion of 'brotherhood' and 'fraternal union' by the desperate struggles of the early trade unions in their heroic age. During the lock-out of 1831, the Whig Home Secretary Lord Melbourne, who had refused to reprieve Dic Penderyn, ruthlessly broke his own law to destroy the new unions, a procedure which was repeated on a national scale in 1834. The transmission of this slogan to the Merthyr of 1906 was then an illustration of that elusive tradition; Brother Len Murray's presence in 1977 seems appropriate.

It was doubly appropriate in that the evidence now available makes it clear that the man who decided the fate of Dic Penderyn, virtually in isolation, was that same Lord Melbourne. What was haunting him in 1831 was the power and drive of what the Home Office called *The Union*, the National Association for the Protection of Labour in the north of England, whose lodges penetrated south Wales after the Rising and which Melbourne mistakenly suspected had been behind the Rising itself. Whatever else he died a martyr to, Dic Penderyn almost certainly died a martyr to the National Association for the Protection of Labour of 1831.

Taliesin's translation, however, fought a losing battle in the twentieth century against more euphonious and oecumenical forms. D. Andrew Davies, Merthyr's Director of Education, made a last stand against this rising and apparently irresistible tide of false consciousness in 1963 when he suggested a version which would be less clumsy than Taliesin's but equally as authentic: Nothing as strong as the bonds of brotherhood or to be succinct: No strength but brotherhood. To be fully authentic, this would need to carry the emotional charge of the 'brothers' of the trade union movement. To be totally authentic to a less sexist age, it would need to run: No strength but solidarity.

Nothing survives of the bite and the challenge of Merthyr's original motto, just as nothing of the NAPL survives in the living tradition of Dic Penderyn's martyrdom. Not force but fellowship: anybody who was affronted by that would be affronted by Motherhood.

It is not entirely true that the Rising of 1831, as opposed to its Martyr, has been forgotten. A special treat in my youth were Sunday evening gatherings at the home of my paternal grandmother, Mary Catherine Williams, a little, tough, black-clad figure whom I suspected had built Gwernllwyn Chapel Dowlais with her bare teeth. Normally she was militant apathy personified. 'What's the worrrld to you, boy?' she'd snap, as she tore the subversive *News Chronicle* from my hands, 'Cere at dy Literature' (Get down to your Literature). Her children, as a desperate measure, once took her to a Chaplin film. She sat unmoved throughout, to comment at the end, 'Druan arno fe' (Pity for him). She was known to have made one public comment on events, when she went to chapel to denounce 'Yr hen Mussoloni na' (that old Mussoloni: her command of Italian was more idiosyncratic even than her command of English). Gwernllwyn Sisterhood duly voted to condemn the Italian invasion of Ethiopia (or Abyssinia as we used to call it).

The real exception for her, however, was The Past. After the chapel 'monkey parade' along twilit streets in ritual sexual tension and the no less carnal delights of cold meat, pickles and Moscow Radio (a concession to youthful fantasy) with its yet more thousands of inhabited localities liberated from the Nazi invader, my grandmother and two venerable companions would rehearse their memories of things past. Often, the talk curled back to 1831. They'd shriek with laughter at the thought of a 'young boy' Abednego Jones, who went about Merthyr during the Rising carrying a 'huge white banner' as big as himself (sometimes twice as big) piping in a choirboy treble, 'Death to kings and tyrants! The reign of justice for ever!'

I ultimately found a huge white banner; workers carried it on the march to the Waun Fair which started the insurrection. I never found the young boy, but I came across an Abednego Jones who had 'carried a banner during the Merthyr Riots' (the phrase recurs repeatedly in obituary and other notices; it marked a man out) and who, I have since discovered, became a Chartist militant. Quite young women in Cefn High Street talked about the Argyll and Sutherland Highlanders marching down the street with their kilts swinging, as if it had happened yesterday. 'Go home and put your trousers on!' the women shouted. A remarkable feature of the folklore of the Rising is the fact that much of it turns out to be sober historical fact.

On the whole, however, it is largely anecdotal and centres almost wholly on the execution of Dic Penderyn. What is absent from it, above all, is any sense of the crisis as a *rebellion*. Working people accepted the description imposed by their superiors — the Merthyr Riots. This terminology in fact stems from a cold-blooded political decision by Melbourne. He was determined to play the crisis as coolly as possible. He had to; the Whig predicament was becoming precarious in the intensifying social and political crisis of the Reform Bill. Melbourne rejected repeated requests from Glamorgan magistrates for a trial of the rebels for High Treason (which was a perfectly proper, indeed the only proper, course of action). Prosecute them for riot, he said. Take the wretched place back into tranquillity and out of the public eye. As far as I know, the first man to give the action its proper name (apart from the republican Richard Carlile at the time) was Harri Webb, the radical and nationalist poet, in his pamphlet on Dic Penderyn published in 1956.

The process by which Dic Penderyn became detached from the Rising can be traced, I now realise, within my own family experience.

The first contact with history I can recollect is a story my mother told me about her grandmother, Sarah Herbert of Tredegar whose brother was a Chartist in Nant-y-Glo in Gwent. Sarah Herbert was an ardent supporter of Henry Richard and an active canvasser in his cause in Dowlais. She once paid no less than 4d to see what was alleged to be Dic Penderyn's ear on display in Dowlais Market (and promptly put a stop to such deplorable goings-on).

This story, so oddly reminiscent of the relic-worship of popular Catholicism, is intriguing from a craft viewpoint. I now think it derives from an entirely false report in the workers' paper *Tarian y Gweithiwr (The Worker's Shield)* of 1884. A correspondent claimed to have met the man who committed the crime for which Dic Penderyn had been hanged; he had met him in Pennsylvania, the man having fled through France. The writer, totally misinformed, said the man had lost an ear and recollected that a soldier who had seen a comrade 'killed' had noted that the 'killer' had lost an ear. No soldier was killed during the conflict and there is no record of anyone losing an ear, but it is at least clear that some kind of Dic Penderyn had lodged in the popular culture of south Wales long before 1900 (Ianto Parker's Pennsylvania confession, which cleared Dic, had been reported in the *Western Mail* in 1874).

More significant, I think, is the fact that an ardent supporter of Henry Richard whose brother was a Chartist of the later, distinctly Liberal persuasion, should also have been a devotee of some cult of Dic Penderyn. For the days of Henry Richard were certainly *not* those of the frontier years. There had been a massive process of realignment and restabilisation, a major advance in Nonconformity and Respectability, a new liberal or radical consensus quite different from the autonomous, radical and rebellious working-class attitudes of the 1830s. These were the days of the 'working classes', whose movements were becoming a marching wing of Liberalism, of a virtual fusion of popular aspirations and Nonconformist democracy. Dic Penderyn had died after a revolutionary insurrection and during a desperate struggle, without allies, for trade union rights, when a working-class identity was established, to reassert itself episodically over the next decade or so, in the teeth of repression, military garrisons in five south Wales towns, an episodically armed middle class (equipped with cutlasses at critical moments), the political hegemony of the ten-pound voters and a press which drowned working people in ferocious abuse and contempt. By my great-grandmother's day, Dic Penderyn had quit the Merthyr Rising and was on his way towards that plaque on the Central Library.

It would take years of back-breaking labour to trace his progress there, as it would to solve the even more fascinating problem of the relative historical *invisibility* of the Merthyr Rising. Some points, however, need to be made.

Since his appearance in 1945, the Dic Penderyn of tradition has naturally developed. His first begetter, Islwyn ap Nicolas, was certainly left wing, but his Dic is a rather formidable character, equipped with an exemplary youth worthy of a Sunday School tract. It would not be too hard to fit him, particularly in Welsh, into that major genre of Welsh writing, the minister's memoir or *cofiant* (where indeed Dic had first put in a coy appearance). Harri Webb's Dic of 1956 is altogether a more racy fellow, fond of his glass and situated in a people's war of liberation against colonial oppression. Alexander Cordell's Dic, brilliantly oblique, moves through that world which his maker, genuinely alert to history and even more alert to historic drama, has so successfully created. At his worst, Alexander Cordell is Silurian Gothic who ought to be published in Nashville. At his best, he can achieve an imaginative 'reality' I have hitherto encountered only among American and French practitioners of popular history or *haute vulgarisation* — and both countries, of course, had the good taste to stage their revolutions during the Age of Reason.

Despite some thunder on the Left, Dic Penderyn becomes ever more visibly a Welsh nationalist. More important, I think, is the tension which afflicts his creators. On the one hand, he has to be presented as a victim of injustice, which he certainly was. On the other, there seems to be an inescapable tendency to make him a leader or at least a person of consequence. Since the context of his execution was a direct workers' attack on soldiers, followed by an armed insurrection which defeated regulars and yeomanry twice, threatened the physical destruction of a military garrison and constituted authority, mobilised 20,000 people from Monmouthshire in potential revolt and collapsed only in the face of 1,000 soldiers despatched against it, these twin but opposite tendencies generate acute contradiction. It is precisely the idea of *rebellion* which is sacrificed. The tensions are very visible in our own day when Dic has been diffused through a rebellious youth culture. We have long had a tough, investigative journal named after *Rebecca*. We now have a *Penderyn*.[2]

¡Que viva Puerto Rico Libre! proclaims *Penderyn* no. 4, as it prints articles on Puerto Rico, the struggle of the Crimean Tartars in the USSR, the General Strike in south Wales, Prison Letters, attacks on Plaid Cymru as 'England's safety valve', the gagging of the Irish

community and Film in Wales. It carries two poems specifically on Dic Penderyn by two of our best-known poets.

John Tripp, accomplished and genial, satirical, Rabelaisian and a fierce polemicist often betrayed by his own innate sense of fraternity, writes a poem which can be placed by a historian without too much travail. Dic has been hanged, cavalry have been disarmed, 'then we put down the Taffs'. All recent writers are alert to the progress of dry-as-dust history (Cordell has worked hard at it); John Tripp is as alert as any:

> The proofs were slender, sir,
> as to his presence at all.
> Now great crowds outside my window
> follow his coffin
>> (Thus are martyrs made)

Then, however, comes a conceptual leap.

> We need Edward's Justices back,
> Thos. Cromwell and Rowland Lee,
>> a few turncoat hanging judges,
> some marcher lords and steel
> To take these rascals' minds off
> their damned Glendowers,
>> ap Gwilyms and God knows who.
> Offa began a problem
>> when he built his accursed dyke.
> These Welsh will make the coronets rattle
> at Windsor before they finish . . .

The revolutionary optimism of the last couplet is as refreshing as a mirage in the reactionary political desert which is south Wales today, but it *is* a curious echo of 1831 itself when government was badly frightened and suspected the loyalty of its own troops (yeomanry were ignominiously defeated and disarmed). Melbourne, writing to his successor at the Home Office eight years later, after the Chartist march on Newport, said 'It is the worst and most formidable district in the kingdom. The affair we had there in 1831 was the most like a fight of anything that took place'.

You will observe, however, that Dic Penderyn is wrenched out of the only historical context which gives his martyrdom meaning and securely lodged in a strictly nationalist pantheon. Presumably rebels who were Welsh must have been objectively Welsh Rebels. The revolt is attributed to some quality of Welshness in revolt against an ancient subjection. Dic was hanged by *rhaff y Saeson*, the *English* rope, sing the pop groups in their *Noson Lawen Dic Penderyn* (Dic Penderyn folknights). John Tripp's litany is familiar; Edward I who hammered us, and especially the 'bards' as hard as the Scots, Cromwell and Tudor repressions, Owain Glyndŵr, the rebel prince and Dafydd ap Gwilym, most human and accessible of our medieval poets. Here, Dic is an incantation in a nationalist curse.

Harri Webb is something else. Though an immigrant and a sophisticate, he visibly belongs to a long line of Merthyr remembrancer-poets stretching back through the eisteddfodau at the Lamb Inn and the Patriot, through Dic Dywyll, Dic Dark the blind ballad singer who kept the Workhouse out of Merthyr for years with his verse, won a prize at an Infidel eisteddfod, wrote on Dic Penderyn and made more money in a week than a furnace manager, back to some of the Jacobins of Aberdare Mountain. Furthermore, Harri Webb has written on the Rising, as he was the first to call it. Here, he supplies a self-consciously 'simple' ballad. Whatever else he is, simple Harri Webb is not, though he is a conscious myth-maker in the Sorelian style — myth as a motor of the will.

> The town was Merthyr Tydfil
> The year was thirty-one,
> Twas there in grim Glamorgan
> That mighty deeds were done . . .

ac felly yn ymlaen, and so on, to quote a characteristic Welsh pulpit style. The nationalism is present but not overly obtrusive:

> The alien lords of iron
> Who ground our people down,
> Took refuge in their mansions,
> And the workers took the town . . .

and, to conclude:

> And the time is surely coming
> When Wales must once more show
> The courage of Penderyn
> So many years ago . . .

What this courage of Penderyn was is not made clear, though some sense of the rebel-leader would surely be felt by a reader. In the poem Dic is simply hanged, though 'Heaven sent its lightnings down'. Moreover, 'Lewis the bold huntsman was banished from the land . . .' Harri Webb knows the story of the Rising and at least mentions somebody other than Dic. He plays merry hell with the chronology of the revolt to serve his purpose but, rare among celebrants of this tradition, *does* indicate that there *were* workers who 'struck' as well as 'bled'.

This truth, however, is negated by what, to me, is the most intriguing and symptomatic verse, about the conflict outside the Castle Inn where at least two dozen people were killed and seventy wounded.

> And at the masters' harsh command
> They fired on the crowd
> And all the gutters ran with blood
> Why are such things allowed?

The sheer bathos of that last line accurately sums up the Dic Penderyn tradition.

More important, the verse itself is not only a travesty of what happened but its exact *opposite*, as the author well knows. It was the *crowd* who attacked the soldiers. The ranks outside the Inn were hemmed in on all sides; their bayonets were pointing straight up in the air; their muskets were not loaded. Their comrades in the Inn's upstairs windows fired only when ordered to by their officers (no master or magistrate gave the order to fire) and this after the crowd had several times broken into the Inn where masters, magistrates and the hated shopkeeper Specials were massed. The discipline of the soldiers was in fact as remarkable as the bravery of their attackers: 'Good God! can't we fire? . . . No, we dare not until we get orders . . .'

It is perfectly true that no soldier was killed and that their firing was literally murderous, but they fired essentially to save their lives. If they had not, they might well have been torn to pieces.

I encountered precisely the same distortion of history in a television programme devised for St David's Day by BBC Wales, in the manner of the Scottish 7:84 popular theatre, to which the Merthyr Rising was a centrepiece. Over my repeated but futile objections, an entirely imaginary scene was inserted in order to throw the initiative in brutal conflict to authority — 'teach this rabble a lesson'.

What is really revealing about this practice is *the terrible reluctance to say that workers were the attackers, the aggressors.* Richard Carlile, the republican of 1831, had no such inhibitions. Authority would seem to have little to fear from revolutionaries of such delicate kidney.

This exemplifies the contradiction at the heart of the Dic Penderyn tradition, with its polarities of Dic as Innocent Victim and Dic as (at the very least) Exemplary Welsh Worker. No matter how fully events are described, it is the *Rising* which is spiritually absent. There is a repeated collapse into the victim syndrome; we are back in the Town of Tydfil the Martyr.

In terms of the historical autonomy of the Welsh working class, in Gramsci's terms, the only ones that matter in this context, this kind of rebel tradition is simply 'gastric juice' (Gramsci again) to its opponents. You will recollect that Society, which took such a hammering in France in May and June 1968, was within weeks peddling plastic paving stones, the student weapon, as souvenirs. It would have even less trouble with this Dic Penderyn.

What is diminished and in extreme cases excluded by this form of tradition is the historical existence and present meaning of the Merthyr Rising of 1831. Even more notably, it turns into an un-person an individual human being who could serve myth-makers perfectly as a symbol of the Rising itself. He was a man much more visible in 1831 than Dic Penderyn, who comes to life only with his death, a man who would have been recognised as a folk hero at any time and any place from the Water Margin of China to the Morelos of Zapata's Mexico.

In 1831 itself in Merthyr, there was a proclamation directed wholly at one man. It was issued by the desperate ironmasters the morning after the shooting outside the Castle Inn, as workers took up arms. An anguished appeal for calm, it was signed YOUR FRIENDS AND MASTERS:

> Good God! that you should have been led on by the Speech of One Violent Man to commit so daring an attack as you did . . .

The One Violent Man was not Dic Penderyn; it was Lewis Lewis, known as Lewsyn yr Heliwr, Lewis the Huntsman and a Village Hampden born.

There is no plaque to *him* on Merthyr Central Library.'

More important, people in Merthyr in 1831 chose to remember Dic in preference to Lewsyn. From the beginning, the victim rather than the hero was singled out. The historical inadequacy of the Dic Penderyn tradition in terms of the historical autonomy of the Welsh working class is thus rooted in a specific historical conjuncture.

We, as people's remembrancers, need to understand that choice. That is why it is necessary to locate Dic Penderyn and Lewsyn yr Heliwr in what-actually-happened. As mere historians we will not and probably cannot succeed. But we have to try.

Notes

1. I have written at length on the Rising and Dic Penderyn in *The Merthyr Rising* (Croom Helm, London, 1978, paperback 1979).

2. We now have *Rebecca* again, as a monthly, with an *Eye-Witness* page which tries to present history as the journalism of the past-in-the-present. I have heard no more of *Penderyn,* though a gossip page under that *nom-de-plume* exists in *Rebecca.*

6 AMBIGUOUS HERO: HUGH OWEN AND LIBERAL WALES*

On first acquaintance, Hugh Owen's face seems as familiar as an old friend. In Meisenbach's celebrated photograph, it looks out upon us from *Young Wales, The Christian Age, The Educational Record* and a select handful of pious memoirs, with its firm jaw, the shrewd but kindly eyes, and that general air of muscular saintliness, which the National Temperance League tried to capture in its commissioned portrait. No less familiar are the manner of men who escorted him to his grave in Abney Park, London, on that bleak 26 November in 1881, riding in carriages in strict order of precedence; firstly, the representatives of the new university college at Aberystwyth, then the National Temperance League, followed by the British and Foreign Schools Society, the Cymmrodorion, the National Eisteddfod Association, the North Wales Scholarship Association, the Finsbury School Board, and Mr Henry Richard. And from every sect and journal in Wales rose the same lament, that, in Hugh Owen, they had lost the one man, above all others, who had been the very fulcrum of that sustained enterprise in educational provision which brought Wales out of primitive isolation into modern society.

'He was not a man of brilliant parts', said Henry Richard, though he had a quick intelligence, sagacity and a superbly persuasive manner. Neither was he an orator; his were the administrator's virtues, a practical, constructive mind, enormous capacity for hard work, the gift of knowing how to choose men and use them. He could clearly be a charmer; T. Marchant Williams remembered 'his beautiful face', and beauty was seldom in the eye of that beholder. People recalled, above all, his monumental persistence; 'a persevering tout on all Welsh matters', according to E.G. Salisbury, whose incessant letter-writing, travelling, committee-packing, made him the personification of what

---

*A lecture delivered at the University College, Swansea in 1962, as one of a sequence of four, later published as *Pioneers of Welsh Education*, ed. Charles E. Gittins (Faculty of Education, University College, Swansea, n.d., I think 1964). The editor, Professor Gittins, was an active and creative man in Welsh and Welsh-language education, who died in tragic circumstances. In his preface, he visibly distanced himself from my contribution, apparently because it was insufficiently celebratory.

Henry Richard regarded as the un-Welsh characteristic of pertinacity. With it went what to a sectarian age seemed an almost incredible freedom from dogma. 'The only Welshman who belonged to every party', exclaimed *Y Genedl Gymreig* (The Welsh Nation), a trifle ambiguously. His presence, added his son-in-law, sanctified the house.

Not that he had no enemies. Dr Thomas Nicholas, ejected from the secretaryship of the university movement, was shrill in his denunciation of 'the arrogant hypocrisy of our Holy Hugh', and David Charles found Owen unprincipled, secretive and dictatorial. He had lured Charles into the university secretariat with a promise that he would be expected to canvass for funds only the upper classes, but what had the victim found? 'I found to my chagrin that there was no such scheme in fact and that I was expected to canvass *all classes*! . . . I pity any man that will have to work under his rule. He is the most unpleasant man I ever tried to work with.' When Robert Davies of Bodlondeb, in 1857, tried to wriggle out of a promise of £1,000 to Bangor Normal College, Hugh Owen crushed him with two hours of sustained moral blackmail. 'We have a work to do,' said Hugh, 'and cannot afford to be put aside by the childish folly of this poor man.' In such enterprises as Hugh Owen had undertaken, ruthlessness was a necessary attribute and could become an occupational disease.

He began in a very proper manner, being born in Anglesey and to Methodist parents. The family was comparatively affluent, with a tradition of fairly easy living, some talent, and status within the independence of the Methodist connection. Owen Owen and his wife settled at Y Foel, near the coast, on the road to Brynsiencyn, where their son William is said to have been the first child christened in the Methodist chapel. Hugh, born in 1804, had been baptized at the parish church. Y Foel was a substantial place, two-storied, with two parlours and a slate porch; visiting ministers stayed there, to be duly astonished at the precocious brilliance of young Hugh. His brother William took over the farm; another, Ebenezer, ended his days, not uncharacter-istically, as superintendent of Norfolk county lunatic asylum. These, and the father, are shadowy figures, but his mother, and how often this pattern recurs, was a formative influence. Charitable and gentle, but with an iron determination, she was imbued with that resolute piety and almost relentless benevolence which later characterised her son.

For Hugh, however, the proselytising rigour of Calvinism was softened by the peculiar character of his first instruction. For his master was Evan Richardson, a refined and scholarly man, whose celebrated schools in Pwllheli and Caernarfon were patronised by the respectable of all denominations. Congregations terrorised by Christmas Evans would call aloud for Evan Richardson to come and comfort them, and Hugh Owen's six years with him left a lasting impression. Owen could certainly appreciate the brimstone manner of John Elias, but this was never his personal style. His was the style of Richardson's sermons which, by all accounts, were not in any way doctrinal or intellectual, or indeed in any way demanding a religion of morals and manners quietly inculcated into a connection which was socially isolated but substantial, a group whose strength was growing and whose exclusion from the sources of power and prestige served only to emphasise its ingrown and inward-looking satisfaction with itself and its values.

They had need of it. In 1823, when Hugh was nineteen, Thomas Clarkson, the anti-slavery campaigner, went on a speaking tour in Wales. As soon as he passed out of the south-east into Cardiganshire, the tone of his diary altered abruptly. Nonconformists, now mainly Methodists, of course, appeared unwontedly timorous and uncertain; the gentry would not sit with them on committees. The social cleavage grew worse as he moved north, and in Caernarfonshire, Clarkson almost succumbed to despair. For, while personal co-operation between Anglicans and Methodists was not unknown, the social gulf was, in general terms, appalling. One of his informants claimed that north-west Wales was the most Tory area in Britain, fifty years behind the south, itself fifty years behind England. Not until Clarkson moved east did the pressure relax, and he immediately prepared a special set of rules to guide his London committee in its dealings with this peculiar district.

This is the milieu which nurtured the young Hugh Owen, which helps to account for the intense *social* awareness of his mature religious outlook, that awareness which informs the remarkable series of private letters he wrote to Thomas Gee, over fifty years later, in support of the latter's campaign in the *Baner*, in 1878, against the growth of 'priestly formalism' within Methodism. In those letters, with forty years' experience as deacon of a London Congregationalist chapel behind him, Hugh Owen returns constantly to the concept of an ardent and controlling *laity* as the essence of the 'Old Corph' the Old Body and, in the alchemy of his memory, the *Old Methodism* of John Elias is transmuted into something akin to the Old Dissent.

For, in Clarkson's diaries, an old, familiar frontier reappears in Wales, given a new dimension by the different chronology of the social growth of Methodism and the Old Dissent, and by the revolutionary redistribution of population effected by industrial society. It was in this precise period that Nonconformity was sweeping forward to numerical superiority, cutting the ground from under the traditional elite. The familar psychology of powerful but excluded groups manifests itself at every turn, particularly among the newer Dissenters of west and north. In fact, the resonance achieved by Hugh Owen's celebrated *Letter to the Welsh* in 1843 is virtually incomprehensible unless one postulates an absence of basic communication between Methodist society and society in general, which was nothing like so patent in the east and south, despite the more radical tone of those areas. Moreover, the educational drive started by Hugh Owen developed largely in response to the needs and aspirations of this particular society which had shaped his own personality; several of the more characteristic institutions of Wales were the direct products of the drive, with the result that they were, at least in origin and early development, geared to one sector of the population only, and that the furthest removed, physically and socially, from the centres of dynamic growth. Distortion ensued.

Two years after Clarkson left Caernarfon, Hugh Owen followed, having learned shorthand and reached the age of 21, off to make his fortune in London. William Bulkeley Hughes, the barrister, found him a stool in the office of a prosperous Welsh solicitor in Hatton Garden; the Methodist chapel in Jewin Crescent, where he met Henry Richard, became his spiritual home. His close friends, all earnest young men, were a distinctive group. Among them were Griffith Davies, FRS, the celebrated actuary who was a leading figure in his profession, and John Davies of the Bank of England, while the pivot of his wider circle was J. Lumley, shortly to be a pillar of the London (later Royal) Statistical Society. In this distinctive company, and as a citizen of the capital, he lived through eleven crucial years, whose central meaning, historians are coming to believe, lay in the formation and articulation of a radical middle-class consciousness.

Symptoms of a decisive change of direction appear in the 1830s. In the first place, he got married. His early biographers introduce his wife as 'an English lady' and then dismiss her until it is time for the funeral. Only Daniel Lleufer Thomas saw fit to give her name. She was Ann Wade who, unable to cope with the Welsh language, became a member at Claremont chapel, Pentonville. Claremont was a stronghold of London Independency, its pastor, the redoubtable John Blackburn, an inspector of Welsh chapels and a fierce antagonist of the celebrated agnostic Richard Carlile. By 1836, Hugh Owen himself had joined; he became a deacon and Blackburn's intimate friend. There is no record of any agonising reappraisal. At the end of his life, Hugh Owen attended a Baptist chapel because it was nearer his home; indeed, in the last month of his life, he was frequenting places which would have startled Thomas Gee. The leaders of Welsh opinion, in sharp contrast to their English confrères, seem to have passed through the shattering crises of conscience of the nineteenth century, not merely unscathed but apparently unaffected. In Hugh Owen's case, one can only note that the undogmatic character of his religious belief seems to have become more marked with the years.

Its social content became all the clearer, for in that same year, 1836, he became a total abstainer from alcoholic liquor. Abstinence was the hallmark of the social missionary and, from this moment on, Hugh Owen plunged into a veritable labyrinth of *improvement*. He became chairman of the National Temperance League; he and his friends formed friendly societies for London Welshmen and London cabmen, served the Thrift Association; he joined the board of the London Fever Hospital, city school societies — the list of charities lengthens with the years. He was, in short, a man of his generation, committed to their ideal of *respectability*, that respectability which meant so much more than its colourless modern synonym, an ideal which was at once a mutation of, and a radical departure from, the older ideal of the *gentleman*. The corollary followed. He would make Wales, too, *respectable*; he would introduce her into modern society.

But, by this time, respectability was not merely a personal vision; it was an objective of government. And, once more in this seminal year 1836, Hugh Owen made his third vital decision. He joined the Poor Law Commission. The story goes that he was interviewed by Edwin Chadwick himself and signed on for his expertise in conveyancing. His official career was smoothly successful. By 1853, he was chief clerk; ultimately his position was virtually that of permanent secretary, and, when the Commission was replaced by the Local Government Board in 1872, he was asked to name his successor. For twenty years, he represented the department at all parliamentary inquiries, including the most delicate, and, in 1867, he and his friend Lumley helped Benjamin Disraeli to prepare his Reform Bill. Mrs Disraeli promptly dubbed them her husband's 'guardian angels', surely a rare distinction among Welsh Liberals. Second in succession as permanent secretary of the Local Government Board was his son and namesake, who had entered his father's office at the age of thirteen. The second Hugh, who won both a knighthood and the friendship of the radical Sir Charles

Dilke, was the compiler of *Owen's Education Acts Manual* which, in multiple editions, became the *Erskine May* of local education authorities. And when the poor law officers decided to form a Masonic Lodge, they designated it, in memory of the father and in honour of the son, the *Hugh Owen Lodge*, consecrated at Frascati's restaurant in Oxford Street in 1896.

The significance of this career needs little elaboration. Hugh Owen, in one sense, was the 'T.J.' Dr Thomas Jones, CH, of his generation. Throughout his life, he stood close to the heart of those movements which, more than any other, were changing the shape of society. It was through him, above all, that those impulses were transmitted to the poor and half-forgotten parishes of Wales. He shared to the full in the spirit of the new and reforming bureaucracy, a list of whose commissioners is a list of the movers and shapers of the realm. One name will suffice — James Kay-Shuttleworth. For education was the heart and soul of respectability and, in London, Hugh Owen seems to have been in the field almost immediately. An attempt to launch schools in Flintshire in 1837 proved a false start, but in 1843, he entered the Welsh lists.

Lists, of course, is the operative word. British education lagged far behind that of the continent, held back by sectarian bitterness; not until 1870 could a *Punch* cartoon direct a policeman against the squabbling divines who blocked the schoolhouse door. From 1833, the government authorised small grants towards the Anglican National Society and the (in practice) Nonconformist British and Foreign Schools Society, but the first real advance came in 1839, when the new committee of the Privy Council, under Kay-Shuttleworth, offered grants towards school building and expenses, in return for the right to inspect. In 1843, a year of intense religious excitement, Sir James Graham's scheme for factory education, under what would have been, in practice, Anglican control, was wrecked by the resistance of Dissent, and the wealthy English Congregationalists threw their weight behind the *voluntaryist* movement, to provide their own schools, entirely free from state control. In the same year, the scope of the government grants was extended, while the Minutes of 1846, imposing the pupil teacher system, established the teacher's certificate as standard, with state augmentation of salaries, giving another impetus to growth, in the context of the most violent sectarian controversy. Into this battle Hugh Owen threw himself, as a spokesman of the British schools system, working towards government grant.

In response to his appeal, Welsh opinion splintered. The state of

Welsh education at this date is painfully familiar, but some qualifications need to be made. Sir Henry Jones, later Professor of Moral Philosophy at Glasgow, once waited, as a boy, for three hours at the roadside, to see a *Bachelor of Arts* walk by, and was so overcome at the majesty of the spectacle that he could not speak. A nice story, it is no doubt symptomatic of many a deep rural area, but it would have no meaning at all in, say, Merthyr, where the Guest schools made Dowlais the 'Prussia of South Wales' and where the sons of grocers went to Bristol schools *en route* to Glasgow University and the Inns of Court. How much meaning would it have in Swansea or Caernarfon or Wrexham? In the more developed areas of Wales, the schooling, while still inadequate, was at least more varied; there was something of a base to start from. One should not overstate the isolation even of the more remote districts. A strong Welsh-language culture enjoyed its extra-mural existence, but it is the degree of isolation, mental, emotional, even fashionable isolation, which distinguished the more from the less developed regions.

Immediately after the Privy Council grants were announced in 1839, the mining areas of Monmouthshire and Glamorgan became the first theatre for one of the famous inspector's reports. From the rural areas of west and north, there was, apparently, hardly a whisper, until Hugh Owen published his *Letter* in 1843; whereupon, the response was explosive. How can one really explain this except in terms of the pyschology of isolation and exclusion? Hugh Owen's letter was simply a monumental statement of the obvious, but, clearly, for the people who responded, the obvious needed to be stated. Radicalism was germinating among them; the *Amserau (Times)* was, somewhat shakily, in print. By nature they were far less hostile to state aid than Independents or Baptists. Yet they seem to have been incapable of believing or comprehending that the state would ever do anything to help them. It was not until one of their own kind addressed them from a government office in London and pointed to an organisation behind him, that they moved, and then only under the spur of acute crisis.

So the familiar frontier reappears. There were, of course, numerous exceptions, but, generally speaking, it was Hugh Owen who carried all before him in the west and north, while it was voluntaryism which set the pace in the south, absorbing the funds and energies of the region, especially after the Llandovery conference of 1844, on the morrow of the Graham imbroglio. This divergence is usually attributed to the difference in outlook between Methodism and the Old Dissent. No-one would deny this, but one should also point to the fact that, in south

Wales, Methodists themselves often caught the voluntaryist infection and that Owen's agent, John Phillips, frequently found the going very heavy indeed among his southern co-religionists. In fact, the distinction is as much regional as doctrinal. The evidence of the Clarkson diaries, the more variegated political life of the south, the locale of the great eviction struggles in later years, all point in the same direction. Society in those areas which more immediately felt the impact, direct or indirect, of industry, was much less monolithic than it was in west or north. Radical their Dissenters certainly were, but their Radicalism had a firm social base, they were more closely integrated, they moved with greater ease. It can be argued that they were more radical because they could better afford to be. Further, they could count as spokesmen, not merely Henry Richard, but John Bright and Edward Baines of the *Leeds Mercury*; in later years they had behind them the force of an educational union with its bases in Manchester and Birmingham. Voluntaryism in the south stems, in part, from greater self-confidence, itself the product of a greater ease and security in society. There was nothing comparable in west or north.

The consequences were unfortunate. It was, primarily, out of the drive led by Hugh Owen that Bangor Normal College certainly, and Aberystwyth University College, to a lesser extent, grew. Inevitably they took their character from the regions towards which the drive had been directed. Locked in its dream of independence, the industrial area, as a region (individuals are another matter), played a secondary part in these enterprises, and by the time voluntaryism had spent itself in the late fifties, or had been transcended by the Forster Education Act of 1870, several characteristic Welsh institutions of higher education had already been established — and on sites remote from the main centres of population and growth. The industrial and semi-industrial areas, more closely integrated into the general economy, had for some time been drawn increasingly into the educational pattern of that economy, and the intensification of their own local effort, at a time when the west and north were being steadily drained of population and were entering on a protracted social crisis, served to aggravate the strain of imbalance. In consequence, the more populous, the richer, and the expansive regions of Wales, were never wholly integrated into a homogeneous Welsh educational pattern. From an early date, the 'gallant barque of Welsh educational endeavour', to employ the favourite metaphor of its pilots, developed a distinct Methodist and north Walian list.

The immediate stimulus in 1843 was the Anglican revival. The

Establishment responded to the onslaught of the radicals after 1832 with a vigorous campaign of church building and school creation. Wales seems to have felt the wind of change around 1837, when Owen made his first abortive attempt to rally Nonconformist opinion. The number of pupils in Church schools, until then fairly static around the 25,000 mark, suddenly rose. According to Sir Thomas Phillips, the Welsh Education Committee of the Church raised £12,000 in three years and numbers in the schools almost doubled. By 1843, at which date there were only two British schools in the whole of north Wales, it has been calculated that, of a total north Walian population of about 396,000, districts holding some 320,000 were already served by a numerically adequate Anglican school system. The energy of the campaign, backed up by the creation of training colleges and the strengthening of Lampeter College, won for the Church a decisive and permanent numerical and financial superiority. The chief argument employed by the clergy against the new British schools a few years later was that they were 'unnecessary'. To many Dissenters, it seemed, as Thomas Rees put it in his history of Nonconformity in 1861, that the Anglican schoolmaster was about to succeed where the Anglican persecutor had failed.

In 1843 came, on the one hand, the extended government grants, but, on the other, the displacement of much Nonconformist effort into voluntaryism. Hugh Owen became thoroughly alarmed. With public opinion in both England and Wales in sectarian tumult, he addressed his first public letter to the Welsh on 26 August. It explained, in detail, how to start schools and apply for government grant, and called for a national campaign. He used his Methodist connections to obtain as wide a circulation as possible and wrote to J.T. Jones, *Gwron*, editor of the *Aberdare Times*, for the addresses of Independent and Baptist ministers. From the latter, the response was tepid, but among Methodists of the west and north, it was electric. He was inundated with letters and compelled to appeal to the British and Foreign Society. In November, they appointed John Phillips as their agent in the north. In deference to the strength of voluntaryist feeling in the south, they refrained from appointing a southern agent. Not until 1853 did they have a man there, in the person of William Roberts, *Nefydd*, of Blaina.

Phillips, however, addressed 150 meetings in eighteen months; within three years, the British Society was boasting forty schools. This rapid take-off ran into severe problems of staffing and maintenance. By 1845, the supply of teachers was causing intense concern, and on 17 March, Owen addressed his second letter to the Welsh. He warned them off any attempt to establish a training college of their own and directed them instead to the British College at Borough Road, London, where thirty Welsh students had already completed short courses that year and had benefited from contact with what he, rather oddly, called 'the more lively and vivacious Englishmen'.

The crisis atmosphere did not slacken. The new teacher's certificate threatened to cut off the rapid supply of Borough Road teachers, Church schools continued to multiply and, in the aftermath of the Rebecca Riots, that Education Commission, which was to become notorious in Welsh annals, started on its work. In August, 1846, as a matter of urgency, the Cambrian Education Committee was set up, with Hugh Owen as secretary. There was widespread fear of an Anglican coup and Owen was in constant communication with the Privy Council, warding off attack after attack by the clergy in the parishes. His fears found expression in his third letter to the Welsh of 17 March 1847. Because of the energy of the Church and the folly of voluntaryism, the benefits of the new system created by the Minutes of 1846 would fall to the Anglicans.

> When the officials now in Wales make their report, their testimony about the great lack of means of instruction there will be such that the efforts which the Dissenters may make to prevent the government from assisting *any party* to supply that need will be utterly ineffectual.

He obviously knew what was coming and his answer was to mobilise public opinion. In the winter of 1846-47, he sent out circulars and petitions to nearly every parish in Wales, calling for a census of Anglicans and Dissenters in the hope of deterring the government with concrete evidence of the numerical strength of Nonconformity. Only the parishes of some areas of west and north responded in any number and, according to Henry Richard, put Dissenters at seven times the Anglicans, a much larger majority than the official census of 1851 was to indicate.

In the meantime, the dreaded Blue Books were published, to be greeted by a deafening clamour of protest.[1] Hardly a year later, the Privy Council inspector made his routine inspection of British schools in Wales, and the difference in tone between his report and that of the commissioners is striking. Up to a point, the commission itself may have fallen victim to what appears to have been an organised campaign by the local clergy, which was certainly in full swing during the winter of 1846/7. Both commissioners and press had been equally offensive many times before, to their own countrymen, and the outcry from Wales seems to have been an unpleasant surprise. In the event, Owen's fears proved groundless. The government was in no position to thrust Anglican schools down Wales's dissenting gullet. In 1849, Kay-Shuttleworth was replaced by R.W. Lingen and the bureaucrat succeeded the social missionary. Pressure relaxed.

From the protest against *Brady Llyfrau Gleision,* The Treason of the Blue Books, Hugh Owen was something of an absentee. He was, of course, implicated; he had given the commissioners many of their letters of introduction. He certainly resented their attack on Dissent; no doubt, he resented the *tone* of the attack on the Welsh language. Whether he resented the *content* of the attack on Welsh may be doubted. In fact, he seems to have shared the belief, common to radicals from Roebuck to Engels, that the Welsh language represented a problem to be solved, rather than a redoubt to be defended. He never taught his sons Welsh. Besides, he belonged to the same species as the commissioners. Once the pressure had relaxed, he went ahead to implement their practical suggestions. By 1852, there were some ninety British schools in north Wales and Borough Road was running courses in Welsh which carried a government bounty of £5. In the late fifties, the British system at last penetrated south Wales, and by the time the board schools took over after 1870, there were over 300 British schools in Wales, with nearly 35,000 pupils. They were still heavily outnumbered by the Church schools and their utility varied, but their value, particularly in the country districts, must have been inestimable. If the voluntaryists had had their way, this generation, the generation of Henry Jones, would have been, in many parts of Wales, a lost generation.

In the course of the campaign, a small but dedicated group had formed around Hugh Owen. As the relatively prosperous fifties got under way, these men felt their interest shift. Once more, it was the movement of English opinion which set the pace, notably the growing middle-class revulsion against popular education. The volume of complaint, of which the reorganisation of the public schools was in part a product, reached a climax in the Newcastle Commission of 1858 and the notorious Revised Code of 1861. In Wales, the grievances had little meaning, but the net effect was to redirect attention to middle-class education and the Principality inevitably felt the tug of the tide.

The non-sectarian Queen's Colleges recently established in Ireland provided a model. In 1848, Swansea tried to establish one. In 1852,

Lampeter was empowered to grant divinity degrees and, shortly afterwards, the Welsh clergy of Yorkshire petitioned for a non-sectarian university in Wales, a plea echoed by B.T. Williams, then resident in Glasgow. Owens College, Manchester, had just been founded on the fortune of an expatriate Welshman. The idea was in the air.

It was in these circumstances that, in 1854, Hugh Owen gathered a circle of friends, who included Lewis Edwards and David Charles, and proposed a Queen's College for Wales. It was conceived entirely in terms of social class. Its object was to serve 'a class daily increasing in numbers, in wealth and importance, which has long been left without any better means of instruction than those which are accessible to the children of the poor'. As he admitted to the Aberdare Committee in 1880-1, Hugh Owen had written off the anglicised upper-middle class of Wales; his aim was the service and, in a sense, the creation of a professional, technical and commercial Welsh middle class, the final goal of national respectability. For that reason, the emphasis was on vocational training in the widest sense, and the scheme was to be a closed system, divorced from elementary education and run on private fees. It was characteristically his own scheme, in its conscious creation of an institutional skeleton for the new order, and in his proposal to nationalise the educational endowments of Wales for this purpose.

The plan was stillborn, killed by the Crimean War and the more pressing needs of primary education. For Borough Road could no longer take the additional strain and, in 1856, Owen, with Robert Forster, set about founding a Welsh training college. Growing directly out of the British school movement, it inevitably found its focus in north Wales and, after prolonged preliminaries conducted with Hugh Owen's customary skill and ruthlessness, the college came into operation at Bangor in 1858, moving into permanent quarters four years later, with John Phillips as its first principal.

In a sense, the history of Bangor Normal is even more of a national epic than that of Aberystwyth. Not that this was immediately evident. At Bangor, reported one inspector, they had not only to polish the stone, but hew it out of the bare rock. Welsh disappeared from the curriculum within five years. Moreover, in south Wales, all sects were affronted at the choice of site and, after the establishment of a sister college for women at Swansea, their financial support dwindled further. A concordat between Bangor and Borough Road, which tried to divert all Welsh students to the northern college, provoked such anger in the south that several young Independents actually learned the Catechism and entered Anglican colleges.

Nevertheless, from the beginning, south Walians attended, and the great expansion which followed the Act of 1870 transformed the college into a truly national institution. It was a college of first-class quality, ranking with the best of the English, and these years about the turn of the century were perhaps its golden age. By this time, it was far more of a national institution than its neighbour, the new university college at Bangor. Rugby football is one unusual but useful index. It was introduced by south Walians in the 1890s; natives who came to mock remained to play and in 1898, the classic Normal *v.* Varsity series began. The latter never won a game until 1913. It was the university which was the local college.

The Normal was characterised by a quite remarkable collegiate spirit and *esprit de corps*, which left its mark on several generations (and not least on the staffing of some Welsh military formations during the first World War). It played a positive role in the shaping of what was to become Wales's characteristic profession. In 1888, the teachers' organisation decided to drop the 'humiliating' *Elementary* from their title and to call themselves instead the National Union of English Teachers. So strong was the Welsh contingent and so violent its outcry that, in 1889, the teachers dropped the compromising *E* altogether and called themselves simply the National Union of Teachers. So the NUT, in title at least, may be claimed as a product of Welsh enterprise. In short, of all Hugh Owen's undertakings, Bangor Normal was probably the most successful, though only in the long run. In the first twenty years of its life, it did little to correct the imbalance in Welsh education.

From the establishment of Bangor Normal to his death, Hugh Owen's prime concern remained middle-class education, the need to equip Wales with a professional and specialised middle class, a type of positivist Nonconformist *clerisy*. This ideal informed the revival of the Cymmrodorion, when he and John Griffiths, *Gohebydd*, tried to turn the society into a hybrid Welsh amalgam of Athenaeum, Rotary Club and Statistical Society. It lay behind his effort to reform the eisteddfod. It was he, above all, who turned it into an organised society, with a hierarchy of membership grades, in a simple but effective design to mobilise permanent middle-class commitment as a nucleus for the more irregular, periodic and shallow sustenance of popular emotion. The ultimate National Eisteddfod Association owed much to his exertions.

Even this reformed Eisteddfod, however, fell very far short of Hugh Owen's ideal. Indeed, it belonged to a different order of being. His own vision, derived directly from that of Henry Brougham, emerges clearly enough from a letter he wrote to William Roberts of Blaina in 1860.

> the Eisteddfod should be reconstituted on a basis similar to that of the Social Science Association and be devoted mainly to the discussion of subjects similar to those embraced by that Association, adding, however, a Department for Poetry and Music and offering premiums as at present, for the best poems on given subjects and for the most skilled musical compositions or performances, but not for the papers by which the various subjects would be introduced.

And what were those subjects to be?

> Education, of the working classes, boys, girls and adults, of the Middle Classes etc., the relation between Employers and Employed in Agriculture, Mining, Slate quarries etc., the health, food and habitations of those employed in each, their morals, their thrift or improvidence, savings banks, benefit societies, co-operative associations etc., etc.

Hugh Owen's Eisteddfod was to be a royal commission in permanent session, an Eisteddfod in which a 'department of poetry and music' was to be an 'addition'. Brougham, Chadwick, Birkbeck, would surely have approved. Indeed, it is difficult to avoid the inference that Owen's mature philosophy was a type of Welsh positivism, Welsh in that it rested ultimately on the social ethos of Nonconformity. 'I shall never rest,' he wrote in one of his letters, 'until the Welsh Educational appliances have been perfected', a fine, clanking sentence, which would have warmed the heart of Auguste Comte.

His attitude to more formal higher education was similar. In the early sixties, controversy over the Revised Code was at its height and public meetings all over England were loud with protest against the neglect of middle-class education. It was in this climate that David Thomas of Stockwell wrote a letter on a Welsh university to his son's new daily, the *Cambria Daily Leader*, which ignited Dr Thomas Nicholas, a tutor at Carmarthen. Nicholas's six epoch-making letters on the subject caught the attention of Hugh Owen, who promptly hauled him before the Swansea Eisteddfod of 1863, summoned his friends, and set in train the process which culminated in the celebrated

December meetings at the Freemasons' Tavern, appropriately one of the three favourite London rendezvous of radical movements of all kinds.

The scheme which emerged from the early addresses and reports seems to have been based on the work of Nicholas and was nothing like as radical, in the clear-cut manner, as Hugh Owen's of 1854; it was an altogether woollier, or, to be more charitable, vaguely liberal, document. Nevertheless, the basic motives were the same. It was the manifesto of a class; the need was to equip the middle classes to a degree proportionate to the charity extended to the poor. The models were London and the Irish colleges; the training was to be basically vocational, with heavy emphasis on science and the need to compete in the industrial and commercial world. All intention to foster a 'merely Welsh nationality' was disclaimed and, as for the Welsh language, 'Let the perpetuation of the vernacular and other peculiarities of the nation be left to the free choice and sympathies of the people, when fully enlightened as to their own interests; but meantime, let the light enter' which has a slightly ominous ring.

There followed the long, heartbreaking struggle against apathy and hostility to establish the University College of Wales at Aberystwyth. Located in a bankrupt railway hotel, it opened its doors in 1872. In the course of that struggle, many of the original ideals seem to have been lost. Wholly dependent on popular support, it relied on a convulsive rally of Welsh opinion. The 100,000 contributions under half a crown, the *Sul y Brifysgol* (University Sundays: fund-raising services in the chapels) the hard-won gifts from quarrymen, miners and commercial travellers were real. Nevertheless, one should point out that most of the funds came from people like the colliery, railway and docks entrepreneur David Davies, hot for his 'mercantile college' and that the largest single group of contributors were in fact the Anglicans, closely followed by the Methodists.

One feature of the movement seems to have been ignored. It is easy to overlook the extent to which it became a social-missionary enterprise directed at an area in economic stagnation. For, while the movement certainly drew support from all quarters of Wales, there was a strong regional emphasis in its thinking. Many of its sponsors, perhaps unconsciously, regarded the undertaking as a linear descendant of the earlier campaigns for the schools and for Bangor Normal. The superb sacrifice of the quarrymen is, in part, explained by this general assumption that the new college would serve the same areas, basically, as the first British schools. This is made clear by Hugh Owen's own evidence before the Aberdare Committee in 1880-1. His committee chose Aberystwyth, he said, because they thought it would be resorted to from all parts of north Wales, and then added, 'it was hoped too that the people of south Wales also would avail themselves of it'. The difference in emphasis, even in the placing of prepositions, is significant. Sectors of the qualified population of the industrial areas were already being absorbed by English redbrick universities and technical institutions, and it was generally believed that these districts would look after their own. In fact, it is perfectly clear that Hugh Owen, certainly, and probably the others, assumed from the beginning that there would be a second college, in Glamorgan. Owen took it for granted that Swansea would be the site.

So that Aberystwyth at first did nothing to counteract the regional divergence; it was itself, in part, a product of it. And, by 1880, it was clearly a failure. A stagnating mid-Wales college, it was threatened with total extinction by the subsequent establishment of Cardiff, and even more, of Bangor, which drained away much of the original dynamism. Its salvation and, after 1885, its rapid growth, still seem miraculous. In the process, it acquired incomparable prestige and built itself into a national legend, the 'university built on the pennies of the poor'.

It is a remarkable story. No less remarkable was Hugh Owen's personal role. His devoted and monumental labour must surely be familiar, if not to Macaulay's schoolboy, at least to Owen M. Edwards's. The opening of the college coincided with the winding-up of his department; he retired and, acting on *Gohebydd's* suggestion, made those famous fund-raising tours all over Wales, with his little black bag, which have fixed him in the public mind. It was to him an intensely distasteful labour, and how paradoxical it seems that this hammer of the voluntaryists should in the end be identified with what was surely the most splendid voluntaryist enterprise of them all. In pursuit of his middle-class college, this man helped to create one of the few truly popular universities in Europe.

It was popular in another sense. Because of the circumstances of its creation, the new college was far more dependent on public opinion and more open to external pressure than many. Hugh Owen did nothing to counteract this; on the contrary, it was on middle-class Nonconformist opinion that he relied. The consequences were not always happy. This display of his manipulative talents in the Thomas Charles Edwards letters, the careful choice of principal, and the handling of such matters as the use of a prayer-book or the abuse of a Joseph Parry, sometimes leave a taste in the mouth.

This was Owen at work in the dust. To see him in calmer, more creative mood, we have to turn to the Aberdare Committee on secondary and higher education in Wales of 1880-1. The formal request for the committee was drafted by Hugh Owen in Lord Aberdare's study. His evidence was crucial and, upon it, we can base an estimate of the man and his work.

He was no pedagogue. On the content of education, his ideas were banal. Beyond the need for technical, scientific instruction, he did not see far. There is a sense of mere propriety about his references to the classics and a liberal education; one is reminded of his handling of the 'poetry and music department' of the eisteddfod. Coupled with this was a rather cavalier attitude towards the academic professions. He accorded them a Welsh respect, but was quite prepared to get his teachers and professors on the cheap. One of his arguments before the Committee was that, Wales being so poor, good teachers could be hired more cheaply. He bandied about the phrase 'cost price of education' with Canon Robinson and, when the latter asked him if he were not aware that headmasters in England could command salaries double what he proposed for the Welsh, he replied, 'No, I am not aware of that fact', a surprising response in the circumstances. The overriding necessity was to keep fees as low as possible, since the Welsh middle class was poorer than the English. In launching his north Wales scholarship scheme a year or two earlier, he had emphasised that it was the school managers who had to be won over; the teachers could be ignored. He was always at pains to conciliate middle-class opinion, even in its most constipated forms. There was a hard core of quiet but intense conventionality in the man. At heart, I think, he was a philistine.

He was not an educator but an organiser of education. Even here, most of his ideas were borrowed. His Welsh university is London transplanted, purely an examining body; his colleges and the general structure of his secondary system he borrowed from Ireland. From one point of view, Hugh Owen was simply an input valve.

It is in the execution of these plans that he shows his genius. As a practical executive, he was superb, and in the service of his rather commonplace ideas, was prepared for administrative revolution. The core of his scheme in 1880 was the Charity Commissioners. Welsh educational endowments were to be nationalised and taken over by the Commissioners, reinforced by a special Welsh officer. They were to create their own inspectorate, for the new secondary schools were to be under their overall supervision. The new schools were to be built on the county rate, their managers to be drawn from a panel of nominees elected by the £30 rate-payers, the selectors being the officers of already existent primary school boards, mayors of towns, chairmen of quarter sessions and, later, representatives of the university. The respectable and largely Nonconformist middle class, in control locally, was thus to be directed by a central authority to which he was prepared to grant wide powers in the remodelling of the school structure. He was quite ready, for example, to close down a school like Ruthin without compensating the locality. What is all this but the Poor Law Commission in new Welsh guise, a logical extension of the principle of his examining, supervisory university? 'We do not want a Somerset House University,' cried B.T. Williams in 1853. But Hugh Owen was, quite literally, a Somerset House man.

The overall scheme, in his own words, was to be a 'harmonious whole'. At the base were the primary schools, then the secondary schools, old ones taken over and new ones built, their control a working compromise between the administrators of the Commission and the representatives of the class for whom the schools were provided. The system was to be run largely on the fees of that class, its prestige maintained by lavish exhibitions designed expressly to catch and hold the interest of these same people. At the apex were to be the two *Prince of Wales's Colleges* at Aberystwyth and Swansea, giving university education almost exclusively to the middle class and submitting candidates to the examinations of the disembodied *Prince of Wales's University*, which was to exercise overall surveillance, in rather a French manner.

There was one complementary feature. Owen estimated the future secondary school population to be 15,000, ten per 1,000 of the population, a good deal less than that of England. It remained to catch the exceptionally bright children of the poor. So each county was to offer scholarships from the rates, one for every 10,000 of the population, making 135 in Wales as a whole. These would be awarded to elementary school children on the results of a competitive examination, and would give a place at a secondary school for two years. At the end of the two-year period, there would be a second round of examinations for a limited number of scholarships, allocated on a regional population basis between north and south Wales, giving a further two or three years at school and, finally, the all-Wales Prince of Wales's Scholarships, which would admit the residual (and possibly somewhat battered) elite to the Colleges.

Such was Hugh Owen's final vision of Welsh education, a vision not without its own grandeur, a logical, decidedly un-English scheme, with recognition of Welsh nationality built into it. What must strike the observer is how resolutely middle-class the whole hierarchy is, and also how reminiscent it is of schemes which were circulating widely in the London of his young manhood. If he were not so Welsh, one would have to call Hugh Owen a Benthamite.

The Intermediate Education Act itself was less logical, less coherent and less radical, but the core was there — the schools themselves — and their creation marks a decisive new departure in the history of Wales. With the Committee of 1880, Hugh Owen's life-work was done. He was knighted in June, 1881, an honour which Wales considered rather tardy, but later in the year his health broke down. He had worked like a slave every day of his life and now succumbed to exhaustion.

To the very end, he does not cease to surprise. The successor he nominated at the Local Government Board was Sir John Lambert, a Roman Catholic; his friend Lumley, who actually drafted the foundation deeds of Bangor Normal, was another Catholic; and in the last month of his life, weary and craving silence, Hugh Owen turned for quiet and meditation into St. Joseph's Retreat, a Roman Catholic sanctuary. In November, on his first real holiday in the south of France, he was taken ill and died. A scholarship scheme and a statue were suggested as his memorial; the committee chose the latter, which was unveiled in Caernarfon in 1888.

And surely, when all is said, Hugh Owen the man remains almost as impenetrable as Milo Griffith's bronze. We meet paradox at every turn, in this Welsh Liberal who was Disraeli's guardian angel, this bureaucrat who organised the eisteddfod, this anti-voluntaryist spokesman of the middle class who created Aberystwyth college, this enemy of popery who welcomed Roman Catholics if they were statisticians, this Welsh Nonconformist whose mind worked like the *Westminster Review*. We have clothed him in the familiar livery of our nineteenth-century champions. He wears it with a difference. Indeed, one wonders uneasily, sometimes, whether it is the right livery at all.

Notes

1. The report of the Education Commission of 1847 was promptly dubbed the Treason of the Blue Books, after the Treason of the Long Knives of the Saxons in the days of Vortigern. Accurate enough in its merciless exposure of educational deficiencies in Wales, the Report moved on to a ferociously sectarian attack on Nonconformity and to a biliously racist onslaught, echoed in the London press, on the Welsh language itself,

whose extermination it advocated. Anglo-Welsh relations have never wholly recovered from this poisonous ego-trip by three arrogant and ignorant lawyers; its immediate effect was to sting a form of Welsh nationalism into life.

Bibliographical Notes

This chapter is an essay in interpretation rather than a narrative in depth. There is no recent biography; the best approach is by means of the summaries by T.I. Ellis in *Dictionary of Welsh Biography* and Daniel Lleufer Thomas in *D.N.B.* The best memoir is W.E. Davies, *Sir Hugh Owen, his life and life-work* (London, 1885). This may be supplemented by letters and other material, including the Clarkson diaries, at the National Library of Wales; particularly useful are two volumes of cuttings, memoirs etc., relating to Hugh Owen and his son, in NLW. Mss. 10613, 10614. Important for Owen's outlook and doctrine are his testimony in *Report of the Aberdare Committee on intermediate and higher education in Wales (1881)* and his correspondence in *Thomas Charles Edwards Letters*, ed. T.I. Ellis (N.L.W. 1952-53).

For Bangor, see the excellent centenary volume, *Bangor Normal College* (Conway, 1958), the relevant section being the admirable survey by Ll.M. Rees. On the university movement, see W.C. Davies and W.L. Jones, *The University of Wales and its Colleges* (London, 1905), *The College by the Sea,* ed. I. Morgan (Aberystwyth, 1928), D.E. Evans, *The University of Wales* (Cardiff, 1953). See also T.I. Ellis, *The Development of higher education in Wales* (Wrexham, 1935) and R.T. Jenkins and H.M. Ramage, *A History of the Honourable Society of Cymmrodorion* (London, 1951).

On the educational background, I have found most useful F. Smith, *The Life and Work of Sir James Kay-Shuttleworth* (London, 1923) and H.M. Pollard, *Pioneers of Popular Education* (London, 1956). Asher Tropp, *The School Teachers* (London, 1957) approaches the subject from a new angle, while Brian Simon, *Studies in the History of Education 1780-1870*, presents a full and balanced study in the sophisticated Marxist mode. For general background, see E. Halèvy, *The Triumph of Reform* (trans. E. Watkins, London 1927), Asa Briggs, *The Age of Improvement* (London 1959) and G. Kitson Clark, *The Making of Victorian England* (London, 1962).

7 IMPERIAL SOUTH WALES*

It is well known (to employ an expression much favoured by the late J.V. Stalin when he was advancing a singularly contentious proposition) that the first official recognition of the existence of a distinctive Welsh people by the modern British state was the Welsh Sunday Closing Act of 1881; a recognition that a Welsh identity at that moment expressed itself in Welsh Nonconformity, which had become almost as much of a national church to the Welsh as Catholicism had become to the Irish.

Britain, however, was not the first modern state officially to acknowledge the existence of a separate Welsh people. That birth-certificate was first granted them by the United States Immigration Service in 1875.

The perspective opened by the Sunday Closing Act of 1881 has been adequately, indeed abundantly, explored by modern Welsh historiography. This was the golden age of Liberal, Nonconformist, radical and Welsh-speaking Wales, when the Welsh 'nation' formed during the heyday of Victorian imperialism broke into political life, with the franchise reforms, the democratic revolution of the 1880s, the county councils, the first state secondary schools, the colleges, the University, the National Library and the National Museum of Wales. These were the creative generations of Welsh academics and preachers and politicians, the time of *Cymru Fydd* (Young Wales), the Welsh Party in the Commons, the great Land Commission and the struggle for the Disestablishment of the Church in Wales. A new Welsh middle class, a new Welsh bourgeoisie, a new Welsh press, drawing on the realities of small town, village and colliery settlement Wales presented the *gwerin*, the classless, Welsh-speaking and cultured 'folk' or *pueblo*, as the most appropriate image and directive myth of a people which

---

*Unpublished. The origin of this chapter was a talk I delivered nearly twenty years ago as a visiting lecturer at University College, Cardiff. I entitled it 'The social and political consequences of Professor Brinley Thomas' and was disconcerted when Professor Thomas turned up in the audience. Fortunately he gave it his imprimatur. Recently I have returned to the theme and elements of this chapter appeared in a lecture to a History Workshop seminar in London in September 1981 and, in more polemical form, in a talk to the Communist University of Wales at Cardiff in October 1981 and an article in *Marxism Today*, December 1981.

had finally come of age, and presented it successfully, moreover, in the face of a rapidly growing and increasingly militant proletariat in industrial south Wales and of a mushrooming industrial society which in fact housed three-quarters of the Welsh as they actually existed and cohabited uneasily, if at all, with this 'nation'. It achieved its appropriately ambiguous symbolic triumph when its most trenchant spokesman, David Lloyd George, finally penetrated 10 Downing Street itself, the first outsider to get there. It seems appropriate that the first volume to be published in the new series of Oxford Histories of Wales opens with a magnificent and magisterial survey of this epoch in consummate scholarship and warm sympathy, and under the title *Rebirth of a Nation.*[1]

To the perspective opened by the decision of the US Immigration Service in 1875, however, Welsh historiography has remained singularly blind. What in Welsh terms was a whole new continent of discourse was opened by the work of a single scholar of immense industry and creative perception, Professor Brinley Thomas, formerly of Cardiff now of Berkeley, California. Professor Thomas's monumental study of the Atlantic economy in the nineteenth century, of the migration of capital and labour, of the interaction of British and American polities, established an entirely novel framework for modern Welsh history.[2] His work looms like an Alpine range across the path of any historian of modern Wales. It is characteristic of Welsh scholarship and letters in the present crisis of identity, however, that what focused attention were some controversial comments on the interplay between industrialisation and the Welsh language which Professor Thomas made, almost as an appendix to his major work.

To quote the *Edinburgh Review* on the Lake Poets, this will not do. Men make their own history, but they do not make it in circumstances chosen by themselves. The work of Brinley Thomas has fixed certain parameters, has established certain fundamental truths about modern Welsh history, notably about the history of the Welsh considered as a biological species, which simply cannot be wished away. He has done this by locating the Welsh within the world, and particularly the Atlantic complex created by the dominance of British capitalism. Considered from that standpoint, the history of the Welsh in the nineteenth century acquires a subtly but decisively different character.

In eighteenth-century Wales, the merchant capitalism of a newly-minted *Great Britain* had already made a marginal country into a sector of an imperial economy. Copper and tinplate, with 90 per cent of British production located in Swansea and Anglesey, a rural cloth trade in north Wales directed at the Gulf of Mexico, the beginnings of iron, lead and slate, were all channelled into export. The 1790s saw the massive impact of the iron industry and an abrupt increase in numbers which turned the Welsh population graph into a right-angle. Until the census of 1841, every county in Wales registered a major population increase, though the rural areas to west and north were already falling behind, while Monmouthshire and Glamorgan, with their population explosions, ran first and third in the growth race among British counties. From 1841, rural Wales entered its long cycle of depopulation, as the industrialising south-east sucked people in, ultimately to lodge nearly four-fifths of the Welsh in that continuously renovating and increasingly English-speaking region. Industrialisation on the north-eastern coalfield, while substantial, ran into stasis, though Gwynedd, in the north-west, with its slate, became another major export centre concentrating 90 per cent of British production. It was iron, coal and tinplate in the south-east which were the pace-makers, to be succeeded by the significant world empire of south Wales steel and rails and by the gigantic world empire of south Wales coal.

Brinley Thomas, in one of his characteristic correlations, graphically illustrates the reality of this new Wales. (See Fig. 1.)[3] This is an attempt to relate variations in income in Wales as a whole to the industrialisation process, by plotting variations in total livestock on the farms (measured in stock units) and in the marriage rate in both Glamorgan (heartland of coal) and Wales as a whole against the selling price of coal. The image which results is striking. From the 1870s at the latest, the graphs move in harmony. The 1870s were characterised by serious strikes in the coal industry. The year 1873 saw the highest peak in coal prices. In 1874, the growth in livestock reached a peak, to climax again in 1891 when coal prices were at a new high. Between the 1870s and 1891 there was an increase of 25 per cent in the total of livestock on Welsh farms and of 33 per cent in acreage under permanent grass. This during the terrible crisis of rural Europe in the 1880s, precipitated by new American competition, when over 100,000 people were driven out of rural Wales. Those emigrants were overwhelmingly farm-labourers; the number of farmers, generally small farmers, remained fairly constant. It was the labourers who went, to industrial Wales during British export booms, to industrial England during British booms in home capital formation.

The year after the peak in coal prices in 1873, the marriage rate in Glamorgan reached a maximum of 22.2 per 1,000 and the birth rate 44.3 per 1,000. Not only in Glamorgan, but in Wales as a whole, the

Figure 1: Wales: Fluctuations in the Price of Coal, Livestock, and the Marriage Rate, 1850-1913

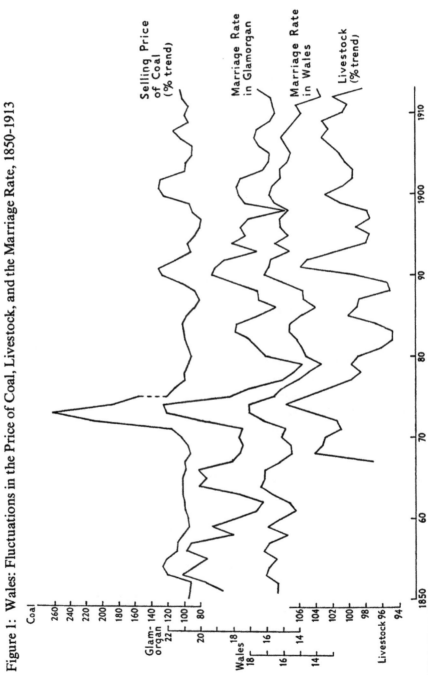

marriage rate closely follows the price of coal which had evidently become the determinant of the general level of prosperity (which would be a major factor in the marriage rate as in investment in livestock) throughout the Principality. The conclusion is inescapable. By the 1870s at the latest, Wales had become an industrial country in the sense that the terrible dominion of the harvest and seasonal cycle had been broken and that it was the rhythms of industry which had become the ultimate determinants of social life.

More significantly still, a critical feature of this whole industrialisation process was the fact that Wales was completely out of step with every other region of the British Isles. What is distinctive about nineteenth-century Wales is the peculiarly *imperial* character of the formation of its industrial society and of the Welsh working class.

The key here is the extension of a market towards a global compass and the centrality of British capitalism to that process. The near monopoly of British industry and commerce through much of the period and Britain's imposition of free trade on the Atlantic basin locked the British and US economies into an Atlantic economy which worked like a push-pull oscillator. Between 1846 and 1914 in that gigantic migration of the peoples which helped to build the USA into the greatest capitalist power on earth, over 43 million people emigrated to the Americas from Europe. Central to the absorptive capacity of the Americas, particularly the USA, was Britain; by 1913 nearly 70 per cent of the £3,500 million she had invested abroad was located in the Americas. There were four major outflows of people from Europe to America. During 1849-53, of two million who crossed the Atlantic, 80 per cent came from Ireland and Germany and were driven to America by the break-up of their own rural economies. The same is true of Irish, Scandinavians, Germans and Italians who went during 1863-73. The 1880s saw the great crisis of rural Europe. The Americans invented the harvester in 1872 and the binder in 1880; they completed their vital transport network (with substantial help from British money). In 1887, on the wheat farms of the US north-west, with wages at 25 dollars a month, wheat could be produced for 40 cents a bushel; in the Rhineland, with wages at 6 dollars a month, wheat cost 80 cents a bushel. The Americans could produce Indian corn in the Mississippi Valley, transport it to Italy and sell it there at a price lower than that of Lombard and Venetian corn, where labourers were paid a third of US wages. In 1885, 77,000 Italian farm labourers emigrated to the USA. During the 1880s, over one and a quarter million people left rural Germany and over half a million quit Scandinavia; Denmark had to rebuild itself. The final peak came in 1903-13, the celebrated 'new migrations' as they were called in the USA, when over ten million Slavs, Jews and southern Europeans flooded across the Atlantic, in a migration which was resuming after the First World War, to be stopped only by the racist American immigration laws of the 1920s.

Central to this process was Britain. The outward pulses of British capital, technological and human export coincided almost exactly with the peaks of European migration. The key was the interaction between Britain, the major investing power and the USA the leading market for investment. During outward thrusts of capital from Britain and people from Europe, the USA experienced a vigorous upswing in capital construction such as railways and building. At such moments, the export sector of the British economy was at stretch while, in relative terms, the British home sector marked time. Conversely, in the downward swings in British lending and European migration, Britain experienced a boom in her own capital construction. There was an inverse relation between fluctuations in the rate of capital formation in Britain and in the countries of new settlement and investment, above all the USA. This is what ultimately governed the flows of the rural population constantly displaced by the earthquake of industrial capitalism. For the Europeans were joined by a quite massive outflow of human beings from the British Isles. To put it crudely, when the British export sector, in capital and goods, boomed, the displaced rural population (with others) followed the thrust of enterprise and the British home sector marked time. Conversely, when the British home sector boomed, its export sector, in relative terms, stagnated and the displaced British population could find a life at home. The peaks of those outward pulses of capital and goods from Britain were 1847-54, 1866-73, 1881-8 and 1903-13.

How does Wales fit? Consider first the external migration balance, achieved (in admittedly rather crude but sufficient terms) by measuring the natural increase in population (the excess of births over deaths) against the actual decennial increase recorded in censuses and expressing the result, whether positive or negative, as a rate per 10,000 of the mean, decennial, home population. Brinley Thomas compares Wales, England, Scotland, Ireland and Sweden, set against the input figures for the USA. (See Table 1.)

Every people has its own variations, of course, but in broad terms, they follow the pattern outlined. With one exception. Every people in the British Isles follows that pattern with the startling exception of the Welsh. Ireland, of course, with its repeated demographic disasters, is

Table 1: Wales, England, Scotland, Ireland, Sweden, and USA:
Rate of Net Loss (—) or Gain (+) by Migration, Decennially, 1851-1957

Period	Wales	England	Scotland	Ireland North	South	Sweden	USA
			Annual rate per 10,000 mean population				
1851-61	— 28	— 16	— 101	— 194		— 7	+ 98
1861-71	— 47	— 7	— 44	— 169		— 37	+ 67
1871-81	— 35	— 5	— 28	— 119	— 127	— 32	+ 51
1881-91	— 11	— 23	— 58	— 108	— 163	— 74	+ 80
1891-1901	— 5	— 2	— 13	— 55	— 118	— 37	+ 37
1901-11	+ 45	— 19	— 57	— 52	— 82	— 36	+ 63
1911-21	— 21	— 16	— 50	— 47	— 88	— 11	+ 32
1921-31	— 102	+ 3	— 80	— 82	— 56	— 15	+ 27
1931-9	— 72	+ 24	— 8	— 5	— 63	+ 9	+ 0.8
1939-46	+ 1	+ 6	— 3	— 23		+ 12	
1946-51	— 18		— 92	— 63	— 84	+ 28	
1951-7	— 19	+ 12	— 53	— 70	— 134	+ 13	

unique in its intensity of emigration, but it follows the rhythm, as does Scotland. The crisis of the 1880s is certainly visible in Sweden. England has the lowest emigration rates (apart from Wales after the 1880s) but the rhythm is clearly perceptible.

But look at Wales. Up to the 1860s, clearly, despite rapid industrialisation, there is a drain of people out. But from the 1860s Wales, unique in the British Isles, breaks from the pattern. The rate of loss starts to fall and goes on falling, irrespective of the British and European rhythms. Where is the crisis of the 1880s in Wales? Rural Wales certainly experienced a crisis; nearly twice as many people quit rural Wales in the 1880s as in any other of the decades under review. But the net rate of loss out of Wales altogether *falls* to negligible proportions. It goes on falling until in the remarkable decade before the outbreak of the First World War, Wales becomes a country of net immigration. In that decade Wales becomes the only country to register a plus in the migration tables outside the USA. In fact, during that decade, in terms of sheer intensity of immigration, Wales, which in this context means south Wales, ranks second only to the USA itself. It was this immigration into the valleys of south Wales which caused a social, linguistic and political revolution and has led some reluctantly to conclude that Wales has become two nations.

The process is demonstrated yet more vividly by a graph. (See Fig. 2.) Observe that before the First World War, England and Scotland

Figure 2: Wales, Scotland, and England: Decennial Net Gain or
Loss by Migration, 1851-1957 (Annual Rate per 10,000 Mean
Population)

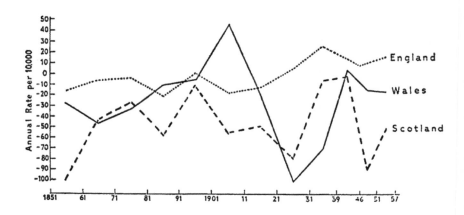

move in harness. From the 1860s, Wales moves out of phase, in a
continuous secular expansion which reaches a climax just before 1914.

Incidentally, it is possible to perceive from this graph just how
catastrophic the post-war depression was in Wales. It was catastrophic
precisely because of the export and imperial character of the previous
growth; the slump hit the very industries that growth was based on. In
consequence, south Wales was deracinated. Nearly half a million
people quit south Wales, a fifth of the whole population of Wales. Not
until 1961 did the Welsh population precariously regain the level of
1921. The industrial valleys of south Wales became and to a large
degree remain a 'problem area' while into rural west and north began
that flow of the largely non-Welsh and largely rentier population
which started their cultural transformation, ultimately to precipitate a
crisis of Welsh-language culture, a crisis of arson and bombs. In terms
of social disruption and identity crisis, the Depression plays the same
role in Welsh history as the Famine in Irish.

In the period before the First World War, however, Wales,
dominated by industrial south Wales, was a region of buoyant and
continuous expansion located in the export sector of British imperial
capitalism, moving out of step from most other regions of the British

Isles. In some ways, its export-orientated character makes it more a sector of an Atlantic than a narrowly British economy.

Turn to the American statistics (See Table 2.) The Irish, of course, stand out. Even in absolute numbers they outstrip the English, whose population was several times larger. Next come the Scots. The numbers of English are small, but the smallest numbers of all are Welsh. In proportion to population, English emigrants to the USA were four times as numerous as the Welsh, the Scots were seven times as numerous, the Irish twenty-six times. Contrary to a widespread Welsh impression, the Welsh have been the least migration-prone of all the peoples of the British Isles. They did not need to emigrate.

Moreover, there is no trace of the rhythmic pulses which characterise the other British peoples. The small-scale Welsh emigration remains remarkably steady throughout. Evidence from a wide range of sources identifies the majority of the emigrants. Farmers

Table 2: United States: Number of Immigrants (With and Without Occupation) from Wales, England, Scotland, and Ireland, Decennially, 1881-1930

Period and country of origin	Mean population of country of origin ('000)	Immigrants to USA (with occupation)	Annual rate per 10,000 mean population	Total immigrants to USA (with and without occupation)	Annual rate per 10,000 mean population
Wales					
1881-90	1,677	5,682	3	12,640	8
1891-1900	1,895	5,005	3	11,219	6
1901-10	2,238	11,708	5	18,631	8
1911-20	2,538	9,988	4	15,379	6
1921-30	2,629	8,402	3	16,267	6
England					
1881-90	25,812	391,118	12	644,680	25
1891-1900	28,861	128,107	4	224,350	8
1901-10	32,061	237,227	7	387,005	12
1911-20	34,440	271,181	8	419,526	12
1921-30	36,290	258,523	7	472,873	13
Scotland					
1881-90	3,881	79,342	20	149,869	39
1891-1900	4,249	28,006	7	60,046	14
1901-10	4,617	86,976	19	133,333	29
1911-20	4,822	100,824	21	164,131	34
1921-30	4,862	177,476	36	293,764	60
Ireland					
1881-90	4,940	382,368	77	655,482	133
1891-1900	4,582	280,054	61	404,045	88
1901-10	4,429	316,340	71	371,772	84
1911-20	4,372	187,902	43	240,041	55
1921-30	4,269	278,794	65	362,921	84

were in fact negligible. Professional and entrepreneurial people of adventurous bent were not negligible. The largest majority and by far the largest were skilled industrial workers. As an export centre of the British economy, Wales and especially south Wales, actually attracted people during those outward pulses which sent so many across the Atlantic; during British home booms, there was absorptive capacity within Britain. Naturally, it was by no means a one-to-one process. Though movement from north to south Wales was more frequent and stronger than has been assumed, the north Welsh would tend to drift into Liverpool and Merseyside or the Midlands. But the evidence overpoweringly suggests that before the critical years around the turn of the twentieth century, the working population within Wales was largely Welsh. The Irish tended to be segregated for cultural and religious reasons, but by 1900 assimilation was rapid. Large numbers of the English (and even the Spanish) who came in, were absorbed so completely that many learned the Welsh language — which explains the existence today of passionate Welsh-speaking Welsh nationalists who bear such ancient Welsh dynastic patronymics as Millward and Reeve. It was the years from 1900 on which witnessed the great shift to the English language in industrial south Wales and this stemmed from a much more complex set of causes than mere number.

The distinctiveness of Wales and, in particular, south Wales, may be demonstrated yet more vividly by looking at the totals for internal migration. Taking England and Wales as a whole, the pattern suggested by the external flows is clearly visible. (See Table 3.) During the 1850s and 1860s, some one and a half million people quit the rural areas. Expanding towns and colliery districts absorb a total equal to two-thirds of that; those leaving the country altogether equal one third. During the 1870s the British home sector is booming. There is a

Table 3: England and Wales: Internal Migration, Decennially, 1851-1911

Net loss by migration (—). Net gain by migration (+)

Area	1851-61	1861-71	1871-81	1881-91	1891-1901	1901-11
Rural residues	— 742,573	— 683,031	— 837,452	— 845,444	— 660,440	— 294,641
Towns	+ 516,789	+ 532,615	+ 604,680	+ 137,760	+ 520,822	— 321,095
Colliery districts	+ 103,467	+ 90,860	+ 84,474	+ 90,303	+ 85,158	+ 113,999
England and Wales	— 327,000	— 206,000	— 164,000	— 601,000	— 69,000	— 501,000

heavy outflow from rural districts, but there is also a marked increase in the absorptive capacity of towns and coalfields. The emigration flow drops sharply. In the 1880s the rural crisis reaches a climax at a time of expansion in the British export sector and of relative stagnation in the home sector. The absorptive capacity of the urban areas falls and there is a massive increase in emigration. The position is almost totally reversed during the 1890s but look at the 1900s. The rural exodus is now slackening but it is still substantial. Moreover this is a climax for European migration and British capital export. Even the towns show a major loss. This is true, also, of the English colliery districts. The net increase for the colliery areas of England and Wales together is 113,000; south Wales alone registered an increase of 129,000. There is another surge of emigration.

Turn now to the figures for internal migration in Wales. (See Table 4.) What is immediately striking is that the south Wales colliery districts in Glamorgan and Monmouth expand most in those very decades when the industrial sector of England and Wales as a whole expand least, the 1850s, the 1880s and, of course, the 1900s. The coalfield in north-east Wales, around Wrexham, starts to lose people from the 1860s, but the holiday areas along the north Wales coast start to grow. The expansion of the south Wales coalfield during the 1860s and 1870s is relatively slow, the population retained within Wales is only a proportion of the rural outflow. During the 1860s in fact the outflow from Wales as a whole was greater than that from the rural

Table 4: Wales: Internal Migration, Decennially, 1851-1911

Net loss by migration (—). Net gain by migration (+)

Area	1851-61	1861-71	1871-81	1881-91	1891-1901	1901-11
Welsh rural areas	— 63,322	— 58,967	— 64,646	— 106,087	— 57,413	— 37,909
Glamorgan-Monmouth-shire colliery area	+ 39,627	+ 11,033	+ 12,213	+ 87,225	+ 40,326	+ 129,295
Wrexham colliery area	+ 2,661	— 1,984	— 1,907	— 1,122	+ 618	— 2,875
Llandudno and Rhyl areas	+ 1,259	— 2,268	+ 2,339	+ 2,190	+ 8,289	+ 5,715
Wales	— 36,271	— 63,005	— 52,139	— 17,794	— 9,350	+ 98,492

Note: The estimated migration balance for 1851-61 and 1861-71 has been arrived at after making allowance for under-registration of births in those decades. The recorded number of births was 4 per cent too low in 1851-61 and 2 per cent too low in 1861-71, according to D.V. Glass's estimates for England and Wales in *Population Studies*, Vol. v, no. 1, July 1951. The figures of net gains or losses by migration in the body of the above table are based on the number of *recorded* births. Hence the discrepancy in the first two columns of the table.

areas; this, of course, was the peak of Welsh emigration to the USA. Over the twenty years as a whole, some 115,000 people left Wales, but the emigration was mainly into England.

It is from the 1880s that the distinctiveness of Wales becomes overpowering. The rural crisis registers very sharply indeed with the maximum outflow of the century, but there is a sharp increase in the absorptive capacity of the south Wales coalfield. In that decade, when emigration out of Britain as a whole reaches its climax, emigration out of Wales falls to a negligible level. In the following decade, the absorptive capacity of south Wales is a good deal less (this is a period of British home boom) but the scale of the rural exodus is much less and the holiday towns of north Wales, Llandudno, Rhyl and their kin, are booming. The rate of emigration out of Wales falls still further.

The final decade, the 1900s, scarcely calls for comment. A net outflow of about 40,000 is overshadowed by a massive inflow into south Wales of nearly 130,000. There is a net gain of nearly 100,000 people. This contrast between the colliery districts of Wales and England is most starkly demonstrated by a graph of the net migration movements within them. Look at it. The Welsh colliery districts (in effect south Wales) are a veritable mirror image of the English; the graphs are almost exactly opposite in their direction. (See Figure 3.)

The consequences of Brinley Thomas's work are clear and have to be faced. Any and every effort to assess the history of Wales in the nineteenth century, to place the 'rebirth of a nation' in full context, has to confront these objective realities. It is a justifiable inference from these truths to assert that if Wales had not been industrialised during the nineteenth century, its people would probably have suffered the same fate as the southern Irish. Since the Welsh were so much fewer, any recognisable entity which could be called 'Wales' would have disappeared in that century, its people blown away by the winds of the world. It is against this massive growth of an industrial Wales of British-imperial character that every other Welsh phenomenon must be set. What has come to be thought of as 'traditional', Nonconformist, Welsh-speaking, radical Wales in particular, that Wales which created so many of the characteristic Welsh institutions, notably the educational, was in some sense a by-product of this industrialisation, in other senses a reaction against it. Its roots and its thinking and emotional life were in or took their rise from (often, however, through the agency of upwardly mobile middle classes who had climbed out of this populist tilth) that rural Wales which was in permanent crisis from 1841 onwards and which lived, in objective

Figure 3: Welsh and English Colliery Districts: Net Migration
Movements, 1851-1911

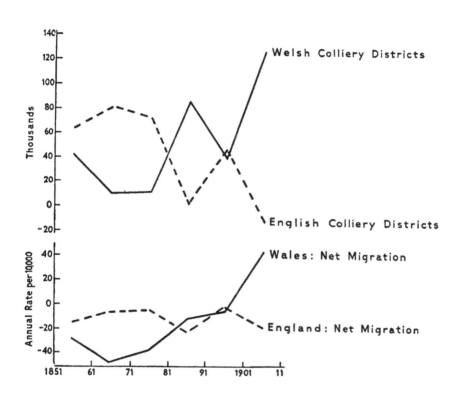

reality if not in subjective spirit, in dependence on industrial Wales.
The 'Wales' of what was at first a very real mind but which increasingly
became a Wales of the imaginative will, was increasingly distanced
from the 'Wales' which actually existed on the ground. This process of
intensifying contradiction was infinitely worsened by the post-war
Depression and, perhaps even more, by the Reconstruction which
followed, and in our own day has become intolerable. One feature
central to the triple vote of the Welsh electorate in 1979 which reversed
two hundred years of Welsh history was a *grand refus* of 'Wales' by the
Welsh as they actually are.[4]

Of no less significance is the fact that industrial Wales — and the
Welsh working class with it — were products of an imperial formation
located in buoyant export enterprise which gave south Wales a world

empire. One striking feature of a Welsh working class which could produce the revolutionary *Miners Next Step* is its boundless self-confidence.

For Brinley Thomas's graphs and tables are complemented by an abundance of evidence which historians whose minds have been commandeered by the computer call 'qualitative'.[5] In 1881, the very year in which Nonconformist Wales won its Sunday Closing Act, the coalowners and shippers of rapidly growing Cardiff, by then the largest town in Wales, raised one of the most mighty public buildings in the country, their merchant palace of a Coal Exchange. Two years later, offered a chance by the Aberdare Committee to unhorse a much more Welsh Swansea in a bid for a new university college, Cardiff's elite grabbed it and got their college in a ruthless and skilful operation conducted with all the power, punch and panache of a bunch of shippers cornering an export market. Cardiff's Bute Street became the jugular vein of capitalist Wales (within which every other Wales had to exist). Not only did John Cory's bunkers straddle the world and south Wales coal keep the Royal Navy afloat, the capital, technicians and technology of south Wales acquired world power.

They helped to distort the development of Spain, wrenching its heavy industry base away from Asturias into the Basque lands where Cardiff and its hinterland were entrenched in Bilbao.[6] South Wales merchants bought up shipping companies and port capital in French and German harbours; Italy, Argentina, Chile and Brazil for years worked to the rhythm of south Wales exports. For years the real economic capital of Chile was Swansea with its waterfront a forest of ocean-going masts. It was south Wales which first launched the iron and steel of the Donetz basin in Russia and of Pennsylvania in the USA.

The greatest editor of the *Western Mail* was one of Cecil Rhodes's men and the new Welsh bourgeoisie in its new Welsh press compared the Welsh to the Japanese as an old people finding a new role. Even Scott's expedition to the Antarctic found a base in Cardiff which, after the Klondyke climax of the First World War, earned the nickname of Lloyd George's City of Dreadful Knights. In the middle of that war, the economist Stanley Jevons could predict a British world hegemony centred on south Wales. This is that 'American Wales' which carried the rest on its indifferent back, that 'un-Welsh Wales' which largely determined the fate of a Wales more familiar to its intellectuals formed by the educational enterprise of the Nonconformist and Radical Nation. This is Imperial Wales, the sense and feel and smell of which, no doubt because of the formative experience of Depression, Socialism and Welsh Nationalism, Welsh historiography seems largely to have lost.

Two cultural symbols of that simultaneously Welsh-populist and British-imperial identity have, however, proved memorable. There was David Lloyd George, leaping like a Magic Goat from the aggressive middle class of north Wales now on the offensive against Anglican landlords and creating a Welsh nation in its own image, into Downing Street and to the pinnacle of British imperialism at its moment of peril. And there was and is Welsh rugby which, after an initial struggle, became the Welsh 'national game' *par excellence*, the only field where it was possible to be simultaneously Welsh and a gentleman, (normally a difficult undertaking), where doctor and lawyer could ruck happily shoulder to shoulder with miner and where Wales, safely lodged as a major directive element within imperial Britain, could express its now self-confident identity in a continuous eisteddfod of Grand Slams and a continuous rugby-dinner chorus of God Bless the Prince of Wales (duly Invested at Caernarfon by a Lloyd George who was as inventive of Welsh traditions as Iolo Morganwg).[7]

It was precisely this fool's export paradise which was brought crashing after 1921 by the Depression which hit the very industries it was based on and whose impact has been so sharp that it now requires an effort of the will to remember that there was once such a Wales.

Yet in many ways, many of the social and psychological forces which have shaped the modern Welsh flow from that imperial experience, not least the working class. The internal contradictions of this polity became tense from the 1890s when a vaulting coal industry ran into problems of geology and profits. Trade unions struck root so rapidly and so comprehensively in south Wales from the 1890s that the least unionised district in Britain became its most intensely unionised district almost overnight. Socialism penetrated in that same decade and the tumultuous battles from 1910 onward in the coal industry started the region on its progression into a semi-mythical Red Belt of the British working class. Through the turmoil of the pre-war, war and post-war years, the leadership of the miners, in a sequence of dramatic shifts, passed from Liberals to Communists in little more than fifteen years.[8] The advance of Labour in the field of parliamentary and local elections was slower and molecular but more firmly rooted; it took the experience of the First World War finally to unhinge Liberalism's grip after a brief post-war Lloyd George honeymoon. In those same immediate post-war years, in the Welsh sector of Europe's 'green revolution' as the great estates finally crumbled, Welsh tenant farmers at last won their long battle and got ready to secure their inheritance.[9]

Another hegemony was shaping here, in embryo a successor to that Liberal hegemony which had been so total that in 1906 not a single Tory MP had been returned from Wales. And despite the manifold differences between that old order and the new, which had made its way in revolt against Nonconformist radicalism and its Welshness and had embraced the English language as the vehicle of rebellion and liberation, there were deep and persistent similarities in assumptions and style and ultimate values; new leaders were often visibly a translation rather than a displacement of the old.[10] The Labour Wales which had struggled to life within the Liberal shell was still the child, even if a bastard child, of imperial south Wales. In 1921 its new power seemed poised to take over a fractured inheritance. Instead, this victorious and populist Wales marched into an economic blizzard which destroyed it.

In one fundamental and rather grim sense, however, we Welsh of the present generation, who may be among the last fully to experience an elusive but all too tangible Welshness as a lived reality, still move in the shadow of the imperial Wales of our grand-parents. For it is the inexorable social and intellectual processes which were set in train not only by the Depression which destroyed it but, paradoxically by the Reconstruction which reshaped a survivor society, which now threaten to eliminate Wales and the Welsh from history.

Notes

1. Kenneth O. Morgan, *Rebirth of a Nation: Wales 1880-1980* (University of Wales and Clarendon presses, 1981).

2. Brinley Thomas, *Migration and Economic Growth* (Cambridge University Press, Cambridge, 1954 and subsequent revisions) and his article, 'Wales and the Atlantic Economy' in the volume he edited, *The Welsh Economy: studies in expansion* (University of Wales, Cardiff, 1962). I thank Professor Thomas for permission to use his tables and graphs. I have tried religiously to follow the argument and conclusions of his analysis; any conclusions which are supplementary to that analysis are, of course, entirely my own.

3. All the graphs and tables here are taken from Brinley Thomas, 'Wales and the Atlantic Economy'.

4. I discuss this contradiction, albeit in somewhat polemical form, in 'Mother Wales, get off me back?' *Marxism Today*, December 1981.

5. Apart from my own work and general reading, I have gained a great deal here from endless and endlessly fascinating discussion and debate with my friend and colleague David Smith of the Dept of the History of Wales at Cardiff, part-author of *The Fed* and *Fields of Praise* (below) and author of many seminal and stimulating essays on

subjects ranging from the Rhondda novelists Lewis Jones and Gwyn Thomas and the Tonypandy Riots to Raymond Chandler and Joseph Conrad.

6. The Spanish population in south Wales is a by-product of this connection as indeed were the south Wales reception of refugee children and the tragi-comic episode of Cardiff captains' attempts to break the Bilbao blockade during the Spanish civil war.

7. David Smith and Gareth Williams, *Fields of Praise; the official history of the Welsh Rugby Union 1881-1981* (University of Wales, Cardiff, 1981).

8. Hywel Francis and David Smith, *The Fed: a History of the South Wales Miners in the Twentieth Century* (Lawrence and Wishart, London 1980).

9. John Davies, 'The End of the Great Estates and the Rise of Freehold Farming in Wales', *Welsh History Review*, vii (1974).

10. An interesting and informative essay here is Peter Stead, 'Working-Class Leadership in South Wales 1900-1920', *Welsh History Review*, vi (1973).

8 WHEN WAS WALES?*

'The Welsh are a race for whom the insubstantial world has always been more real than the visible one': so Bernard de Voto, an idiosyncratic but superbly evocative historian of the American continent, commenting on the legend of Madoc, that Welsh prince who was said to have discovered America in 1170 and to have fathered a tribe of Welsh Indians; a myth which proved the most potent and persistent myth of American westward expansion and whose revival in the late eighteenth century triggered the birth of the first modern nation in Wales, the Jacobin nation and its millenarian migration to the USA:

> The Welsh are a race for whom the little people have always shaken their milk-white arms in a ring by moonlight and the towers of Avalon have always glimmered in the sunset . . . and a people who, though they have always gone forth to battle have always died . . .

Clearly, I am one of the Little People. It is some time since I saw milk-white arms shaking in a ring by moonlight, though one lives in hope. The only white arms in a ring I recollect were those of undernourished pitch and toss gamblers on the tips during that Depression which snapped the mainspring of our people in its industrial heartland, dispersed half a million of them and precipitated those multiple crises of identity in which we now live.

I strongly suspect that Bernard de Voto may have become hopelessly confused among his Celts. He did however, pinpoint a truth. The Welsh are difficult to identify.

The frontiers of a Welsh nation have rarely coincided with the frontiers of a Welsh people. A Welsh nation has frequently been a

---

*The BBC Wales Annual Radio Lecture (the thirty-first) broadcast on BBC Wales/Radio Cymru on 12 November 1979 and re-broadcast on BBC Radio Three on 29 February 1980. The pamphlet, published by the BBC, was apparently sold out in a couple of weeks, but despite requests, the Corporation would not print any more. I have corrected three errors, my own and the printers', and have eliminated one unwarranted editorial insertion, but have otherwise left the text unchanged, except for one footnote added in explanation.

189

fraction of a Welsh people, often a small one though never of course a vulgar one. Nations have not existed from Time Immemorial as the warp and woof of human experience. Nations are not born; they are made. Nations do not grow like a tree, they are manufactured. Most of the nations of modern Europe were manufactured during the nineteenth century; people manufactured nations as they did cotton shirts. The processes were intimately linked, as peoples called non-historic invented for themselves a usable past to inform an attainable future, under the twin stimuli of democratic and industrial revolutions. In the precociously unified monarchies of Britain and France, they began to manufacture nations earlier; a British nation emerges from the eighteenth century, in the union of England and Scotland around the armature of merchant capitalism, world empire and liberal oligarchy. The ongoing and increasingly revolutionary processes of capitalism are now radically restructuring and remodelling the nations they conjured into existence, eliminating some, transcending some, fragmenting some. The British nation and the British state are clearly entering a process of dissolution, into Europe or the mid-Atlantic or a post-imperial fog. Britain has begun its long march out of history.

How ironic it seems then, that in Referendum, General Election and European Election during 1979, it was the Welsh who registered their country as the most passionately and totally British of all the regions of the United Kingdom of Great Britain and about a half of Northern Ireland. We Welsh look like being the Last of the British. There is some logic in this. We were, after all, the First.

When did we begin? When was Wales? 'Hwn yw y gododdin. Aneirin ae cant.' This is the Gododdin. Aneirin sang it. The title line of what is generally accepted as the first Welsh poetry to survive. Written no later than the sixth century, one of the oldest literary traditions in Europe and itself the heir of an even older civilisation. Still accessible, moreover, to a modern reader of Welsh in a way that early English is not to a speaker of modern English. Historic immobility, even stagnation, perhaps? But that is what one calls a tradition, you agree?

But what tradition does it celebrate? It is a British tradition, in the British tongue. The poem is about a battle in modern Yorkshire between Northumbrians and the defenders of Romano-Celtic North Britain. It was written in what is today Scotland, as were the battle poems attributed to Taliesin. The first Welsh poetry written in Scotland about battles north of Trent? At much the same time, our patron saint, whom no other church recognises, emerged, his shrine at a hub of that complex of western sea-routes along which Celtic civilisation and the great Irish mission church pulsed. In the seventh century, a Welshman could serve as bishop in Spanish Galicia; lives of the Welsh saints were written in Brittany. St David was possibly as Irish as St Patrick was Welsh.

What do such words as Irish, Welsh, English mean in that dark and dramatic time when the British Diocese of the Roman Empire shuddered apart into multiple piratical kingdoms of warring tribes? They mean nothing. When Offa of Mercia cut his great dyke in the eighth century as an agreed frontier, he drew a line between two peoples, each of whom was old and between two embryonic nations, each of whom was new.

The people to the west of that line knew where they were; they were in Rome.

Catamannus Rex: Sapientissimus, opinatissimus, Omnium Regum: so runs a memorial pillar to a seventh-century king in Anglesey. In Glamorgan they were still Roman in the eighth century, four hundred years after the legions had left. A Welsh leader Emrys, ringed by his 'bawling bards' chanting praise in intricate word-play, his rule reaching no further than his sword could reach and his stolen gold shower, could call himself Ambrosius Aurelianus and wear the purple. The last Roman monument in the western world is in Penmachno. The longest and most fecund of Welsh traditions, running an elusive thread through Mabinogion and poetry, and given a European stature by Geoffrey of Monmouth, is the British and Arthurian complex of stories, legends, mythical history and redemptive prophecy stemming from the historic Arthur, last of the Romano-Britons. As late as the tenth century, the polemical poem, *Armes Prydein*, written in opposition to Hywel Dda's pro-English policy, was directing anti-Saxon minds not to a Welsh but to a British identity. It took centuries for the peoples west of Offa's Dyke even to conceive of themselves as Welsh.

What defined the Welsh in the end were the English. In the open lowlands a strong, unifying monarchy emerged early, to become almost unique in the Europe of its day and to be strengthened still further by the injection of Norman power in the eleventh century. The relatively rapid rise of a powerful England turned the Welsh, almost from birth, penned as they were in a harshly poor upland economy staked to a bony mountain spine, into a marginal people. Talented but marginal, the talent probably a function of the marginality, light of foot, light of spirit, light of plough, they lived by their wits, the Jews of the British Isles.

The Welsh as the English called them, succumbing early to their deplorable national habit of addressing natives as foreigners, the Cymry as about half of them called themselves, emerge into history from the wreck of Roman Britain as highly self-conscious heirs of the British. There was a profound divergence between the historical experience of north and south, possibly the root cause of their divergence in the use of the Welsh language.[1] The romanised Commonwealth of the Silures generated a kingdom of Gwent-Morganwg, heavily Roman in its style and climate, living close to Celts in the south-west and Brittany, who were excluded from the Cymry who defined themselves in battle in north Britain. Ringed by immigrant kingdoms of Irish origin fusing, largely through the David evangelical style of Christianity, into the ramshackle confederation of Deheubarth, Gwent-Morganwg, for centuries an extension of the civilisation of Salisbury Plain, seems to have settled relatively easily behind the Wye even as Gwynedd, under its north British dynasty of Cunedda, defined itself in the struggle for North Britain before falling apart in the eighth century as Powys emerged as the survivor kingdom of an extensive Romano-British polity on the Severn. Hardly had these piratical little kingdoms defined themselves as British and Christian than the internal breakdown of their inherited Roman superstructure coincided with a need to reshape settlement and tenurial patterns in the teeth of a voraciously land-hungry church at the very moment when the terrible scourge of the Vikings broke on them, to drive their new High Kings of all Wales generated by this internal crisis into the shelter of the new English Crown focused on Wessex. In a battle of the traditions, the old British ideology of Nennius and *Armes Prydein* against the new Britain of Hywel Dda in which the Welsh were a junior partner, Welsh social structure and polity were shaped by Hywel's Laws in political dependence on the English Crown, even as many Welsh princelings became half-Vikings themselves within the cultural world of the Irish Sea, that mini-Mediterranean of the north.

Hard on the heels of English and Vikings, came the Normans who ripped half the country away into a rich and hybrid Welsh-European civilisation, projected Welsh culture into Europe, thrust European modes into the semi-independent west and north and dragged the Welsh out of the Celtic-Scandinavian world into the Latin. In response, the Welsh around the survivor kingdom of Gwynedd struggled to build a miniature Welsh feudal state, to win a brief success under Llywelyn ap Gruffydd, first and last Welsh prince of Wales, who was broken by armies largely Welsh in composition and by a Welsh aristocracy in revolt against Llywelyn's ruthless abrogation of Welsh tradition, marshalled by Edward I who revolutionised English military society in order to destroy Gwynedd. The colonial centuries which followed were ended by the Rebellion of Owain Glyn Dŵr, a war of national liberation which like all such wars was also the greatest of Welsh civil wars, to be followed by the seminal Tudor century, when the Welsh gentry climbed to power over the ruins of principality and aristocracy alike, when the Welsh were hoisted to a temporary pinnacle of prestige, when the old British ideology of the Welsh became a new British national mythology and when Welsh society was absorbed wholesale into English. That century witnessed that characteristic Tudor contradiction, a Protestant Welsh Bible to direct and service the survival of the old language on the one hand, official discrimination against and social scorn for that language on the other. Even as the old culture stammered before the Renaissance as Protestantism rooted itself in Welsh soil, the long and rich tradition of Welsh writing in the English language was born as the Welsh language began its slow recession into a sacerdotal tongue, a sacred language, and lost contact with the fullness of modern secular living.

The century of turmoil which followed the Tudors decimated the lesser gentry of Wales, a product of its kindred social structure and critical to its separate identity and expelled it from public life, even as its landowners were clasped into the hot and clammy embrace of the broad, open, astute and ruthless oligarchy of the new Great Britain and its unprecedented mercantile empire of the eighteenth century.

The alternative society in Wales was born no less of that new mercantile Britain with its Atlantic dimension: an evangelical drive for literacy which turned a majority of the adult population technically literate in Welsh for a stretch of the eighteenth century, a Calvinistic Methodist movement independent in its origins from English Methodism, stirrings of rationalist and radical movements among the Old Dissent created by embattled Puritanism and an upsurge of interest in Welsh history and antiquities powered above all by the London-Welsh, surrogate capital of an invertebrate country. The entry of this alternative society into history was explosive. From the eighteenth century, the new industrial capitalism thrust into Wales. Over a hundred years it quintupled the population, sucked most of it into the modernising and English-speaking south-east, provided the money and the power and the will for a Welsh revival and the insidious processes which cut that revival down in its prime. Over little more than two generations, the Welsh went on their Long March out of

Establishment and into the spiritual world of Dissent, even as south and east began theirs into West Britain. A further surge of growth built south Wales into an imperial metropolis of the new British world economy even as, in response, a new and semi-political Welsh nation clawed its way into half-existence, displacing and dismissing into limbo the half-formed Jacobin nation of the 1790s, to form along a language line and a religious line which was also a class line, to claim a monopoly of Welshness in the late nineteenth century even as a new industrial civilisation blossomed in the imperial democracy of south Wales and there was a massive, buoyant and innovatory immigration into that south Wales second in intensity only to immigration into the USA itself. And after a Klondyke climax to this new American Wales in the First World War, the terrible Depression of the 1920s and 1930s burned through this complex and contradictory Wales like radioactive fall-out from a distant holocaust. The Depression which plays the same social role in Welsh history, I think, as the Famine in Irish, unhinged this Welsh polity, devastated its communities, dispersed a quarter of its people and thrust a community of survivors, struggling to rebuild consensus in a precarious post-war prosperity into those crises of identity and those bankruptcies of rooted political traditions which plague our contemporary experience.

In such a people with such a history, the problem of identity has been desperate from the beginning. In recent centuries we have progressively lost our grip on our own past. Our history has been a history to induce schizophrenia and to enforce loss of memory. Professional history, history as a craft, is even more recent a phenomenon in Wales than in England. Half-memories, folklore, traditions, myths, fantasy are rampant. We are a people with plenty of traditions but no historical memory. We have no historical autonomy. We live in the interstices of other people's history.

Our survival has been a kind of miracle. What is immediately clear, from even a cursory survey of our broken-backed history, is that the tiny Welsh people, for we were always very thin on the ground, have survived by being British. Welsh identity has constantly renewed itself by anchoring itself in variant forms of Britishness. The phrase British Empire was invented in 1580 and by a Welshman, Dr John Dee, mathematician and magician, navigator and scientist of European reputation like Robert Recorde of Pembrokeshire before him, enchanter and dabbler in the occult and intellectual mentor to the exploration, colonial and piratical enterprises of the age of Drake, chief scientific adviser to that 'red headed Welsh harridan' Queen

Elizabeth I. It was in British empire that a Welsh intellectual could find fulfilment in the sixteenth century. That pattern has proved recurrent.

The historic British nation was generated in Anglo-Scottish mercantile capitalism in the eighteenth century, to assume quasi-permanent ideal form and to persist until the third quarter of the twentieth century. There are nationalists among Scots and Welsh who deny the existence of this British nation. Their organic conception of nationality and nationalism requires them so to do. They are taking as an axiom what in fact they have to create. It is necessary for them to do this; in their own terms it is proper for them to do it. When they deny the historical existence of a British nation, however, what they are actually doing is asserting the power of the human will against objective historical reality. This is not to create a historic will, such as Antonio Gramsci, the Italian marxist who was the most creative marxist since Marx himself, called for, himself preoccupied with the problem of nation-making. They are erecting human will into an anti-historic force and therefore into a myth. They are trying to shout down history to its face; they are spitting in the winds of the world.

The existence of a historic British nation, dominated by but qualitatively distinct from the English polity, is a central fact in the modern history of these islands. The history of the Scots and of the Ulster Protestants is inconceivable without it. The history of the Welsh is totally incomprehensible without it. The Welsh, the original British, have survived by finding a distinctive place for themselves within a British nation.

This is what makes the present predicament of Welsh people who wish to be Welsh so painful. The form which Welsh nationality assumed in the nineteenth century, the pseudo-nation of a 'Nonconformist people', has proven to be, historically, an instrument of middle-class modernisation. Its limited objectives attained through Liberalism, the husk fell away, leaving Labour to inherit. The residual and tougher nationalism which has today displaced it, reverted to the standard European form which the first Welsh nationalism had assumed in the 1790s. In essence, it was a form of linguistic nationalism which, in Europe, grew into a species of modern tribalism and exclusivism. The application of a strict Welsh linguistic nationalism today, of course, would mean instant death to the Welsh people as a distinct people. Some individuals have followed the logic of this predicament into an historic bunker under permanent siege which would require massive invasions of civil liberty to sustain itself. On the other hand, the form of Welsh personality which historically and genuinely has existed within a British identity seems to carry all the stigmata of the historically transient; it becomes a question of style, of accent, of historically acquired manners, of half understood hymns sung on ritual occasions, a question of trivialities. It may simply prove a station on the road to historical extinction. Central to this predicament is precisely that British nation which hegemonic British capitalism created and of which modern south Wales was not merely an element, but a central directive force.

I do not think such a history can be interpreted effectively in terms of the currently fashionable concept of internal colonialism. This, while it has now created a school of historiography in its own right, derives ultimately from one marxist interpretation of history, that first seriously applied by Andre Gunder Frank in a study of South America and the relationship between metropolis and satellite in the Third World, extending within state frontiers. It has been erected into a global analysis by Immanuel Wallerstein and has recently come under attack from Robert Brenner in a sustained controversy in both academic and marxist journals. The thesis locates explanation in the extension of a market and the transfer of a surplus from satellite to metropolis with all the relations of production, social relations, ideological, intellectual and spiritual forms which follow. It is very often perceptive in terms of its analyses of the social and psychological consequences of the rapid advance of capitalism over the globe; this is precisely its strength in Wales, but in truth it derives from Adam Smith rather than Marx, it misses the centrality of a mode of production in all its social complexity. It singles out one element only, the market, from that mode of production, which embodies the transformation of human attributes and human creations into commodities in the complex class relations which derive from that process; it mishandles the central reality of uneven development and it therefore often reads consequences as causes.

The industrial development of Wales was imperial from birth. Copper around Swansea and Anglesey was a world monopoly, directed in particular at the West Indies; the rise of the massive iron, steel, coal, and later tinplate industries was geared directly to the mushroom growth of British commercial empire based on Atlantic slave power during the long French wars and riveted to British industrialisation in the free labour epoch which ensued. From the 1840s Welsh industry secured another world empire in railways, incorporating the Welsh working class as a junior partner in the process, after the storms of the frontier years. The incredible world empire of south Wales coal is familiar. But this was much more than a simple matter of coal export. South Wales capital, south Wales technology, south Wales enterprise, south Wales labour not only fertilised whole tracts of the world from Pennsylvania to the Donetz basin; they were a critical factor in world economic development. The growth of Spain was completely distorted by the power of south Wales, which wrenched its natural heavy industry base from the Asturias to the Basque provinces; south Wales merchants bought up the shipping companies of French ports and of Hamburg; Italy, Argentina, Brazil worked to the rhythms of south Wales trade. In consequence a whole new industrial civilisation grew up in the south; the Welsh Outlook Press could compare the Welsh to the Japanese as an old people finding a new role; the most creative editor of the *Western Mail* was one of the Cecil Rhodes's men. At the height of the First World War, Stanley Jevons, professor of economics, could envisage a post-war British global hegemony centred entirely on south Wales. That this metropolis was characterised by mass poverty and exploitation and working-class struggle is nothing unusual. This is par for the course for capitalism. Indeed the mushroom growth of south Wales into a major centre of the British labour movement from the 1890s, its transformation into a seminal power in that movement, followed a natural American and Atlantic pattern. The nickname American Wales in fact identifies a structural truth; the nearest and most obvious comparison is with Catalonia, another region of distinctive personality which experienced an American and Atlantic pattern of growth and slump to become a metropolis of the wider homeland of Spain.

The use of the term internal colonialism to describe this historical conjuncture precisely reverses the reality; it is the contradictions of an imperial capitalism we are dealing with, not those of one of its satellites.

In our modern history, it is possible to detect three central characteristics. The first is marginality. The original marginality, of course, was that of poverty, a cramped and pinched community of small commodity producers unable to generate capital, living in bleak and back-breaking poverty and in unremitting colonial dependence, its most vivid symptoms the great droves of skinny cattle and skinny people seasonally tramping into England to be fattened. That marginality was ended and ended decisively by the establishment of industrial capitalism. Towns, a middle class, a proletariat were created, the population was forcibly relocated; by the 1870s the marriage rate even in Merioneth was dependent on the price of coal. American Wales had emerged and the rest of Wales had to adjust; rural Wales lost over 800,000 people. The economy, however, remained marginal in one fundamental sense. The south Wales economy which enabled the country to sustain its phenomenal population increase and to retain it within its borders, was geared almost wholly to export. It worked to exactly the opposite, inverse rhythm to every other industrial region in Britain. In the first decade of the twentieth century as British industrial decline registered visibly everywhere else, south Wales reached a climax of frenetic expansion and drew in migrants at a rate second only to the USA. The Depression therefore was all the more catastrophic. What remained was a derelict society of survivors. In our own day, the continuing elaboration of capitalism has multiplied professions and white-collar industries; most of us work for multi-national corporations or in the tertiary sector of bureaucracy and services; a precarious prosperity is slithering into crisis as all life is sucked away to those coasts which are becoming a coastal fringe of Europe, draining Wales's hollow heart to the point of vacuum.

A second factor has been diversity often amounting to division, itself a product of this type of capitalism, a diversity which has been able to find coexistence only within a British identity. Apart from the familiar divisions between Welsh and English speakers which, despite heroic efforts, seem to be getting worse, Wales has always been a patchwork of cultures, and industry at first intensified the divergences. The massive restabilisation of the middle years of the century, after Chartism and Rebecca, which incorporated both a working class and the new Nonconformist populism around its preacher-journalists, achieved a kind of synthesis in radicalism, which masked deep divisions and which served in historical terms as an instrument, what Gramsci would have called a gastric juice of modernisation; this synthesis fell apart with the rise of Labour out of the brash new civilisation of the south during the boom years of an imperial democracy.

These variant forms of Welshness all required the power and the presence of the new Britain to be effective. This was as true of those standard hero movements of our textbooks, the builders of colleges and schools and eisteddfodau, their efforts increasingly directed as rescue enterprises to a rural Wales in permanent crisis, as of the new plutocracy of the American boom towns of the south, the new professional classes and of the new and abruptly politicised working class cadres who to combat capitalism looked for international and in practice British muscle. Two phenomena characterise the situation, I think; the emergence of Welsh rugby as a simultaneously Welsh, populist and British imperialist force and the catapulting of David Lloyd George and his Welsh populism into an imperial power.

The Depression, killer of nations, destroyed the integument which held this complexity precariously together. The massive growth of Labour, despite the fervour of a religiose ILP and the challenge of a Communist minority, was essentially a tribal defence mechanism against the slump, a warm rough blanket against the winds of the world. It could not restore that integument, by its nature it could not. Its social democracy was essentially British. And today, of course, its social democracy is as bankrupt as the parliamentary democracy which was its instrument.

A third determining factor, I think, is historic melodrama. Our recent history has been sheer melodrama. After centuries of slow almost imperceptible growth, a coral-growth when the Welsh were never more than 400,000 strong and frequently much fewer, industrial capitalism tore into Wales, quintupled its population, doubled the life-span of its people, powered and then neutered a Welsh revival, planted communities and uprooted them, in a breakneck pellmell growth, endlessly revolutionising everything it touched, to climax in the middle of the slaughter of the War and then to smash up in cataclysm. We are living through the morning after a night before which lasted four generations; a psychological factor, I believe, in the present equation.

No wonder we are driven to ask when was Wales? When did we begin? We are living through what may be our end. The end of Wales and the Welsh as distinct entities.

It is apparent that Wales and the Welsh, as distinctive entities, cannot survive the capitalist mode of production in its present historic phase. A tiny Welsh nation may survive in a marginal and impotent bunker; a vivid Welsh-language culture should survive if only in aspic. But the continuous reproduction of Wales and the Welsh over generations requires the elimination and the transcendence of the capitalist mode of production. If capitalism in the British Isles lives, Wales will die. If Wales is to live, capitalism in the British Isles must die.

A vocabulary of structural dissidence is as widespread in Wales as in Britain; a movement of structural dissidence is as absent in Wales as in Britain. This was a predicament familiar to Antonio Gramsci and his generation in the 1920s as they tried to remake Italy and the west in socialism. The parallels are apt, for the Welsh, until the recent divergence, were in structure and spirit, a European people; all the valid comparisons are with European peoples of the Atlantic world. The Europe to which we belong is not the Europe of Saunders Lewis; the Europe of Saunders Lewis's *Brâd (Treason:* a play) is our enemy. Our Europe is the Europe of Rosa Luxemburg and Anton Pannekoek, of Karl Korsch and Victor Serge, of Fernando Claudin and La Pasionaria; above all of that Aneurin Bevan of Italian communism, Antonio Gramsci the little hunchback who was one of the greatest creative spirits of this Europe, who was done to death in Mussolini's jails and who worked to the motto borrowed from Romain Rolland, *Pessimism of the intelligence, optimism of the will*, to make a socialist society and an Italian nation.

The human will was central to Gramsci's marxism, but it was an historic will, geared to the objective realities of history. To quote the eighteenth century, freedom is the knowledge of necessity. Such freedom is grounded in the mastery of history. No freedom is possible unless we conquer an historical autonomy, unless we can stand up among the giant cogwheels of history. History is more than a word, more than a footnote on a printed page, more than a tired smile in a shadowed study. The corpses of the dead generations do weigh like an Alp on the brains of the living. This is why we must assimilate their experience if only to get shot of them. Gramsci accurately perceived that the historic will derived from an act of choice which probably lies beyond reason.

To the question when was Wales, it is possible to return several answers. One could say, with a measure of truth within narrow limits, that Wales never was. It is equally possible to say, with equal truth within equally narrow limits, that Wales always was.

In reality, Wales is now and Wales has always been now. Wales is not an event, it is not a moment, it is not a mystical presence ubiquitous through our history like some holy ghost. Wales is none of these things. Wales does not exist and cannot exist outside the Welsh people as they exist and as they existed, on the ground, warts and all, *wie es eigentlich gewesen es*, as it actually happened. Wales is not a thaumaturgical act, it is a process, a process of continuous and dialectical historical development, in which human mind and human will interact with objective reality. Wales is an artefact which the Welsh produce; the Welsh make and remake Wales day by day and year after year. If they want to.

It is not history which does this; it is not traditions which do this; that is Hegelian mysticism and infantilism. History does nothing, said Karl Marx, it is men who do all this. Men make their own history, but in the terms and within the limits imposed on them by the history they inherit; always provided, of course, that they master that history and make a choice. To make history, to win historical autonomy, it is necessary to make a choice in historical awareness.

There is no historical necessity for Wales; there is no historical necessity for a Welsh people or a Welsh nation. Wales will not exist unless the Welsh want it. It is not compulsory to want it. Plenty of people who are biologically Welsh choose not to be Welsh. That act of choice is beyond reason. One thing, however, is clear from our history. If we want Wales, we will have to make Wales.

Note

1. I have employed this clumsy expression because of misinterpretation. A reviewer in a Welsh-language journal apparently read the original 'divergence in language' as meaning a divergence between the Welsh and English languages! Only an idiot would talk of the use of the English language in sixth-century Wales; only an idiot, I have to add, would think I was.

INDEX

Milton Keynes UK
Ingram Content Group UK Ltd.
UKHW022248021224
451945UK00007B/25